A SKYE FULL OF STARS

Sue Moorcroft writes award-winning contemporary fiction of life and love. *A Summer to Remember* won the Goldsboro Books Contemporary Romantic Novel award, *The Little Village Christmas* and *A Christmas Gift* were *Sunday Times* bestsellers and *The Christmas Promise* went to #1 in the Kindle chart. She also writes short stories, serials, articles, columns, courses and writing 'how to'. She is the current president of the Romantic Novelists' Association.

An army child, Sue was born in Germany then lived in Cyprus, Malta and the UK, and still loves to travel. Her other loves include writing (the best job in the world), reading, watching Formula 1 on TV, hanging out with friends, dancing, yoga, wine and chocolate.

If you're interested in being part of #TeamSueMoorcroft you can find more information at www.suemoorcroft.com by clicking on 'Street Team'. If you prefer to sign up to receive news of Sue and her books, go to www.suemoorcroft.com and click on 'Sign me up'. You can follow @SueMoorcroft on X (formerly Twitter), @suemoorcroftauthor on Instagram, or Facebook.com/sue.moorcroft.3 and Facebook.com/SueMoorcroftAuthor.

A Skye Full of Stars

Sue Moorcroft

avon.

Published by AVON
A division of HarperCollins*Publishers* Ltd
1 London Bridge Street
London SE1 9GF

www.harpercollins.co.uk

HarperCollins*Publishers*
Macken House, 39/40 Mayor Street Upper,
Dublin 1, D01 C9W8
Ireland

A Paperback Original 2024
3
First published in Great Britain by HarperCollins*Publishers* 2024

A catalogue copy of this book is available from the British Library.

ISBN: 978-0-00-863684-5

This novel is entirely a work of fiction. The names, characters and incidents portrayed in it are the work of the author's imagination. Any resemblance to actual persons, living or dead, events or localities is entirely coincidental.

Set in Sabon LT Std by HarperCollins*Publishers* India

Printed and bound in the UK using 100% Renewable Electricity at CPI Group (UK) Ltd

MIX
Paper | Supporting
responsible forestry
FSC™ C007454

This book contains FSC™ certified paper and other controlled sources to ensure responsible forest management.

For more information visit: www.harpercollins.co.uk/green

Acknowledgements

After visiting the Isle of Skye in summer to research the first of the Skye Sisters trilogy, *Under a Summer Skye*, I was delighted to make the corresponding winter trip for *A Skye Full of Stars*. It felt like a completely different island, with short daylight hours and icicles clinging to roadside rocks. I loved it.

In this book, Scandinavian characters take major roles – especially impetuous Mats Larsson and his lovely kids Astrid and Alvin. Enormous thanks are due to Pia Fenton for not only answering a host of questions about Sweden and the Swedish but reading the full manuscript and helping get every detail right.

Thanks also to Gill Stewart for performing the same role for the Scottish characters and Scotland. She's been invaluable, as has Roz Macaskill who lives on the Isle of Skye and could even check whether superyachts ever sail up the Sound of Sleat. (They do.)

Lisa Timoney generously chatted to me about being an adoptee, and several of her insights made it into Ezz's reactions and thought processes.

If you've already read *Under a Summer Skye*, you'll know why I had to find Dev a new job. Jess Shanahan gave me fascinating oversight on media training for young athletes and mentoring them through their hunt for sponsorship.

Since he retired, my brother Trevor Moorcroft has been super-useful in performing factual research for me (and for several of my author friends). My thanks to him as always.

Gratitude for authorly chat and support goes to Pia Fenton, Myra Kersner, Mark West, and many members of the amazing Romantic Novelists' Association. Talking about publishing never gets old.

Further appreciation to:

The members of Team Sue Moorcroft for their support and for helping me choose character names (if you like my novels, you can join the Team via my website at www.suemoorcroft.com); and Teamster Janina Simpson for once again lending me her dog Daisy to live with Thea. Everyone who follows my social media accounts – especially if you send me nice messages or spread the word about my books by sharing my posts. Online groups where readers gather to talk about books. And Bookbloggers, who review my books and join my blog tours, earning a special place in my heart.

A *Skye Full of Stars* is my twenty-fifth published novel. My writing life changed when I teamed up with agent Juliet Pickering of Blake Friedmann, who sold the ninth of those to Avon Books UK, HarperCollins. Since then, Avon has taken me to number one in the UK Amazon chart and made me a *Sunday Times* bestseller. The team at Blake Friedmann has sold my books in different languages and in many countries. Juliet and all at Blake Friedmann; editor Helen Huthwaite and the Avon team – you're awesome.

And thank *you*, dear reader, for picking up this book. That makes you awesome too.

In memory of my grandparents

Grandad Joe Moorcroft
Grandmother Elizabeth Moorcroft née Parr
Grandad Sidney Holmes
Granny Edna Holmes née Pickering

Chapter One

Ezzie Wynter, manager of Rothach Hall, had the best job in the world at one of the most beautiful spots on the Isle of Skye.

Through the tall, elegant windows of her panelled office, lawns and gardens glittered with November frost. Beyond that lay the parkland, the silvery waters of the Sound of Sleat and then the mainland's green and purple mountains, already dusted with snow. But what kept drawing Ezzie's attention from checking over the Christmas decorations for the hall's public rooms was a tall man in his sixties huddled into a shapeless, dated black overcoat and woollen hat. He stood where the drive broadened before the semi-circular steps, his hesitant gaze on the big double doors like a child unsure of his welcome at a party.

Skye didn't draw as many winter tourists as it did from spring to autumn, so Rothach Hall was staffed sparingly at present. Orla from reception was off for a few days, and the new assistant manager wouldn't arrive until February, so today Ezz had been the one to put out the sign saying *Public rooms open*. Now pride in the hall prompted her to offer further encouragement to their lone winter visitor to enjoy the public rooms' polished wood and pink-streaked Skye marble. She put down a box of red baubles on tartan ribbon, grabbed her long, tailored coat from its hook and tip-tapped over the tiles of the lofty reception area past the mahogany reception desk. Opening the doors, she stepped out into the bitingly cold air with a bright, professional smile. 'Good morning. Were you hoping to come in? We're open.'

The man looked startled, and he was either given to old-fashioned gestures or hot flushes because he removed his hat to show a closely shaved head. As he gazed up at her, at the top of the steps, his lips formed a slow half-smile. 'Thanks. Are you a guide?'

Skye attracted visitors from around the world, so she was unsurprised that his accent placed him somewhere in the middle of England, though further west than Suffolk, where she'd grown up. 'I'm the manager, Esmerelda Wynter. I'm afraid the public rooms aren't big enough to warrant guides. There are interesting information cards, though, prepared by a historian.' She hoped he didn't have a reading issue like her sister, Thea, because there was no aural alternative. Her blonde, shoulder-length hair blew annoyingly across her face, silky, yet poker-straight, and she pushed it back.

Finally, he began to tread slowly up the steps. But he didn't gaze into the panelled lobby, where the dogleg staircase soared up to the next floor, instead pausing to give her a shy smile. 'Have you been manager long? It looks a lovely place to work.'

'I've worked here for over nine years, but as assistant manager till a few months ago. The public rooms are to the left and also up these stairs.' She indicated the way to the first tall, gracious room at the rear of the lobby and then the imposing wooden staircase. A large glossy white door to their right was marked with an uncompromising *Private*, because it accessed the Larsson family's own quarters. They owned Rothach Hall and were due to visit for Christmas this year. Previously, their visits had fallen in spring or summer, so one of Ezz's current preoccupations was waking the hall from its customary winter semi-hibernation. Hoping to encourage him indoors so she could return to her desk, she added, 'The public room furniture predates the hall's restoration and there are framed examples of the fabric and wallpaper of the historical décor. There are also fine, traditional Skye marble fire surrounds and mirrored overmantels.'

'Thanks.' He continued to smile.

He didn't set off her 'unwanted attentions' radar, but it seemed good sense to make it clear that she wasn't alone, although it sometimes seemed as if she staffed the entire place by herself in winter. 'Both the gardeners are here today if you have any questions about the grounds. Enjoy yourself. I'm afraid I'm expected on a video call.'

With a nod and a last smile, he ambled across the lobby towards the public rooms with their faded tartan upholstery and watercolour paintings.

Back in her office, she hung up her coat and switched her attention from investigating the Christmas decorations for the upcoming decking of Rothach Hall to the computer on the antique walnut desk. Earlier, she'd been searching for the standard operating procedure files. Unfortunately, her predecessor in this lovely office, Tavish

MacBetha, having departed on bad terms, had provided no job description or handover notes. Ezz frequently had to formulate files and records from scratch because he'd apparently deleted random items as a you-can-kiss-my-sweet-backside-goodbye gesture.

The management of the building and staff was no problem in view of her years as assistant manager, but so far as her interaction with the Larsson family went, she was feeling her way. Tavish had dealt with the family himself wherever possible and given the impression of possessing special skills. From what Ezz had been able to glean whenever watching him in action, he not only did just whatever Erik, Grete and family required, but he also did it unobtrusively and obsequiously. He'd hinted at holding vital qualifications in five-star hospitality and having experience in a 'private household'. As he'd passed on none of his knowledge, since taking over as manager in July she'd paid for online tuition. This placed great emphasis on 'high-level service' and 'an impeccable say-yes attitude', which recommended phrases such as 'you need only tell me what you'd like' rather than bombarding employers with direct questions.

Clearly, the polite-and-helpful manner that had served her as assistant manager required adjustment now she was manager – or 'estate manager', which, apparently, she should have been calling herself. Her dark suit remained the same, but colourful manicures had been replaced by clear polish, and her at-work make-up was discreet – which was a shame when she had bright blue eyes to make the most of.

The course termed owners of 'substantial private households' as 'globe-trotting elite', and she acknowledged that the Larssons fell into that category. Their fish processing plants in Sweden and Norway might not be glamorous but generated the money to restore Rothach Hall as the family's retreat and a visitor attraction on an island off the west coast of Scotland. The hall provided salaries not just for Ezz but also for her sister Thea and the rest of the full-time staff, and seasonal staff from May to October. Despite all this, Erik and Grete had genial, down-to-earth manners – if you didn't cross their boundaries on matters such as how other members of staff were treated – as Tavish had discovered to his cost. Ezz was more wary of their children and grandchildren, who'd been born into wealth and private education.

Now, it was Grete who'd be video-calling her, probably to give instructions regarding festive celebrations. Ezz ran her eyes over the notepad where she'd made notes about things like Christmas trees and menus, then checked her suit and hair before joining the call, professional smile at the ready.

The screen flickered, then an image formed of a smart, older woman, silver-framed glasses matching her silver hair. Ezzie's smile widened. Grete was a powerhouse despite her seventy-or-so years. Her management style consisted of telling people what she wanted with a twinkling smile and expecting it to be done. Now, her eyes crinkled to slits and her soft Norwegian accent emanated from the machine. 'Ezzie! How are you?'

'Very well, thank you,' Ezzie answered. 'And you?'

'Good, good. We must speak of Christmas.' Grete's English was good, much better than her Swedish husband Erik's. Their children – Mats, Jonas and Maja – spoke fluent English in what sounded to Ezzie like a lightly American accent, perhaps from attending international school. She'd investigated the term and found it meant

5

multinational students, multilingual instruction and global perspective, which sounded like a privileged start in life.

'Of course. You only need to tell me what you'd like.' Ezzie poised her pen over her pad.

But instead of providing details about the family visit, Grete asked, 'How far are you with plans to make a Christmas attraction at Rothach?'

Ezzie did a mental swerve to meet the unexpected question. 'The lantern walk around the grounds and gardens will be easy to create, and Dilly at the Nature Garden Café has agreed to extend café opening hours for events, with a Christmas snack menu. I've been working on the programme starting next winter,' she added cautiously, hoping she hadn't got something horribly wrong and was supposed to be ready with a full winter wonderland already.

Grete propped herself comfortably on her elbows. 'We did say next year. But I have wondered whether we can do anything this winter.'

Ezzie sought a positive way of saying that there was no time to advertise, and that interest would take a while to build. She licked her lips. 'Of course. I'll work on where best to find our customers.'

Grete's eyes twinkled. 'Ezzie, I know you cannot produce a few hundred visitors to Skye in December when it is already November 7th. But I have the idea that we should talk to the island's bigger hotels and offer a short event for their guests. Many hotels advertise winter breaks with Christmas menus. A small-scale event would test the market.'

Relief at this eminently practical plan made Ezzie brightly enthusiastic as she scribbled notes. Her online course had advocated developing the memory of an elephant rather than writing things down, but that sounded risky. 'I can certainly look into that for you.'

Grete nodded. 'I will work with you on making Rothach a Christmas attraction. It will be a new project for me. I plan to arrive at Rothach in two days and stay until Christmas to enjoy Skye. I'm leaving Erik with the fish,' she added wryly.

Ezz smiled at the small joke and hoped that nothing in her expression gave away her astonishment that instead of arriving around three weeks before Christmas as previously planned, Grete was arriving *soon* and apparently intended to spend a couple of months on Skye. She focused on logistics. 'I'll make Gwen aware, so she has your suite ready.' Maintaining her anything-is-possible air she asked, 'Will you want the family areas decorating for Christmas, for when you arrive? The public rooms will be decorated soon.'

'But for the family rooms, not until December.' Grete propped her chin on her fist. 'For the first evening, perhaps Gwen will prepare my favourite Scottish meal – haggis with . . . Tell me again the name.' Her smile became anticipatory.

'With tatties and neeps – which is potatoes and swede,' Ezzie supplied promptly.

'Ha, yes.' Grete beamed. 'With also chocolate dessert. Not Scottish, but it is what I like.'

Ezz noted that on her pad. 'I look forward to seeing you at Rothach again on . . .' she glanced at her calendar '. . . Saturday. You need only tell me if you'd like meeting at an airport.' They often flew into Inverness, but Glasgow was also feasible.

Grete hesitated. 'Let me return to you on that.

Meanwhile, I will send Gwen a shopping list. Oh, and Esmerelda, Mats will also contact you very soon with his own arrangements.'

Ezzie hesitated. Gwen filling the cupboards and fridge as requested was nothing new, but Mats calling Ezzie directly was. The eldest of Grete and Erik's children, he was active in the family business. She'd interacted with him, his wife Inger and their children when the family spent summers at Rothach, but only superficially. Mats was tall, fair and good-looking. Inger was so polished and beautiful that she'd made Ezz feel like a conker husk, and habitually issued orders for her family without even looking up from her phone. Though Ezz wondered what 'arrangements' Grete could be alluding to, she didn't want to break the rule of questioning her employer so said calmly, 'Of course.'

Grete ended with a brisk but friendly goodbye. Then Ezz was free to arch her eyebrows and let her face reflect her thoughts – which were: *Why is Grete coming to Skye for so long without Erik? And why would Mats Larsson want to speak to me?*

As she had no choice but to wait and see, she stacked the boxes of Christmas decorations to the floor for now and began to research quality Skye hotels that they might work with on Grete's new project.

In a good suburb of snowy Gothenburg in south-west Sweden, Mats Larsson stared from his apartment window watching his children, three-year-old Alvin and five-year-old Astrid, skipping around the gated gardens belonging to his apartment block. Alvin's snowsuit was green and Astrid's purple with silver stars. Their nanny, Josefin, who was happy to act as if she were five rather than fifty-five, kicked snow into glistening arcs that made the children scream with laughter as the spicules blew back into their pink-cheeked faces.

Mats smiled. Nobody could fail to be cheered by laughing children. Alvin plopped backwards into a miniature snowdrift and Josefin swooped him up, turning a bumped bottom into something else to giggle over. Josefin was a prize – overpaid, judging by what he knew other parents shelled out, but worth every krona. He'd gone for a Swedish nanny this time, though one with good English. He, his brother Jonas and sister Maja had all been brought up to be bilingual, and were each doing the same for their children.

He moved his gaze to the phone in his hand, rereading his mother's message of five minutes ago, informing him that she'd told Esmerelda Wynter, the manager at the family's second home in Scotland, to expect his call. Mats and Grete had made their travel plans despite frowns from his larger-than-life father – amiably bossy, lovingly impatient, and always mercurial – Erik. At forty-six, Mats was more than capable of running his own life, but he didn't often disregard his dad's opinion quite as directly as he presently was.

Mats tapped Esmerelda Wynter's number in his phone's contact list. As he listened to the calling tone, an image sprang to his mind of the efficient, blonde, blue-eyed Englishwoman in neat heels and a severe uniform that flattered her tall, slender figure. Dad had sacked the last manager, unctuous Tavish. His parents had told him the story, but this year had been so stressful that it had fallen through the cracks of his mind, especially as Ms Wynter seemed a nicer person than Tavish and his parents held her in high regard. He watched Astrid, Alvin and Josefin heaping up snow that he judged would soon become a snowman, patting handfuls of it onto the fat white body. Every face wore a smile.

A smooth, female voice echoed in his ear. 'Ezzie Wynter. Good afternoon.'

'Good afternoon, Ezzie,' he answered briskly, glad she'd reminded him of her preferred name. 'This is Mats Larsson. I'm calling to say that I'll be arriving at Rothach Hall on Saturday with my two children and their nanny.' Then he wished he'd thought to begin with, 'How are you?' as he would have if he didn't have so much on his mind. She was a pleasant, polite person and he didn't mean to be aloof. He continued, 'I know my mother's already contacted you. We'll be arriving together. I hope you'll be able to find my nanny, Josefin, a room close to the children – one that won't be needed when the rest of the family arrive for Christmas.'

'Of course,' she replied serenely. 'Everything will be ready for you.'

'So, that's three adults and two children arriving on Saturday, November 9th,' he emphasised, in case her controlled response arose from not grasping the imminence of the visit. He pictured her behind the desk in the manager's office, sharp-but-pretty features composed as she agreed with all he said. Tavish would have managed to convey a hint of reproach in his polite replies, letting Mats know that everything *would* be ready, but that not every employee would be capable of such wizardry. 'Can somebody meet us at Inverness Airport if I send flight details? The seven-seater Volvo will be spacious enough, with the roof box for luggage.'

'Of course,' she repeated.

He watched Astrid knock Alvin into a snowdrift and

Alvin decide to laugh rather than cry. The little boy staggered to his feet in his tiny green snow suit, then brought up a handful of snow and squashed it into his sister's face. Mats grinned with parental pride, both because Alvin had evidently been planning his reprisal while he was down and because Astrid squealed with laughter, rather than getting upset. Yet somehow, the sight of his children being adorable, sparked anger – not at them, of course, but at Andreas who'd uncaringly split up Mats' family over a year ago without apparently worrying about the effect on the children. There had been no point remonstrating with Inger for not trying harder at a marriage they'd both known wasn't working, but her affair with Andreas had also been a blow to Mats' pride.

He sighed. A sojourn in the Isle of Skye would be a distraction for Alvin and Astrid and provide Mats with some much-needed peace. The children usually saw their loving grandmother every week or two, but her holidaying with them for a couple of months would be a bonus. Then, in a few weeks, their grandfather, uncles, aunts and five cousins would descend to play Christmas games and eat Christmas goodies and share in the mountain of Christmas gifts.

'Mr Larsson?' The tentative voice in his ear reminded him that Ezzie Wynter waited patiently on the other end of the phone.

'Mats,' he corrected her, feeling unreasonably pricked at her formality. He cast around for something he could have been mulling over to account for his silence. 'I hope it's possible to have toys delivered to Rothach?' In all the upheaval, he hadn't yet bought a single Christmas gift.

'Of course,' Ezzie replied. 'Delivery times are usually a little longer than to the mainland, that's all.'

'Good,' he said. 'Then we'll see you on Saturday.'

'It will be a pleasure to see your family back at Rothach Hall,' she responded with extreme courtesy, before they ended the call. Although Mats understood why his dad had promoted Ezzie, her decorum was overdone for his taste. Tavish had been the same. Larsson Fiskeri did business in the UK and, judging from that experience, other Brits spoke normally.

After a glance outside to check the children still played happily and were unlikely to come up to the apartment in the next five minutes, he dialled again. After a moment, he heard the familiar gruff, '*Hallå*, Mats.'

Automatically, he switched to Swedish. '*Hej*, Pappa. Just letting you know that we've confirmed our arrangements to leave for Skye tomorrow. We'll be waiting for you when you come for Christmas.'

Erik gave a disapproving snort. 'This is unnecessary. You have Nanny Josefin to look after your children. I don't see why you're taking a long leave. You're so impetuous, Mats.'

Mats rubbed his forehead. It wasn't the first time he'd been called that. 'I want to be with my children at a difficult time for them, Pappa. I don't approve of Inger taking an extended holiday away from the kids any more than you do, but getting engaged to Andreas, a rich man, has gone to her head. The kids will miss her while she's on a superyacht for three months with Andreas and his friends. They've had too much to deal with this year. I'm needed more as a father than as chief financial officer of Larsson Fiskeri.' Josefin valiantly divided her time between Inger's house and his apartment just as Astrid and Alvin shared their week between the two, but since the breakdown of his marriage, Mats had become a more hands-on dad.

12

Bath-time bubbles and book-time cuddles had quickly shown him what he used to miss out on every time he was late home from work. He took a breath and softened his tone. 'I work hard enough to justify a rare long leave, don't I? I have an efficient deputy and I'll be contactable by phone or email, just as you are when you're at Rothach. I'll return in January. The children aren't even at *dagis* here. Next year, Astrid will begin compulsory education and the opportunity will be gone.' There was no point in sending the children to *dagis* – day care – when they had a nanny.

Half-heartedly, Erik grumbled, 'I'll never retire if my children don't take the company seriously.'

Mats smothered a laugh. 'If all our family members resigned tomorrow, Larsson Fiskeri would sail on with others in our roles. That's how business works, and you created an exceptional business.'

'Hm.' Erik sighed. 'At least your mother will have your company. Travel safely.' Then he was gone, Mats' quirky, growly dad, who'd worked so hard all his life that he was finding it hard to stop.

Mats checked outside again, squinting against the glare of the snow to locate his two blond cherubs, smiling as he caught the bubbling sound of Alvin's laughter. His priority was those two figures in colourful snowsuits. Everything else came second – even the family business. He'd leave it if he had to.

An hour later, Ezzie's usual calm had deserted her and she slapped her hands on her desk until her palms stung. 'Shit, shit, *shit*!' Each drawer in her beautiful desk had been upended, her computer subjected to every search she could think of, but there was no sign of what she knew had once

13

existed – the plan of the Larssons' section of Rothach Hall, with notes on which family member occupied each room.

Irritably, she reached for her phone to call the housekeeper. Gwen was friendly and bright, sailing through her sixties like Captain Imperturbable, a font of Rothach Hall knowledge. 'Hello, Ezzie.'

Ezzie felt reassured just to hear her musical Scottish lilt. 'Gwen, do you know where each of the family sleeps? I'm afraid the plan's gone missing.'

Gwen laughed. 'Missing? Ach, amazing how certain things mysteriously vanished when Tavish took himself out the door. Yes, dear, I know most, I believe, and we can confirm with Grete. We've plenty of time before they arrive for Christmas.'

Ezzie didn't sigh, because not even with this trusted colleague of over nine years would she be anything but cool and professional. 'I've just learnt that Grete, Mats, his two children and their nanny are arriving on Saturday and staying up to and including Christmas, so we need to have those rooms ready straight away, I'm afraid.'

Gwen earned points in Ezzie's book by not breathing a word of dismay or anxiety. In fact, she sounded delighted. 'Oh, really? Then we'd best get on.'

Ezz grabbed her pad and pen. 'Can you meet me in reception to go into the family side and draw up a fresh plan?' The private quarters were often referred to as 'the family side' by Rothach Hall staff.

'I'll be right there.' Gwen ended the call.

Two minutes later, Gwen arrived through a small door marked *Staff Only*, which accessed the mud room, staff facilities and then the rear courtyard. Her uniform was a black and grey striped dress with flat black tie-ups, her dark grey hair in a smooth bun. She glided like a galleon

14

under sail. 'I've told Georgia and Peony to go in once we're done,' she said, referring to the other housekeeping staff, who communicated mainly with each other and seemed happy to live their quiet life in the staff accommodation behind the hall.

Ezz unlocked the big, glossy white door marked *Private*. The family side was silent, as if waiting for the people it belonged to rather than Gwen and Ezz, the smell of lemon polish on the air. At the far end of the corridor, the kitchen was more farmhouse than grand house, with waxed wood cabinets and worn marble surfaces. All the downstairs walls wore coats of emulsion rather than posh wallpaper, even the main lounge and the home office, and the floor tiles had been refurbished during the hall's restoration, rather than ripped up and replaced. The furnishings were a mixture of traditional pieces that the family had bought with the house more than a dozen years ago, plus modern additions. Ezzie strongly suspected the latter had come from IKEA and that Erik and Grete would have enjoyed assembling them, Erik laughing until his cheeks glowed red and Grete's eyes crinkling to slits above her broad smile.

Gwen moved towards the staircase. 'Shall we go up?'

Ezzie followed her bulky figure over sage green carpet. Every brass stair rod gleamed, because Gwen, Peony and Georgia kept the place spotless whether it was echoing emptily or ringing with happy Larsson voices. On the first landing, Gwen sailed across a capacious area where the last of the daylight poured through the massive windows that characterised the hall, then halted at a pair of doors. 'This is Grete and Erik's suite, of course.' She opened the doors and Ezz saw a giant bay window framed in blood-red velvet, a couple of comfortably creased cream leather chairs and a low table.

Gwen waved towards the door set into the left-hand wall. 'Bedroom with twin en suites.'

Ezzie's pen flew over the page of her pad she'd headed *1st floor*, sketching and scribbling. She could draw a more careful version later.

Back on the landing, Gwen led the way down a corridor. 'Mats and Inger stay in a turret room.' The room was round and decorated with dazzling silk fabrics.

Ezz halted, pen poised. 'Mats didn't mention Inger, so I presume she'll come later. He said it would be him and his children, with the nanny, Josefin. She's not the same nanny who came the summer before last. Her name's spelt with a J but it's pronounced like a Y – Yosser-feen. The youngest child will be three or so now.' She made a note to work out all the children's ages – helpful for when arranging Christmas trees and other possible hazards. 'Where do the children sleep? Mats requested that Josefin be found a room nearby, but not one that other family would need when they arrive for Christmas.'

Gwen nodded. 'When they came last, the two rooms between the master suite and the turret were used. The wee boy slept with the nanny they had then – an American lass. She always talked to the children in English and Astrid was already swapping between Swedish and English as if it was the most natural thing in the world.'

'All the Larsson children I've met speak English as well as Swedish. It makes me ashamed of my own language skills.' Ezz took out her phone and began to text. 'I'll check Mats' preference about sleeping arrangements. Who else sleeps on this floor?'

'The room down the end is a playroom, but everyone else sleeps on the floor above.' Gwen's quick, flat-footed stride soon carried her to the playroom, a long room with uncurtained windows, two blue sofas, a group of tartan beanbags, a big TV and plastic drawers for games and toys. A bookcase displayed books in English and what Ezz presumed to be Swedish. Or Norwegian.

A ping of her phone signalled Mats' reply. Ezz read it aloud. '"Astrid and Alvin will share a room. No doubt we can make changes if they suddenly want one each."' She replied, *Of course*, then added to her plan Astrid and Alvin in the room next to the turret and Josefin in the one after.

They climbed a smaller staircase to confirm who lived where on the second floor, and, finally, put their heads together to try and remember the names of the children. 'Astrid and Alvin belong to Mats and Inger,' said Ezz, to recap.

'Jonas and Ebba have Emil and Filip,' Gwen added. 'They're the eldest of the cousins, I'm sure. Then Maja and Nils have Liam and Walter – he's lively, that Walter.' She smiled fondly.

'They have another,' Ezzie recalled. 'In the summer, Erik and Grete told me they were grandparents again and the baby was about six months.'

'Maybe walking by now then,' Gwen suggested. 'Not that I have my own wee 'uns, but my sister has enough grandkids for us both.'

They trod back downstairs. It was nearly five, and a luminous blue dusk was rapidly darkening the windows. Before Gwen retired to her apartment at the back of the hall, she paused. 'No doubt they'll be seeing in the bells with us?'

In Scotland, Hogmanay – known to the rest of the world as New Year – was celebrated even more than Christmas, with parties, ceilidhs, festivals and the enthusiastic

17

rendering of 'Auld Lang Syne'. Ezzie paused on this sinking reminder that this year, because the Larsson family would be in residence, she wouldn't be able to go with Thea to see their eldest sister Valentina for Hogmanay. Now she was Rothach Hall's manager, she'd probably be expected to be on call. Though Valentina and family had recently moved from Edinburgh to Inverness, it would still be too far away if Ezz were needed.

'I believe so.' She made a note to consider a Hogmanay event next year, when they started a winter programme for the public. Maybe the Nature Garden Café could serve the haggis, neeps and tatties that Grete loved, with an alternative of stovies – which looked to Ezzie like a disassembled cottage pie.

Gwen rested her hand on the door to the reception lobby. 'Georgia and Peony are taking leave over Christmas, so we might need a seasonal or two.'

'If we can,' Ezzie said drily. She hadn't been impressed with Georgia and Peony wanting Christmas and New Year off when the family were to be at the hall. Evidently, they hadn't done her online course, which said household staff should forget any such expectation, but Tavish had agreed it, apparently – *just* before he'd left. There hadn't been much Ezz could do.

'We can,' Gwen answered with a broad grin that creased the weathered skin around her grey eyes. 'My sister's granddaughter Caitriona has already said she'll be home from university and is keen to reduce her overdraft with a wee job.'

'That sounds perfect.' Diplomatically, Ezz added, 'We'll have to be flexible this Christmas, with the family being here.'

Gwen shrugged. 'I would only have visited my sister on

Christmas Day. Her shower are so noisy that the hall will be more restful, even with folk to feed.'

Ezz smiled, envisaging Gwen tying her black apron over her striped dress and whipping up Christmas dinners on demand. 'Thank you.'

When Gwen had departed, Ezz headed for her office, phoning her sister Thea as she went. 'Hey, Head Gardener. Just letting you know of the imminent arrival of family on Saturday. Grete, Mats, two children and the nanny.' Her online course would have had her refer to them as 'Madam, Mr Mats Larsson and his children,' but they'd told her to use first names, so she did.

Like Gwen, Thea dealt with the situation. 'OK. I'll delay the planting of the tulip bulbs so Sheena and I can get the garden vac on the pathways.' Sheena was the assistant head gardener. She worked daylight hours only from November to February, unless Thea was off. As Skye winter days were short, that usually meant nine-thirty a.m. to three-thirty p.m., or maybe four.

'Great. Thanks.' Happy that Thea had everything under control, Ezz settled to working on a neater floor plan. As she wrote names into boxes representing bedrooms, she mused on all the empty rooms. By her count, even when all the family arrived, that would still leave around eight rooms unoccupied – mind-boggling to someone living in a two-bedroom cottage in Rothach village, nestling below the hall in a bay that looked to have been scooped out with a spoon.

But she felt no envy. The Larssons could afford an enormous house, partially open to the public, with a café and a car park in the beautiful grounds, but she was rich in other ways, like having two fantastic sisters, Thea and Valentina, and this job that she loved.

She paused on a sliver of regret. She did feel a tiny bit isolated this winter, as Thea was now part of a couple with lovely Deveron Dowie. And in the summer Thea who, like Ezz and Valentina, had been adopted when very young, had found her French birth mother, Ynez. Understandably, Ynez and her partner Jean-Jacques occupied some of Thea's time with calls and video chats. They even planned to buy a cottage on the mainland, and Thea and Dev had visited them in Brittany in September. Adding to her slight loneliness, Ezz had paused her dating apps after the last man she'd met, Henry the auctioneer – she thought of him that way because he announced his profession so frequently – had been a bit weird.

But her heart lifted as she remembered that Valentina, husband Gary and lovely son Barnaby would be squashing into Ezz's house over Christmas, Thea's spare room being too small. Even if Ezz's duties took up some of the time, there would still be some to spend with them.

Who needed eight spare rooms, when the one you had was full of family? Family meant love.

Chapter Two

Ezzie had finally found time to complete checking the stock of Christmas decorations for the public rooms and ordered fresh ribbon and extra Christmas swags online, when Thea popped her head around the office door. 'Can I get a lift home?' When the days were long in summer, Thea would walk home through the copse, but in winter that gravel path was lonely and pitch-dark.

'Absolutely.' She smiled at her petite sister, bundled up in a green fleece beneath her waxed jacket, with a woolly hat pulled over her dark hair. Her work boots were a snug, waterproof black.

Thea, who'd started work at Rothach at the same time as Ezzie, came in and flopped into a chair, rubbing her hands. 'I love Skye when it's frosty and there are icicles everywhere, but I also love your car's seat heaters.'

'They'll barely have time to warm before we reach the village,' Ezz objected.

'Warmer than my bum after a day outdoors,' Thea confided.

Ezz protested. 'Eww!' They laughed as she closed down her computer, put on her black coat and changed into boots, as her office shoes weren't much protection against a frosty evening. Thea just did up the buttons on her waxed jacket.

Outside, they crossed the courtyard, mindful of the uneven paving. The outside lights would dim automatically at six, leaving just enough illumination for anyone moving between the hall, staff accommodation and the car park behind the big wooden-framed greenhouse. On the way home sometimes, Ezz liked to switch off the lights and wait until she could see a million, billion, trillion stars, glittering down. Maybe she'd add silver star-shaped decorations to her online order tomorrow. They'd look amazing dangling from the pendant lamps in the public rooms.

As she beeped her car open so Thea could get in while Ezz scraped glistening white frost from the windscreen with a satisfying rasping noise, she wondered how the Larssons would like Rothach Hall in winter, with just six hours of daylight. It was a big change from summer, when dawn came at four and daylight lasted till around ten p.m. The pattern might be similar to Sweden, but here they were on holiday, with leisure hours to fill. The cinema was an hour's drive away in Portree, and the only McDonald's on the island was Murray McDonald's Vehicle Repair Garage.

She scraped her windscreen then scrambled into the driver's seat, gave the wipers a couple of swishes to clear the last sparkles of frost, and took the service drive through the back of the estate, headlights flitting across bushes and seed heads wearing glittering white jackets.

She followed the drive past the playthings that saw few children clamber over them in winter, and the Nature Garden Café that, until spring returned, would only open between ten a.m. and three p.m., mainly for local meet-ups like Knit 'n' Natter and Rhyme Time. Strings of flickering white lights outlined the café door and a row of illuminated icicles hung from the roof.

'Pretty,' Thea observed. 'But I prefer the real icicles Jack Frost hangs all over Skye in winter. We had a lovely home in Suffolk with Mum and Dad and their crazy musician friends dropping in all the time, but I adore Skye. And if I hadn't come here, I wouldn't have met Deveron.' Satisfaction rang rich in her voice.

'You and Dev are sickeningly loved up,' Ezz teased. Actually, she couldn't have been happier for her little sister now Deveron, a seasonal gardener at the hall until a couple of months ago, had moved into Thea's pretty, thistle-purple cottage. Not wishing to highlight that Thea's newfound happiness meant Ezz spending more evenings alone in her Chapel Road home, she responded to Thea's other comment. 'If it wasn't for that car accident in Suffolk, we'd never have moved here.'

'Ugh. Don't rake that up.' Thea made a cross with her fingers, as if warding off a vampire.

The automatic gates opened, allowing the car to turn onto Manor Road, which villagers referred to as 'the road above', and it was indeed higher than the village cradled in Rothach Bay. Ezzie drove cautiously as frozen puddles edged the road and there were no streetlamps. Amongst the scrubby hedgerow, her headlights picked out an outcrop of rock decorated with a curtain of icicles. 'We're forecast a particularly chilly winter on the island this year. I don't know if it's my imagination, but Skye

23

seems to have become more wintry in the past few years.' Ezz steered around a curve.

'I'd better get on with digging up the dahlia tubers in that case.' Then Thea's phone buzzed, and she fished it out as Ezz turned right into Low Road marked *Rothach Village*, slowing for the undulating, mainly single-track lanes where shrubs lolled over stone walls. She smiled at a yellow notice reading '*Border collie crossing*', though she'd yet to see a dog in the road, and an honesty box beside a tree stump where, in summer, someone sold eggs and garden produce.

'Valentina's texted. She wants to FaceTime us both as soon as possible.' Pleasure rang in Thea's voice. But then her tone altered. 'I hope everything's OK.'

Ezz glanced at the dashboard clock. It wasn't yet six p.m. 'Now?' Low Road became Chapel Road, and she drove past her own front door. The landlord had painted the cottage 'dawn blush'. Ezz thought that whoever had named the gingerbread colour had never witnessed the soft pink of a Skye dawn. Electing to avoid the steep slope of Creag an Lolaire as rivulets frequently froze across it, she bore right to Bridge Road.

'I'll ask.' Thea tapped her phone screen. She was easily overwhelmed by dense blocks of text or long forms, so short phone messages were more her style. Ezz negotiated the humped stone bridge, then the slope up Glen Road and into Loch View. Thistledome, Thea's cottage, stood at the top. In daylight, you could see over the cottage roofs to the crystal waters of Rothach Bay far below. In the darkness, the view was of the star-strewn sky above a spangling of streetlights, dwindling to the pinprick mooring lights of boats wintering in the shelter of the bay.

Ezzie drew up outside Thistledome, its cheerily lit

windows suggesting that Deveron was home, just as Thea received another message. 'Valentina says now's good,' she reported. 'Maybe she's working from home. She doesn't usually leave the office this early.' Valentina was a lawyer in a big corporation and worked long hours, racing home to spend time with six-year-old Barnaby and usually only starting dinner once her beloved boy was safely in bed. Even then she worked on emails while it cooked.

Spectres of illness or similarly bad news assailed Ezzie, but she kept them to herself as she hopped from the car and scurried up the path behind Thea, huddling into her coat as the freezing air nipped her skin. The front door opened, and a bundle of pearly grey fur and bright eyes greeted them with a joyful, 'Arf, arf!' Daisy, Thea's noisy little dog, who Dev had rescued in the summer, considered herself the guardian of Thistledome.

Behind Daisy, a male voice boomed in a Scottish burr, 'Come here, yer scrumptious woman.' Then, as the tall, dark, curly-haired owner of the voice came fully into view, he added in sheepish, more natural tones, 'Oh. Um, hello, Ezz.'

'Hi, Dev,' Ezz returned with a broad grin, crowding into the brightly lit home so she could shut the door on the frigid evening. 'Sorry to play gooseberry. Hello, Daisy!' Ezzie waited out Thea and Dev exchanging greeting kisses by fussing the little fluffball, who looked as if she might have a healthy dose of poodle in her pint-sized make-up. Ezz had once scandalised Thea by observing that Daisy was like a dust bunny with legs and ears.

Finally, Thea broke away from Dev, and the little dog abandoned Ezz in favour of treating her beloved mistress to a wiggle-dance of joy.

'I'll make coffee,' said Deveron, and Daisy promptly

changed allegiance again to scamper along with him. It could have been that Dev held a special place in her heart after he'd scooped her half-drowned from the burn last summer – but more likely, it was the mouth-watering smells emanating from the kitchen.

Thea took Ezz into the tiny lounge, where flames danced cosily in the woodstove, and they shared the sofa while Thea set up FaceTime on her phone. Seconds later, Valentina appeared on the screen in a blouse and skirt, her dark hair swept up. Straightening her hair was one of Valentina's things, as if no one would take seriously a female lawyer with natural ringlets. None of the sisters looked remotely like the others, each being separate adoptions, but they didn't need to be connected by blood. They were connected by their hearts.

'Are you all right?' Ezzie demanded, at the same moment Thea asked, 'What's wrong?'

Valentina's dark eyes twinkled. 'Am I not allowed any good news?'

'Spill it then,' Ezz demanded, instantly relieved. 'I put a meal in my multicooker this morning and it'll be turning to mush.' She and Valentina were the sisters who occasionally sparked off each other, though most of that had been left behind since they'd lost their mum and dad.

Valentina beamed. 'We've bought a holiday home. It's something we've been thinking about. I sold some shares, which did unexpectedly well, and also got a salary bonus. I wanted to invest in property and have somewhere to rent out when we're not using it ourselves.'

Ezzie stared. 'Wow. That's quite an announcement. But where compares to your three-bedroomed, two-bathroom apartment looking over Moray Firth in Rosemarkie Bay?' When Gary had been head-hunted by a company in

26

Inverness, Valentina hadn't wanted to live in the centre, when there were pretty places just outside the city.

Valentina's beaming smile only grew broader. 'It's number 1 Fishermen's Cottages on the Quays in Rothach Bay.'

Ezz felt a jolt of delight. '*Here?* Seriously? You'll be here for holidays?'

'Epic,' Thea breathed. 'That's fantastic.'

Gary slid his face into view, wearing a conservative haircut and a wry smile. 'I tried to talk her into somewhere warmer, preferably somewhere that wouldn't need gutting and starting again, but she's being stubborn.'

Valentina gave him a little shove. 'Stop raining on my parade. I wanted that cottage.'

Ezz's brain was ticking. 'If you've bought it already, this has been going through for ages and you haven't said a thing? Have you visited Rothach without telling us?'

'Of course not. I've done video walk-throughs with the agent.' Valentina made jazz hands. 'Ta-dah! I wanted it to be a surprise.'

This time, Gary grimaced. 'And she thinks she's going to arrange all the building work remotely.' His tone was sceptical.

'She will,' Ezzie defended her sister stoutly.

They chatted for twenty minutes, then Valentina checked her smartwatch. 'I have to collect Barnaby from his friend's house.'

A lot of husbands might have protested, *I'll go, darling. You chat with your sisters.* But Gary, never the most thoughtful of men, just nodded.

Once the call was over, Ezzie retrieved her coat from the back of the sofa, her mind buzzing. 'Won't it be awesome that they have a place here? We'll see more of Barnaby, as well as Valentina. And Gary,' she added. 'He didn't seem

27

excited for Valentina, did he? Maybe because she's the one funding the cottage.'

Thea's nose wrinkled as she followed Ezz into the hall. 'He and his brother William were spoilt by older parents. They've grown up competitive and self-orientated.'

'True,' Ezz conceded. 'It makes Gary a successful careerman but a less successful human being. Maybe he'll be all the better for playing a supporting role this time.' Ezzie popped into the kitchen to say goodbye to Dev and was soon picking her way down the icy path to her car, pausing to gaze at the neighbouring cottages sloping away from Thea's, their pastel colours muddy in the golden glow from old-fashioned streetlamps.

It was impossible to pick out Fishermen's Cottage down beside the rocky beach, but she still stared into the darkness and tried to fix the likely location in her mind. As the cottages stood right at one end of the bay, she usually saw them from the beach or from Harbour View. They nestled at the foot of the cliffs beneath Rothach Hall, on the Quays beside Causeway and Harbour View. No fishermen now lived in the row of four small residences, as far as she knew.

Ezzie hugged the knowledge that soon the sisters could be together more often. She climbed in her car and texted Valentina. *If you ever want to work remotely from Rothach, I'll help where I can with childcare on days off. Xx* Barnaby adored the rocky beach, and Ezz, never having had kids of her own, enjoyed scrambling around with him. It would bring fun into days off that were often spent on solitary walks or even wasted on chores.

Then she eased her little yellow car down the frosty lanes to her cosy cottage feeling happier than she had for ages.

Chapter Three

Unexpectedly, Mats was enjoying the journey from Sweden to Scotland. It wasn't a massive stride across the planet, but there were no direct flights. To make things easy on Alvin and Astrid, they were overnighting in an Amsterdam hotel, ready to continue on Saturday. Maybe Andreas would have chartered a flight – or maybe he had his own plane? – but that was a bit rich for Mats' blood.

Josefin had taken the children to bed after burgers and fries, so now he and his mother were relaxing over their wine while around them in the lounge bar was the chink of glasses and the hum of voices. 'This is restful.' He raised his glass to toast her. 'It's not often that it's just the two of us, unless we're at the office or one of the production plants.' Those caverns of ice, fish and stainless steel seemed far away already.

She returned his salute, the bar lights reflecting from the lenses of her spectacles as she settled deeper into her upholstered chair. 'It's good to finally step off the treadmill.'

He absorbed the comment. Grete had worked tirelessly at his dad's side for decades. Erik was a workaholic, rarely seeing the need to recharge his batteries, but it seemed Grete was tiring of it. It was a change that was understandable, but out of character.

Casually, he probed, 'Was Dad OK when you left?' He wiped a condensation ring from the light wood tabletop that was in keeping with the beige and blue décor in the bar. They spoke in Swedish, though her native Norwegian was perfectly comprehensible to him. She'd been married to a Swedish man and lived in Sweden for so long that she used more Swedish words than the average Norwegian.

She pulled a rueful face. 'He's wounded because I told him that if he never retires, he'll go to the next world directly from his desk.' She took several sips of wine.

'Oh,' he said, inadequately, trying to imagine that conversation and whether Erik had been startled by his usually supportive wife's blunt observation.

Perhaps the wine had loosened her tongue as Grete went on. 'We used to talk about travelling in our retirement, but it's never happened.' She twirled her wine glass by its stem. 'We're so lucky. We own a mansion on a wonderful island and yet we hardly visit it. Your pappa and I spent a couple of weeks there in summer this year and the rest of you went elsewhere.'

His brows rose. 'I didn't take a holiday. I was getting myself sorted out after getting divorced.'

'It must have been harder than it looked, then – a service moving you into that nice apartment you've rented.' She smiled to show she was teasing.

Drily, he returned, 'The upheaval was emotional. You

haven't been through a divorce.' An urge hit him to check she wasn't considering one. But what if she said yes? No matter his forty-six years, he really didn't want his parents to split up. 'But for me there was relief as much as sadness and disbelief,' he admitted. 'It's nice not to have to consider anyone but Alvin and Astrid. Inger's a bit of a princess.'

Grete looked troubled. 'I wish she hadn't gone away for so long. The children don't understand. I'm afraid she'll regret going dotty for Andreas eventually. He's cocooned by inherited wealth, spending much of his life in indolence, whereas working for Larsson Fiskeri, earning everything you have, has made you a strong, balanced person. Same for Jonas and Maja.' She smiled ruefully. 'Your father began with a fish stall and grew it into a successful organisation. Perhaps I shouldn't be surprised that he seems incapable of leaving it.'

Mats frowned, thinking of his dad, ruddy-faced, a shock of brindled hair, an enormous, booming, 'Har, har, *har*' of a laugh, often at his own unsophisticated sense of humour. Mats hadn't had any trouble choosing between the family firm and his children, but what if Erik had one day to choose between the company he'd nurtured and the wife who'd been with him every step of the way?

Would he get his priorities right?

Next day, they disembarked at Inverness Airport in the early afternoon. Astrid clutched a toy mermaid and Josefin's hand. Alvin was tired of planes and rode in Mats' arms. His hair, still the thistledown of babyhood, tickled Mats' chin.

Ezzie Wynter met them outside the arrivals gate, impeccable in her dark coat over her suit and impressing Mats by giving the children wide smiles and saying, 'It's such a pleasure to see you back in Scotland,' even before shaking hands with Grete, him and Josefin.

'Hello.' Astrid smiled sunnily, her fair hair waving about her head.

'*Hallå*,' Alvin echoed, after unplugging his thumb from his mouth.

'We're going to speak English a lot while we're here, aren't we?' Mats reminded him gently, and Alvin obligingly amended it to, 'Hello.'

Ezzie stacked their luggage on a trolley then steered it through the bright airport and out to the pick-up zone where the big grey Volvo that his parents kept at the hall waited. It was an overcast, windy day, and her blonde hair flew around her head as she pitted her slender frame against the vagaries of the trolley.

'I can do that,' he began uncomfortably, but Ezz just smiled, and as Alvin was now dozing in his arms, he couldn't press the point.

However, when they reached the Volvo, Ezz halted, expression dismayed as she looked from the suitcases to the luggage box – which was clearly out of her reach.

'No problem.' He let Grete and Josefin get the children into their car seats then he slid the suitcases into the capacious box while Ezzie looked mortified. 'It's no problem,' he repeated, hoping she'd be a bit less uptight about her duties.

Grete took the front passenger seat, Mats and Alvin settled in the middle row and Josefin and Astrid in the rear. Ezzie hurried to the driver's seat. Alvin had briefly roused but dropped off again. As Astrid and Josefin were engrossed in a game involving the colours of cars, Mats texted Inger to reassure her that the children were safe then watched the countryside around the airport and the waters of Rosemarkie Bay. He checked emails until Alvin woke up and wanted entertaining for the remainder of the two-and-a-half-hour trip. Together they gazed out at beautiful scenery, where the road wound first between agricultural fields and then narrowed to carry them through craggy hills that, in winter, were little more than pine and rocks. Still stretches of water like Loch Luichart boasted a few sailing boats for them to talk about, even on a raw winter day.

As they neared the end of the journey he said to the children, 'Watch out for the bridge. It takes us right over the sea and onto the Isle of Skye.'

Moments later Ezzie pointed through the windscreen at the graceful arches that gave way to an impressive arc against the blue-grey sky. 'We'll be going over in a moment.' She drove competently through the busy little town of Kyle of Lochalsh, then swept left to take the bridge.

'Boats,' Astrid shouted as the Volvo climbed, while Alvin gleefully waved to vessels approaching the bridge from both directions, foaming the steely grey sea into white wakes. They crested the bridge and drove onto the Isle of Skye, passing the white houses of Kyleakin on their left and soon heading over the moor to the Sleat Peninsula.

Twenty minutes more then Grete called, 'Here we are,' from the front seat as they bumped over a stone bridge and up the drive to Rothach Hall. Winter had bared the branches of the deciduous trees dotted among pine and spruce, but otherwise it looked exactly as it did last time he'd been here, the summer before last. He'd forgotten how much grassy parkland lay either side of the drive, studded with stands of trees, before the formal area. There, the hedges and conifers of the knot garden were so neatly trimmed that they looked like sculptures. The walls of the walled garden rose up to the left and the south lawns to the right before, finally, they drew up before the curved steps to the grand double doors of a gracious grey-stone building with tall windows and a turret.

Ezz said, 'Welcome back to Rothach Hall.'

Excited, the children couldn't wait to tumble from the car. Mats had time to heave out suitcases and bags from the luggage box before catching sight of his little blondies racing away over wet grass, quick and cute in shoes that wouldn't keep their feet dry. 'Astrid, Alvin,' he called, hastily thrusting the luggage box keys at Ezz as he and Josefin ran to corral the excited children and usher them towards the granite steps.

'I don't remember this place,' Astrid shouted, bouncing up the stone steps like a kangaroo.

'I do,' Alvin shouted back, having to climb the steps one at a time.

Mats laughed. 'You can't possibly, Alvin. You were tiny.'

'I do,' he maintained, but giggled at his own fibs, blue eyes dancing, and tiny white teeth flashing.

Heart full for his little boy, Mats swept him up and did kangaroo jumps up the steps like Astrid, who instantly began to kangaroo down again.

'Wait for me, I can't jump.' Grete laughed, hurrying after them. Josefin grabbed the children's bags and followed.

Mats felt a surge of excitement as the group poured across the lobby and into the private quarters. 'What do you think, Astrid and Alvin?' he asked, gazing around the lofty interior flooded with light, its white paintwork gleaming.

Astrid was already running for the big staircase, one arm out of her coat and her hat behind her on the hall floor. 'I'm going to see my room,' she cried. She paused. 'Which is my room?'

Mats raced after her, hampered by Alvin in his arms. 'Wait, Astrid. We'll find your room together.'

'Wait', 'stop', 'slow down' were phrases to which Astrid was deaf and she was on the first floor, trying to get into his parents' suite by the time Mats caught up with her.

'Astrid.' He injected calm reproach into his voice. '*Wait*. And do *not* use your feet to open a door. That's not your room. I'll show you where you and Alvin will sleep. Let's walk nicely.'

He took each of his children by their hands – stooping because three-year-old Alvin was still tiny – and escorted them decorously to the room beside the turret, which he'd agreed with Ezzie would be the children's. It was painted the pale blue of a winter's morning. Astrid gave a delighted shriek and threw herself on one of the single beds. Alvin emitted an ear-splitting yell of his own and took a run onto the same bed.

'This is my bed,' Astrid declared.

'*Nej*, my bed,' Alvin implored, eyes filling with tears as he gazed at Mats for support.

Mats encouraged them both off it. 'I think I'm going to let Alvin choose his bed first, because you were a bit rude, weren't you, Astrid? Which bed, Alvin?'

Alvin gazed around the tall, airy room with blue panels painted on the walls and blue curtains at the tall windows. The beds were identical. He glanced at Mats, then Astrid. Maybe out of contrariness or perhaps to appease his sister, he walked over to the other bed. 'This one.'

'That was nice of Alvin, wasn't it Astrid?' Mats asked gently.

'Yes,' she agreed, hurling herself back onto the bed she'd wanted all along.

Mats exchanged grins with Josefin, who'd followed

with the children's bags. 'This should be your room through here, Josefin.' Politely, he opened a white-painted door that led into a similar room but decorated in shades of yellow. 'There's a bathroom for you and the children across the corridor.'

Then he glanced out of the window and saw the big grey car still at the foot of the steps.

Ezzie Wynter was perched on a stool heaving the last suitcase from the luggage box, blonde hair and black coat flying in the wind. The rest of the baggage was neatly lined up at the top of the steps. Guilt stabbed him. There was he trying to instil a gracious attitude in his daughter, yet he'd thrust the keys at a member of staff without a please or thank you and left her to struggle when his height would have allowed him to reach the suitcases easily. That he'd been trying to keep the children in check wasn't much of an excuse. He'd only needed to say, *Josefin, please take the children while I see to the luggage*.

Gravity took the suitcase she was tugging, making her teeter backwards. He drew in a sharp breath, a vision of a split head flashing before his eyes. Then, regaining her balance, she calmly stepped down from the stool and then carried the suitcase up the steps to join the others.

With a word to Josefin to keep Alvin and Astrid with her, he raced back down the way he'd come. But when he opened the door to the reception lobby, he found the luggage already in a neat line of green and grey, and Ezzie nowhere to be seen. The sound of an engine suggested the car was on its way to the parking area behind the building, so he assumed her to be at the wheel.

Annoyed at his own lack of consideration, he began to take each suitcase inside.

Ezz, after an inner debate, had elected to work the day after the Larssons arrived, though, before learning of the current visit, Sunday and Monday had been her planned rest days. Tavish had made himself available to the family when they were in residence and taken accumulated days off after they'd gone. This time the family was here for two months though. By the time the new assistant manager came to take work off Ezz's hands the Larssons should be back in Sweden.

So, Sunday morning, she made one of her first tasks to fetch a sack barrow from the mud room to wheel the boxes of Christmas decorations into the downstairs public room, parking it in the doorway. Her phone was in her pocket, and she also kept a keen ear out for any member of the Larsson family who might call her name.

She glanced appraisingly around the lofty, panelled room, graced with furniture and paintings from earlier centuries. Glass cases held exhibits of lace, sketches, journals and other artefacts that Rothach's long-ago occupants had left behind in dusty, damaged attics. Her first task was to put up a stand utilised only at this time of year. Its information card read:

Although present-day Rothach Hall loves
Christmas, the hall's history encompasses the
Scottish Reformation in 1560 under the protestant
leadership of John Knox. In the following decades,
Christmas celebrations became associated with
Catholicism and increasingly frowned upon.
Christmas was banned by Scottish parliament from
1640 to 1712, and not widely celebrated for a
further couple of centuries.

However, Christmas Day was declared a Scottish public holiday in the 1950s, and so now we're happy to welcome our winter visitors with festive decorations in the public areas – but elegant and low-key to respect our long and diverse history.

After a moment to check the effect, she turned to a cupboard concealed in the panelling that provided her with a stepstool, and soon she was hanging silver stars from each pendant lamp, the words *star of wonder, star of light* from the 'We Three Kings' Christmas carol wandering through her mind. Once down from the stool, she admired how each cluster glinted in the light from the windows. Next, she used the tartan ribbon on the red baubles to attach them to Christmas garlands of artificial greenery and pinecones, then arranged them carefully on windowsills and atop glass cabinets. She didn't know the age of the beautiful old panelling, but it wasn't the kind of thing you stuck pins into.

As she worked, she mulled over whether she could manage some days off by asking Orla to be available to the family when Ezzie wasn't. She'd suggest it. Grete was approachable and Orla capable.

In the quiet, she caught a squeak, a whisper and a scuffing of feet, and she glanced up. A faint footstep, then the two little Larsson children stood on the threshold of the large room, holding hands and regarding her through sea-blue eyes. A smile took charge of her mouth. With their wavy hair, they were like sweet little pixies. 'Hello,' she said, putting down a garland and joining them near the doorway so she could cast a quick eye over the contents of her sack barrow and check there was nothing there that could hurt them. 'How are you today?'

The little boy, Alvin, gazed at the stars hanging from the lamps. '*Jul*. Christmas.'

The eldest, the girl called Astrid, kept her solemn gaze on Ezz. 'Alvin doesn't like mash,' she announced in her startlingly fluent English.

Oh-kay. Barnaby had accustomed Ezzie to gamely joining in conversation, no matter how apparently random, so she gave the subject due consideration. 'Not even with gravy?'

Astrid asked her little brother a question in Swedish before turning back. 'No. He likes fries.'

'So do I,' Ezz answered agreeably.

Alvin spoke up. 'Chyckling. And *reece*,' he declared firmly.

Astrid giggled. 'He's trying to say chicken and rice, but he's jumbling up Swedish and English words.'

'Chicken and rice are good, too.' Then, noticing that Alvin had a boot on one foot but only a sock on the other, Ezzie said, 'You're not going outside, are you? Because it's frosty and your toes will turn to ice.'

Astrid shook her head. 'We're not allowed, unless someone takes us.'

'That's good.' Even though the hall stood well back from the cliffs, there were woods and all kinds of places in the grounds for small children to get lost. Then she heard an exclamation and Mats Larsson loomed behind his children, tall, blond and fearsomely good-looking, his dishevelled hair just long enough to flop either side of his forehead. Ezz realised that his children's eyes were the colour of a summer sea, whereas his were more of a match for the sea in winter. His self-assurance bore the gloss of money and education.

'There you are, children.' He sounded half annoyed and

half relieved. 'Do you remember what I said about not leaving the apartment without an adult?'

Astrid's expression became self-righteous. 'You said not to go *outside*. We're inside.'

One side of his mouth tugged up. 'I suppose that's true. But I meant not outside the apartment.'

Astrid considered this. 'This isn't an apartment. It's a house. It has upstairses.'

The corner of the mouth twitched again. 'I was using "apartment" in the sense of one section of a building being separated from . . . Never mind. What have you been talking to Ezzie about?'

He shot Ezzie an apologetic look.

Astrid nodded emphatically at her father. 'That Alvin doesn't like mash. You told Farmor that Alvin didn't like mash, and you were going to speak to Ezzie about it.'

Mats' fair skin flushed. He took his children's hands and drew them away. 'OK, you could have left this to me, but thanks for your help. Say goodbye to Ezzie.'

'Bye,' they chorused obediently.

The trio vanished, Alvin asking something in Swedish and Mats replying in English. 'Perhaps you can make Christmas decorations with Josefin.' Then came the sound of a door opening and Mats raised his voice. 'Josefin?'

Ezzie remained where she was, rerunning the conversation in her head. *You were going to speak to Ezzie about it.* A complaint already? Crap.

She'd begun returning cardboard boxes to the sack barrow when Mats reappeared alone, and still flushed. 'Sorry that my children took it upon themselves to bother you. It's just that Alvin's got this thing about only eating food that's clearly identifiable.'

'Of course,' Ezzie said, feeling her own cheeks heat.

40

'Your mother requested neeps and tatties, but I should have asked if there were other requests.' She paused. Then breaking the rule of not asking non-essential questions, because she really ought to be sure she understood what was being said, asked, 'Sorry, but when Astrid said "Farmor", did she mean your mother?'

When Mats smiled, his eyes creased and twinkled a bit like Grete's. 'Yes. Literally, it means father's mother. In Sweden we differentiate between our grandparents – father's mother, mother's mother, mother's father and father's father. Farmor, mormor, morfar and farfar.'

Ezz followed this with interest. 'Thank you. How incredibly practical. If you'd like to give me a list of favourite foods, I'll make sure Gwen gets it.'

He'd resumed his usual complexion. 'Mum had put plenty of Alvin-friendly foods on the shopping list, but didn't think to tell Gwen about dinner. My children like most plain foods, really, especially fish.' His thick sweater looked expensive, stretching over his chest as he thrust his hands in his pockets. 'I think Skye has plenty of that? I've seen fishing boats chugging up and down the sound.'

'Of course.' She made a mental note of *plain foods, especially fish* and suppressed the urge to tell him all about the fertile inner sea between the east side of the island and the mainland, the Sound of Sleat at the south and the Outer Hebrides to the west. She'd developed a deep love of Skye in the nine years she'd lived here, but she was here to fulfil his requests, not chatter.

His gaze roved over the room behind her, now ready for any visitor who liked to be welcomed by pretty Christmassy things. 'Very nice.'

Ezz thanked him with a smile, pretty sure he hadn't come back to praise the Christmas garlands.

41

He hadn't. 'There's something else I'm hoping you can help me with. A favour.'

She hesitated. A favour? She was an employee. How the hell was she supposed to answer that? She fell back on, 'Of course.'

That silvery gaze rested on her as if detecting her reserve. 'It's nothing onerous. Josefin has been very good about spending a protracted time here, including Christmas, but there's not much to entertain her. Would you take her to the village pub? From the couple of times I've been, it's a friendly place.'

Ezz froze. He wanted her to take Josefin *drinking*?

Frowning when she didn't reply, he added, 'In working hours, obviously. I'm not asking you to give up your time off.'

'Of course,' she repeated, summoning her professional smile, though her lips had dried. Should that have been *Of course not*? She hesitated, feeling a hot rush of anxiety.

'I'll send her out to you.' He glanced at his watch; a big-faced black smartwatch that screamed *expensive*.

'Of course.' Ezzie maintained her smile, not wanting her off-balance moment to be construed as prickliness as he turned to leave, and she prepared to carry boxes up to the public rooms upstairs. Well, actually . . . she did feel a smidge prickly at being sent to the pub – not because he was disposing of her time as that was what she was here for, but because a person's relationship with alcohol could be tricky. No doubt he'd assumed that hers was healthy. Or, more likely, hadn't considered it at all.

She tried hard to be the perfect employee, but now she was dealing with Mats Larsson rather than his straightforward parents. When she'd helped Grete and Erik through the formalities of the old manager's resignation and then been offered the job, she'd felt she'd received the seal of employer approval. But Grete and Erik would tell you if you displeased them. What you saw was what you got: a self-made couple who loved their family and the business they'd built.

Their son Mats was different. She couldn't read him, yet she didn't feel she'd handled the last few minutes to his satisfaction.

Her job, which only days ago had felt both fun and secure, suddenly seemed a bit less of each.

The Jolly Abbot Inn looked like a big white cottage with a slate roof. The tables that stood outside in summer had been stowed away and a Christmas tree twinkled beside the black-painted front door. Most people would think the pub was a pleasant place to spend Sunday lunchtime, especially in working hours and at someone else's expense . . . but Ezz was the only person in a suit. Rosamund behind the bar wiped her hands on her jeans and pushed up the sleeves of her knitted top as she teased Ezz. 'My, we don't get many office clothes in here.'

As Rosamund and son Brodie were Ezz's neighbours, living as she did across from the pub here in Chapel Road, Ezz joked back, 'I'm raising the tone. This is Josefin, the nanny from Rothach Hall.'

Rosamund beamed all over her round face. 'Welcome, welcome, Josefin. What would you like to drink?'

Josefin chose wine, fitting right in in jeans and a marmalade-coloured jumper that went with her short salt-and-pepper hair, rosy cheeks and ready smile. 'I like it here,' she pronounced, nodding approvingly at the red banquettes that lined the white walls and the wooden tables and chairs in the centre. Christmas lights had been

43

twined around the optics, so the ambers and auburns of whisky and brandy lent their glow to the clear liquids of vodka and gin. Josefin pulled a wry face, fingering the cutlery rolled up in napkins that was a precursor to the Sunday lunch they'd ordered. 'But I do not understand what everyone says.'

Ezz tried to relax. The nanny seemed friendly and keen to make friends, which Ezz was too, now she thought of it. It certainly wasn't Josefin's fault that Mats had asked for her to be brought here. 'Some people are speaking in Gaelic, that's why. I understand that about forty per cent of the island is Gaelic-speaking, though I'm afraid I've never tried to learn. Your English is excellent, and everyone on Skye speaks that as well.' Josefin had a Swedish accent, but otherwise spoke English perfectly. 'Ah, here are my sister's neighbours, Maisie and Fraser.' Ezz waved at the octogenarians who'd just entered, rubbing their hands and well wrapped up against the cold, pausing at the bar to order drinks before ambling over.

'May we join you?' Fraser had abandoned the tam-o'-shanter he wore in summer in favour of a blue woollen beanie, and his long silver hair flopped out when he removed it.

Maisie wore a red fleece hat with ear flaps. When she pulled it off, the Christmas lights shone on her neat silver bun. She'd never wear her hair loose and windswept as Fraser did. 'Hello, Ezzie.' Her beaming smile took in Josefin, too, and Ezz again made the introductions.

'Where's your wee sister?' Fraser demanded as he lowered himself creakily onto a vinyl-covered stool, his grimace suggesting that the cold weather had got into his joints.

Josefin looked interested. 'You have family here, Ezz,

though you are English and not Scottish?' She sipped from her large glass of red wine.

Ezzie, who'd ordered orangeade, was glad Josefin was chatty, making her easy company. 'Yes, Thea's the head gardener at the hall so you might meet her there, even if she doesn't come to the Jolly Abbot today. She usually works Monday to Friday in winter, when the grounds staff don't need seven-days-a-week coverage. She lives at the top of the village in Loch View.'

'I like this village.' Josefin sipped from her wine glass again and smacked her lips appreciatively. 'The houses are so many pretty colours.'

Maisie lifted her gin and tonic. 'You'll not find that commonly on Skye, because most of the houses are white. So far as I'm aware, only Rothach and Portree have the colours. My cottage is lemon yellow,' she added proudly.

The level of Skye Ale in Fraser's glass was going down rapidly. 'Ach, it's daft,' he said irascibly. 'My house is white, as tradition intends. And white's cheaper than colours.'

'Mine's a sort of gingerbread colour. I'd probably choose pale green, if I owned my own house.' Ezzie felt almost relaxed as their delicious-smelling Sunday roast arrived. As they ate, Maisie and Fraser set about educating Josefin on 'Sleat' being pronounced 'slate' and that Rothach was 'Roth*arsh*', the *ch* not getting caught in the back of the throat as in so many other Scottish words.

'I'm from the south of Sweden, and we have a similar sound in words like "usch". It means "yuck",' Josefin volunteered between disposing of bites of roast potatoes and beef.

Ezz enjoyed her meal while Maisie and Fraser told Josefin about Fairy Glen at Balnaknock. 'They say it's where the fairies hide in the dells,' Maisie expounded mysteriously.

'Och, it's a landslide that left a funny-looking landscape,' Fraser contradicted.

Then the elderly pair told the tale of Flora MacDonald rowing Prince Charles Edward Stewart from Benbecula to Skye, disguised as an Irish maid called Betty.

Fraser wagged a horny finger in Josefin's direction. '*That* story's no fairy tale. Clan MacDonald of Sleat, they lived at Armadale Castle and feuded with the MacLeods of Dunvegan.'

Her meal disposed of and a second drink drunk, Josefin looked hugely entertained as Maisie and Fraser continued to 'blether', as they would call it. Ezz soon began to wonder how long the social occasion was expected to go on. Should she suggest to Josefin that they wind it up? Or was a nanny so much like a member of the family that she'd expect to call the shots? When Mats had asked her to bring Josefin here he hadn't set a time limit. Ezz would much rather be at her desk than in the pub, where everyone but her seemed to have an alcoholic drink. Having decided that alcohol had no place in her life even before she came to Skye nine years ago, she was becoming restless. She rarely came into the Jolly Abbot. But . . . maybe that was why she sometimes felt she lacked company? She put the thought away to examine later.

Finally, as Josefin ordered her third large glass of wine, Ezzie ventured, 'Are you looking after the children later?'

Josefin only relaxed further into her seat. 'No, I have the rest of today off.' Her ruddy cheeks were even rosier now, and her eyes glittering.

'Oh. OK.' Ezz settled down to listen to Josefin tell Maisie how different Skye was to the seaport city of Gothenburg.

Then Thea and Dev burst in on a blast of cold air, cheeks rosy and eyes alight. Ezz greeted them gladly. 'Here's my sister Thea and her boyfriend Deveron. Thea, Josefin's the nanny for Mats Larsson's lovely children. He suggested I bring her here and introduce her to the village.'

One of Thea's eyebrows twitched, and her dark eyes met Ezzie's, clearly understanding Ezz's discomfort over the assignment. 'Great to meet you, Josefin,' she cried. 'I hope you like Rothach Hall.'

Soon, she and Josefin were chatting happily. After a while, Thea suggested, 'Would you like to come with Dev and me while we walk our dog? We can show you the footpath through the copse in case you ever want to come down here without a car. The drink-drive rules are strict in Scotland.' She glanced at Ezz's feet. 'Ezz isn't wearing her walking shoes—' ignoring the fact that Ezz's home was only a few yards away so she could have changed her footwear in a minute '—so she'd better drive back.'

'Yes, yes,' cried Josefin, flushed with bonhomie and shiraz. 'I would like to.'

Barely sparing a quick 'Are you sure?' Ezz made good her escape, sending Thea a silent but heartfelt 'Thank you,' from the doorway before she whisked out.

She drove her yellow hatchback through the winding, narrow lanes. At Rothach Hall the family door was firmly closed, so she settled back at her desk.

Her first job was to phone Gwen. 'Mats has mentioned the children's meals.'

'He talked to me,' Gwen said comfortably. 'Today, I'm to cook a plain meal for the children at about five p.m. Grete and Mats want stovies, later. Josefin and I will share getting the children's meals through the week.'

'Great, thank you.' Ezz ended the call feeling like a fish secure in her own little pond again.

An hour later, Josefin traipsed through the lobby, waving

to Ezz and looking rosily relaxed. 'I'm back. Thank you for taking me.'

Waving back, Ezz returned, 'You're welcome.'

When nobody had emerged from the family area to request anything by five-thirty, nor phoned or emailed, she switched off her computer and was soon following the beams of her car's headlights along the familiar roads home.

Indoors, she made herself coffee – she'd treated herself to hazelnut latte pods ready for Christmas – and curled up on one of her turquoise sofas to catch up with schoolfriends and past work colleagues on Facebook while she drank it. Once she'd commented on a skiing party in the Dolomites, a new baby and a winter wedding, she put her phone and empty mug aside. The boiler in the kitchen gurgled but, otherwise, the silence of the cottage pressed down on her as if to emphasise her solitude.

Glad that the village was so safe that dark, wintry walks weren't out of the question, she jumped up and ran upstairs to change into fleece-lined jeans and her favourite boots. Back down in her hallway she pulled on her ski jacket, gloves and a purple hat and then set out into the dark evening. Heading down the steep lanes towards the sea, she enjoyed the refreshing sting of freezing air on her cheeks as she passed cottages lit from within like pumpkin lanterns at Halloween. Once in Harbour View, the streetlamps cast a net of light that allowed her to see the beach, where frost-spangled pebbles tumbled, and rockpools sported lacy edges of ice. Until she'd spent winters in Skye, she'd believed that salt water couldn't freeze.

A row of cottages faced the beach, and a boat waited on worn wooden stands, its mast angling out from the tarpaulin. There wasn't another person in view, which wasn't uncommon in the village, especially in cold weather. She settled her hat more cosily over her ears and followed the bay's curve to Fishermen's Cottages, where Harbour View met the Quays above Causeway.

When she reached number 1, she halted, experiencing anew the joyful thrill of Valentina's surprise announcement. She'd see so much more of her eldest sister now she owned a holiday home in the village. Although she'd seen the cottages hundreds of times, she examined number 1 with fresh eyes. It was the end terrace, closest to the rocks at the end of the Quays. A side window looked over Rothach Bay to the peaks of Knoydart on the mainland, which she'd seen dusted with snow earlier today as if from a giant sugar shaker. 'It's certainly a fixer-upper,' she murmured to herself, surveying the tiny dwelling. In the light of the streetlamps, she could just about see that the cottage had once been pale blue, though much of the colour had flaked away. There was no more paint left on the wooden window frames or the door than there was on the walls, lending the place a neglected air. When she cupped her hands against the filthy glass, she could see only darkness, but on brushing encrusted salt from a wonky sign, she saw someone had once cared enough to bestow the name Overlook Cottage.

Fishermen's Cottages were among the smallest in the village, under their slate roofs. They had no front gardens, though each boasted a rectangle of cobbles where she imagined past fishermen spreading their nets. A couple of decorative lobster creels stood outside the house next door, and its windows were brightly lit behind its curtains, as if to demonstrate to Ezz how cute and cosy Overlook Cottage could be with love and attention.

Impulsively, she pulled out her phone and called Valentina. 'I know you're probably busy, but I'm standing outside your cottage and feeling excited for you.'

Valentina's laugh echoed down the line. 'You ratbag, you're making me jealous. Send me a pic.'

'It's pretty dark down this end of the bay.' But Ezz held up her phone to take a view of the cottage. As she sent it, she commented circumspectly, 'It needs a bit of work. Did you know it's called Overlook Cottage?'

'A *lot* of work – and no, what a charming name,' Valentina enthused. 'But look at those rotten windows.' She was obviously studying the photos Ezz had just sent. 'Some won't close and two at the back are broken. The agent says we'll be able to replace them, as long as we have the same style.'

'You'll have to buy a boat,' Ezz announced solemnly. 'And row out to sink your own lobster creels in the bay.'

'Not likely.' Valentina laughed. 'Once the renovation's complete, Overlook will be for us to relax in. I can't wait to pick up the key. Actually, I was wondering . . . Could I stay with you on the weekend of the 23rd and 24th? Gary's parents are hosting a gathering in Warwickshire because cousins and aunts are over from America. I could easily cry off that and let Gary take Barnaby.'

Ezzie's heart soared at the idea of two whole days with her big sister. 'That's not even two weeks away! Do come.' Then reality intruded and she added, 'I might have to work chunks of the weekend, though. I'm not sure if I can get time off when there's family in residence.' Then she shivered, a sea mist stealing up Causeway and trying to slither its chilly fingers into the collar of her coat. 'Brr, it's getting cold. I'll walk home while we talk. I'm ready for a hot meal and TV.'

'Speaking of TV,' Valentina said. 'Are you watching *My Ghost Kingdom*, about adopted children and their birth families? The last one's on tonight. I hadn't even heard the term "ghost kingdom" referring to the adopted person's imagined birth family, but I can relate. As a kid, I used to imagine that I shared blood with royalty or famous actors.' She laughed. 'Whereas I expect my parents were just ordinary people coping with an accidental, inconvenient pregnancy.'

Ezz began retracing her steps. 'Compulsive viewing, when you're adopted, isn't it?'

Valentina agreed. 'And heart-rending sometimes. Some birth mums were treated shamefully.'

Ezz skirted a particularly frosty patch of road that seemed to glitter a warning of its potential treachery. The village lanes didn't have many pavements. 'Although I take the reunions with a pinch of salt because they only seem to show the cheerful, successful ones, it's fascinating watching people's stories unfold. One minute I empathise with those who say their adoption affects their sense of identity but the next I side with those who say they've no need to know who created them. And that segment on the prevalence of teenage moodiness in adoptees made me think of Thea's difficult patch at school. Is your birth family on your mind?'

'Mostly I'm too busy to worry about it,' Valentina confessed, 'but it does float into my mind sometimes who my birth parents were. Why they didn't keep me. Who my siblings and cousins might be – especially when Gary's family has a giant get-together. He explains all these first and second cousins to me, and I don't really get it. He and his parents can talk about family relationships for hours. It makes me aware that we don't even have our adoptive parents anymore.'

51

'I still miss Mum and Dad, even though they died when I was twenty.' Ezzie crossed Harbour View and began up the dogleg slope of Creag an Lolaire, gasping when her feet almost shot from under her. Freezing sea mist could polish the ground to a glassy sheen. 'Particularly lately, because I'm at a bit of a loose end,' she confessed, turning right into Chapel Road and spotting the light that shone outside her cottage to welcome her home. 'Well,' she corrected hurriedly, not wanting to prompt a worried Valentina to call Thea to talk over Ezz's isolation. 'I might start dating again, but the last one put me off.' She stopped to catch her breath. Above the mist, the moon rode in a star-bestrewn sky. Giggling, so Valentina wouldn't get how much it had upset her, she admitted, 'He had a bit of a quirk.'

Valentina's tone sharpened. 'Quirk? Or kink? He didn't hurt you?'

'No, no,' Ezz soothed. 'He was great at first and after a couple of dates I went home with him.' She wasn't coy with her sisters. 'And then he announced he had special pleasures. Honestly, I just stared at him, because, you know . . . special pleasures? He said he liked to pretend he was an army officer, giving orders.' She giggled, though it had been far from funny, being alone with Henry in his house as he tried to coax her upstairs. 'When he said he called his man-part Major Magic, I left.' She hoped she'd made it sound funny, because at the time it had made Ezz feel vulnerable and she'd driven home too fast in the dark, imagining him pursuing her. At least she'd never told Henry where she lived.

'Ezz!' Valentina sounded as if she didn't know whether to be amused or appalled. 'You will call the police if you feel threatened, won't you?'

'Yes, yes, lawyer sister,' Ezz breezed. 'Any minute now you're going to ask why I can't settle down with someone like that nice Ramsay I used to live with in Suffolk.'

'I do feel slightly like that,' Valentina acknowledged ruefully. 'You're forty-four and I want you to be happy.'

Ezz snuggled into her coat, cold yet unwilling to deprive herself of the enchantment of the dark, frozen evening. 'Ramsay didn't want to relocate when I wanted this job in Skye. You know that.' And her doing something really hard, like giving up alcohol, had not received his support at all – a case of a hard drinker not appreciating a reformed drinker, she supposed. He'd felt criticised when she talked about not missing the hangovers or putting herself or others at risk during drunken escapades. For that and other good reasons, Valentina had never been told the full story of Ezz and Thea uprooting from the English countryside and replanting themselves on the beautiful Isle of Skye. They'd thought she'd be happier not knowing. 'I don't think Mum and Dad would have liked him much anyway.'

A fresh wave of nostalgia for their parents Maxie and Vince swept over her. Two musicians who'd adopted three girls and then had to leave them on the threshold of adulthood when something as mundane as a hotel's faulty heating system had taken their lives. Her laughter deserted her. 'We were so lucky. Mum and Dad put us at the centre of their busy lives. I suppose the advantage of being adopted is that the authorities check your potential parents are good people. With natural parents, you get what you get.'

'Too right.' Valentina sighed. 'What if our birth parents are horrible? One of those stories on *Ghost Kingdom* was about a man who discovered his father had been a gangster.'

With a shiver, Ezzie took a step towards her cottage. 'Nobody could live up to Maxie and Vince.' The street lighting just here was sparse, letting her look up at a galaxy of stars, asteroids, comets, space dust and whatever else the Earth floated in, like a million diamonds flung on black satin.

Valentina was silent for several beats. 'I get what you mean. Thea's glad she's found a birth parent now, but it wasn't plain sailing, and it doesn't mean our parents would be as OK as her mother Ynez. Even if we're not the result of rape or incest, we were almost certainly dirty secrets. Our birth mums probably dealt with the emotional conflict decades ago and might not thank us for stirring it up again. Their current families might not know we exist, and by searching our birth mothers out we'll expose their past disgrace.'

'True,' Ezz acknowledged.

Valentina went on. 'I'm not sure I want to know that I was originally called Jessie or Mary-Anne or Nelly. I'm *Valentina*. Mum and Dad were my mum and dad. You haven't applied for your original birth certificate either, have you? It's the first step on a road that might lead anywhere.'

Ezz tugged her hood over her hat. 'Agreed. But if I ever started the process, I'd treat finding my birth family like dating via an app. I'd exchange messages. Then maybe I'd chat on the phone. Eventually, if we all wanted to meet up, I'd do it in a public place so I could leave whenever I wanted. If they bothered me, I'd block them – like I blocked Henry. Without my home address, they'd no longer have access to me.'

'Wow,' Valentina said slowly. 'You've thought about this.' She hesitated. 'I've put a DNA testing kit on my

Christmas wish list, but it's mainly about health, because – as Gary's mother Pearl pointed out – if there's anything in my genes to be concerned about, it'll affect Barnaby. And there's also ancestry. Thea's discovered she's half-French, which is a nice thing to know. You're so blonde, maybe you have Nordic forebears. I can be interested in where my ancestors lived without needing to meet any relatives the test might throw up.' Then Valentina rounded off hastily. 'Oops, Barnaby's shouting for me. See you soon, I hope.'

'OK, I'll go home and get warmed up. Give Barnaby a hug from me.' Ezz's frozen toes were beginning to curl inside her boots, but before she finally turned towards her cottage, she lingered for one long last look at the night sky. She liked the stars and had downloaded an astronomy app in a fit of enthusiasm, where constellations like Cygnus were shown by dotted lines drawn between the stars.

She'd soon grown tired of the app but thought, fancifully, that she was like one of those twinkling stars within a constellation named Birth Family – part of something bigger, whether she acknowledged those lines or not. Other people shared her DNA. Out there. Somewhere. Valentina had Barnaby who looked like her and Thea had Ynez. *I don't have someone else with blonde hair, blue eyes and a pointy nose,* she thought.

But then she shrugged. At various times of her life, she'd wondered about her birth family. She'd done nothing about finding them before and doubted she ever would.

Chapter Four

On Monday morning, Mats read to the children on Alvin's bed, having luxurious amounts of dad-time while he was in Skye. A video call was due from Inger. The three of them lolled together on a mound of pillows decorated with planets. Alvin and Astrid, hair brushed and cute faces gleaming, kept switching their gazes from the book about a fox and a mole to an iPad, screen blank, propped up against an obliging blue teddy bear halfway down the bed.

Then: 'I want to hold it,' Alvin bellowed in Swedish, hurling himself over the book and seizing the iPad. The teddy bear somersaulted to the floor.

Astrid gave an outraged gasp. 'You're too little, isn't he, Pappa?' She tried to wrestle it from his hands.

'Not, not,' howled Alvin, his tiny fingers reddening as he clung harder.

'Hey, hey,' Mats crooned soothingly, lifting Astrid off Alvin and prising all fingers but his from what had been a freshly polished screen. 'Nobody's going to hold it. We propped it up against bear so it wouldn't get broken, and everyone would be able to see when Mamma calls.' He leant sideways to retrieve the toy, and then propped up the iPad once more. 'Astrid, we might have to chat about your behaviour concerning your little brother. And both of you should remember we're trying to talk English while we're here,' he added, remembering the fact. 'So "Daddy" in English, OK?'

Astrid pointed at the toy bear without addressing her sistering skills. 'He's not called Bear, he's called Åke.' She resettled herself against the pillows, her recently brushed hair now escaping from its scrunchie.

'I not little,' Alvin added inaccurately.

Mats was relieved when the *bee-boop, bee-boop* of an incoming video call hit the air.

'Mamma!' Alvin shouted, trying again to hurl himself at the iPad.

Mats scooped him up. 'Sit nicely, and I'll answer the call.' His arms were long enough that he could reach the tablet without letting the children up from their pillows.

Inger appeared, relaxing on the curved seating of what was obviously the sumptuous deck of the superyacht she was living on. She smiled, and the whole screen seemed to light up. 'Astrid, Alvin,' she cooed in Swedish. 'How lovely to see my darling babies. How are you? Are you having a nice time?' Inger's dark hair blew back from her face.

'*Hej*, Inger,' said Mats, not bothering to ask that she conduct the call in English. The children would speak more naturally to their mother in their native language. A quick smile, then he retired to lounge on the floor, content to watch his children's eager faces while they chattered. After a while he'd get Josefin to look after Astrid and

Alvin while he and Inger discussed anything the children didn't need to hear.

'We're in a place called Skye,' Astrid boomed, adding in English, 'But not that sky.' She pointed upwards.

'And we're in our bedroom,' Alvin declared, not to be outdone. 'Josefin's bedroom's next door. And Farmor's here, too.'

'She's downstairs. We came on planes, and we stayed in a hotel,' Astrid put in.

'There's lots of outside here,' Alvin added. Mats laughed aloud at this description of Rothach Hall's extensive grounds.

From the iPad screen, Inger laughed too. 'I know where you are. I've been to Rothach with you, when you were younger. You just don't remember.' Brightly, she added, 'We're cruising up the coast of Egypt. It's sunny.'

Astrid looked at her big bedroom window. 'It's sunny here.'

'But here it's sunny and *warm*,' Inger pointed out.

'Here we have icicles, just like at home,' Astrid countered. The call proceeded with details of the children's day so far – largely eating and watching TV, according to them, with no mention of getting fresh air while kicking a ball around the lawn or using their brains by doing puzzles with Farmor. Josefin came to the door and Mats beckoned her in. Once in the room, she angled her head beside the children's. '*Hej, hej,* Inger. Nice to see you. Astrid and Alvin have been excited about talking to you.'

'I've been excited about talking to them,' Inger claimed, although Mats wondered why she didn't do it every day, in that case, or why she'd chosen to be away from them so long. He knew the answer of course . . . Andreas. Before he'd brought Inger into his circle, she hadn't been quite so remote from her children. Mats hoped that after the cruise she'd have more time for them again.

After twenty minutes, the children's attention began to wander. 'Can we watch *SpongeBob SquarePants*?' Astrid asked Inger, as if she were in the room.

'I should think so,' Inger replied. 'Is Josefin still nearby? Perhaps she'd put it on for you while I talk to Pappa. But don't leave without blowing me kisses.' When the children made 'Mwah! Mwah!' sounds and kissed their fingers, she laughingly returned their salutes.

Then the two little people raced through the bedroom door towards the playroom.

Mats took up the iPad and settled himself against Alvin's bed. 'They miss you,' he said, because no matter how much he was enjoying so much time with his kids, he felt it should be said. It would be the first Christmas the children wouldn't see their mother.

'Don't, Mats,' she said with affected weariness. 'I know you disapprove of my holiday, but the children are fine and I'm getting the experience of a lifetime.'

'You are, aren't you,' agreed blandly, without commenting on her immediately leaping to her own defence when he mentioned the children missing her. 'But it's what you changed partners for, right? I had enough money for you, but not enough time. You blamed that when you fell for Andreas.' And she'd always refused to acknowledge that Mats' long hours spent earning money meant only a few weeks a year for idling around on luxury holidays. Mats still winced when he remembered the day Erik had overheard her telling a friend that Mats' family 'made their money out of fishcakes. Fishcakes! I'd almost rather it was urinal cakes.' Stung to find himself looked down upon, Erik had flamed with indignation.

'Anyway,' Mats said, as raking up old grievances was unproductive. 'I'm glad you were able to chat to the children. They're fine, and when the rest of the family come for Christmas, they'll be even better.'

Evidently seeing this as a barbed comment she answered, 'We'd already agreed that the children would spend this Christmas with you on the Isle of Skye,' as if him taking them away for what had originally been planned for three weeks had been the sole reason that she'd accepted an invitation for a cruise that lasted three *months*. Her hand loomed briefly then her image vanished.

He sighed at the abrupt end to the call, carried the tablet back to his room next door and shoved it onto his bedside. Inger's default setting was to make herself feel good by shining a light on what she saw as the faults of others, but the exchange had left him ruffled and resentful. He'd hoped to get a clearer idea of when she intended to return home to Sweden. His gaze strayed to the windows in this room they used to share and where they'd enjoyed happy times, in the early days of their marriage. The curtains Inger had chosen were of wildly expensive fabric, but he thought the views through them were far more beautiful. One window looked over the lawns and drive to the glittering Sound of Sleat, with a lone fishing boat drawing an arrow on the calm water. Another window showed rippling greensward. Pivoting, through the last two he could see the family garden and the copse beyond. As Alvin had said, there was 'lots of outside here'.

On a sudden fit of energy, he jogged down the hall to the playroom, bursting in on Josefin helping Alvin build a Duplo tower while Astrid was glued to *SpongeBob* on the TV.

'Who wants to come exploring?' Mats cried, in the manner of one offering a humungous treat.

'Yeah!' Alvin bellowed, leaping to his little feet and scattering the Duplo tower as he raced headlong for Mats.

Astrid peeped out of the corner of her eye. 'I'm watching *SpongeBob*.'

Mats swung Alvin up onto his shoulder. 'OK. You girls stay indoors, and we men will go out—'

'Coming!' Astrid declared hurriedly.

Josefin began to climb to her feet, her big smile filling the space between her round cheeks. Mats halted her. 'You have an hour to yourself, Josefin. I'll be fine with the kids. After all, you're missing Christmas with your sister and family this year and deserve extra downtime at least.'

Surprise flickered over her face. 'If you're sure.' She subsided onto the floor and began to gather up Duplo bricks: red, yellow, blue and green.

He hoped he hadn't offended her. Being a nanny was an odd position. It was *almost* family. *Attached* to the family. But not family. Josefin had few external ties other than friends in Sweden and an adult son in California, and he almost said, 'Unless you'd like to come?' But part of the attraction of his leave of absence was spending more time with his children, so he called, 'Boots and jackets on,' swinging Alvin to the floor. 'Don't run on the stairs.' Astrid was already sprinting up the corridor.

'I faster than Astrid,' Alvin cried, which, as he was panting in her wake, was demonstrably untrue.

Downstairs in the cloakroom, they began the process of dressing in outdoor clothes, which took at least twice as long as necessary.

'Don't want that yacket,' declared Alvin.

61

'It's a *jacket*,' Astrid corrected him. 'Those aren't my boots.'

'Can I have yellow scarf? I lost a *strumpe*-sock.'

'That means sock-sock! I don't like mittens. Where are my gloves?'

'I don't need help. I do it MYSELF.'

'I need a wee. I'll just take my coat off . . .'

'I need a wee, too.' In an instant, two children were bickering over who'd go first, and coats, boots, scarves and gloves were shed across the cloakroom floor. Mats thought ruefully that Josefin would have asked who needed the toilet before even thinking about outdoor clothes.

Finally, finally, they were suited and booted and in the crisp outdoors under a blue sky scattered with towering clouds. Mats said, 'Hold my hand down the steps, please.' And then they were all running across the grass in air so cold and fresh it made him giddy as he breathed the scents of pine needles and the sea. Mats took one of Alvin's hands and when Astrid grabbed the other, his little red boots barely touched the ground.

Astrid's giggles floated from her mouth like bubbles of joy. 'We can run fast, can't we, Daddy? We can run a long, long way.'

It turned out they could run about a hundred metres before the breathless children wanted to pause to examine worm casts in the lawn and then fling themselves on the grass and wriggle, pretending they were worms themselves. Mats took a philosophical attitude. Children and dirt went together. The washing machine would take care of it.

Surrounded by the giggles of happy children, he looked back at the house, admiring the grey stone that somehow never looked cold, and the turret under its conical hat. The wind combed the grass from side to side like a giant hand stroking green velvet. Then he turned his face towards the sea, letting his hair blow back. Across the sound, it was hard to tell which dark humps were the mainland and which were clouds. They piled up together on the horizon like a heap of grey, purple and white duvets.

When the children abandoned the worm game and meandered down the sloping grass, he strolled behind. The visitors' car park was empty today and he was glad. Whenever he'd visited Rothach in the summer, the public had roamed the major part of the grounds while his family kept to their allotted areas in hall and gardens. Rothach Hall being a visitor attraction helped with the costs of an enormous, expensive property but it was great to have the place to themselves.

He remembered that the old donkey and pony Grete had allowed to retire here had been joined by new friends recently. 'Hey, I have something to show you.' With Alvin on his shoulders and Astrid skipping beside him, they battled the wind down to near the stone hump-backed bridge over the stream – or 'burn', as that was the Scottish name for it.

'Horsies,' Alvin squealed from his vantage point on Mats' shoulders, as the paddock come into view.

Mats grabbed Astrid so she couldn't blast up to the paddock and frighten the animals. 'Small horses are called ponies. Three are ponies, and one's a donkey.' They drew near enough for him to read the notice on the metal gate. 'Look, that sign says: "Mary Pony and Clive Donkey". I remember your cousins Emil and Filip painting it. That's Clive Donkey, with the funny sticky-up mane, and Mary Pony with grey around her eyes. Farmor told me about the other two ponies. They're called Haggis and Scotch.'

63

'Which is which?' asked Astrid, gazing from a stocky bronze-coloured pony to a shaggy, friendly-looking one with a body the colour of the froth on hot chocolate but a darker face.

Mats considered. 'I'd guess the bronze one is Scotch, because it's roughly the colour of whisky.'

Alvin, who Mats had thought would be out of mischief up on his shoulders, suddenly flung up his arms and shrieked an ear-splitting 'Yah!'

Mary and Clive tossed their heads, snorting like dragons and rolling their eyes, while Scotch and Haggis cantered away over the rough grass. 'Alvin,' Mats reproved. 'That's not nice behaviour.'

He swung the little boy down to solid ground. Though the reproof had been mild and his descent to earth gentle, Alvin burst into tears. 'I want to see Mam-ma,' he sobbed, reverting to Swedish in his upset.

'So do I,' declared Astrid, looking suddenly unhappy.

Mats crouched down to encircle both children in his arms. 'You've just seen Mamma. You talked for ages.'

Astrid's lips trembled. She looked a lot like Inger when she did that. 'We want to see proper Mamma. Real Mamma. Not on the iPad.'

'Oh, dear.' Mats hugged them harder. 'We can try to talk to her again on my phone, if you want.' But the children only knuckled their eyes and sniffed, looking small and vulnerable in the magnificent landscape of grass and rock, sea and trees.

'Playthings, then,' Mats said, swinging Alvin back up onto his shoulders. 'I'll bet we have them all to ourselves.'

Astrid looked up through the dirty circles that had appeared from rubbing her eyes with grubby hands. 'What kind of playthings?'

'Wait and see,' he said mysteriously, and led the way, chattering about how tall the pine trees were and that the formal bit of garden was called a knot garden, which Farmor liked, then past the bare twigs that graced the walled garden, and there it was – a playground made of wood, which would swarm with visitors in summer but was now still and empty.

'Swings,' Astrid cried, dropping his hand and beginning to run.

'And me,' Alvin shrieked urgently, kicking against Mats' chest as if he was urging on one of the ponies.

'Ouch.' Mats laughed, swinging him down to the damp ground. 'Let's go see that wooden fort.'

Astrid, hearing this, changed course for the fort. 'We can be soldiers.'

The log fort was so substantial that even Mats clambered up onto it, as there was no one to see him ignore the signs that said the apparatus was for under-fourteens. He could only take two strides before making an about-turn, but Astrid, bossier than any drill sergeant he'd encountered when on compulsory basic training in Sweden, gave him so many contradictory orders it was easiest to march on the spot. Hair blowing crazily in his eyes, he shouldered an imaginary rifle and marched with a jerky gait to make the children giggle.

And then Alvin shouted, '*Hallå!* Hello!'

Mats spun around to see Ezz with a member of staff he knew to be the head gardener and Ezzie's sister, and his buffoonery faltered.

'Hello,' both women called back, wearing polite smiles. Thea was buried in an enormous fleece, cargo trousers and work boots. Most of her dark hair was covered by a green woolly hat. Ezz was wrapped in a stylish black coat with twin rows of buttons and her blonde hair flew around her head.

Mats felt like a prize fool but prepared to style it out. 'Um, hello.'

'We been to see horsies,' crowed Alvin, his tears of a few minutes ago forgotten.

'Aren't they fab?' Ezzie answered. 'This is my sister, Thea. She's one of the people who feeds the ponies and the donkey in winter.'

'Your *sister*?' the children chorused in tones of disbelief, as if adults couldn't possibly have siblings.

Astrid turned inquisitor. 'Do you live in the same house? Or do you live here at the hall?'

'Different houses, but the same village,' Ezz answered gravely.

'What village?' she demanded.

'Rothach village,' Thea said. 'It has a beach.'

'Quite a rocky beach,' Ezz chimed in. 'The sand isn't great for sandcastles. Our nephew likes the rock pools though. Enjoy the playground,' she added to the children – presumably – and then they said goodbye and hurried away towards the hall, Ezzie's smart black ankle boots tapping on the path.

A few drops of rain blew suddenly against Mats' face and automatically he turned to the children to pull up their hoods. 'Time for hot chocolate, I think.' He felt oddly deflated that Thea and Ezzie hadn't lingered to chat but sped away as if he'd offended them.

Abruptly, he remembered inadvertently leaving Ezzie to climb on a stool to empty the luggage box when they'd arrived from the airport and he glanced after her. He'd meant to apologise for that but had forgotten when he'd asked her to take Josefin out and for a split second she'd looked appalled, before her usual courteous mask had slipped back in place.

The appalled look had made him curious. He was sure it had been a glimpse beneath the bland, professional mask Ezzie Wynter habitually wore, a clue to the inner life of the pretty, composed woman.

Yet he hadn't understood that look at all.

Chapter Five

Ten minutes after Ezz returned to the hall and was working peaceably in her office, Mats, Astrid and Alvin half-fell into the lobby, unwinding scarves and dragging off hats. The children gambolled up to her office door and chorused, 'Hello!' as if they hadn't seen her with Thea only minutes ago.

She smiled at their cute rosy faces. 'Did you have fun?'

Two heads nodded emphatically. Alvin bounced in his red boots. '*Ja*. Now we have hot *choklad*.'

'Want some?' Astrid asked hospitably, licking her lips, as if anticipating a hot-chocolate moustache to savour.

Ezz assumed an expression of mock sorrow. 'I'm afraid I'm working.'

'C'mon, children.' Mats' voice floated from just out of sight.

The two little poppets spun around and scurried off and Ezz returned to the staff rosters, wanting them laid out until mid-January so she could pass further updating over to Orla, who'd be back at work tomorrow after her days off.

She went on clicking on headshots of the staff to allocate them to shifts. The wind rattled the window. The sound of a door opening reached her and this time when she glanced up, she found Josefin advancing into the room, a steaming red mug in her hand.

'Astrid worries that you are missing out on hot chocolate,' she said, smiling, and placed the mug on the coaster on Ezz's desk.

'Oh!' Ezz was charmed. 'How lovely of her. And how kind of you. Thanks to you both.' Appreciatively, she sniffed the sugary-scented steam.

'You're welcome.' Josefin smoothed her caramel-coloured top. It almost matched the pale brown of her eyes. 'I come also for information. The children wish to visit the beach in the village tomorrow. As Alvin is so small, I think I should drive them. Do you think yes?'

Ezz considered Alvin's short legs. 'I do. The roads are narrow, but it won't take you long in the Volvo. Let me show you.'

She opened an online map on her computer and chose satellite view, and then swivelled the monitor so Josefin could see. 'Here's Rothach Hall, look. This line—' she traced it with her finger '—is the main drive. You can take that or the service drive at the back. They both lead to Manor Road. The first turning right is into Low Road, which becomes Chapel Road, where the Jolly Abbot is. Then take Creag an Lolaire into Harbour View, where you'll be able to park at the side of the road.'

Josefin straightened up from viewing the screen. 'Perfect. Thank you.' She sent Ezz an appraising look. 'I enjoyed visiting your pub. I have the evening off. Would you join me there again?'

Ezz's first reaction was to gracefully decline, just because it was the pub. But then she remembered her last visit to the Jolly Abbot with Josefin, when she'd fleetingly reflected that avoiding the pub meant missing opportunities to socialise. And there was only another solitary long winter evening on her horizon as Thea would be with Dev. No amount of being glad for Thea's happiness made Ezz feel any less alone. Josefin was a kind, ordinary, friendly woman. When Mats had instructed Ezz to escort her to the Jolly Abbot it had felt like an imposition, but to be invited by Josefin herself felt like a hand of friendship. To accept would be a *choice*, not an obligation forced on her. It was always easier to deal with a choice and pubs sold drinks completely free of alcohol, didn't they? 'Thanks. I think I'd like that,' she said.

That evening, Ezz didn't take a great deal of trouble over her appearance, just to cross the road to the village pub: jeans, a sweatshirt and her blue hiking boots, which she liked particularly with tartan laces.

Josefin arrived at eight. '*Hej, hej*,' she cried, huddled in a green Puffa coat that, in the light from the outside lamp, made her look like a cheerful chrysalis.

Ezz pulled her ski jacket around her and they hurried across the road to the Jolly Abbot. Its Christmas finery of white, red and green twinkle lights were a beacon of bling, a reminder that Christmas was just over six weeks away. 'Whoo,' Ezz cried, as the wind stood her hair on end.

Josefin laughed as her own mousy crop tossed wildly. 'At the hall, it is worse. The wind whines around the building like a ghost.'

70

'It's usually more sheltered in the bay.' Ezz glanced around, trying to spot the Rothach Hall Volvo or even the pick-up. 'You didn't walk?'

'I did,' Josefin maintained. 'I have a torch on my phone.'

'Blimey. It must have been dark and steep beneath the trees.' Ezz opened the heavy wooden door. They were hit with a wave of beery warmth and the lights from the indoor Christmas tree in its dress of shiny baubles and glittering tinsel. Four thirty-something men at a table looked up and smiled. In her mind, Ezz called them the Regular Drinkers as on the rare occasions when she visited the pub – such as Maisie or Fraser's birthdays – she always saw them at the same table and Rosamund and Brodie behind the bar seemed to know them.

Josefin reached the bar first. 'What would you like? We could share a bottle of wine.'

'I'll have Irn-Bru, please,' Ezz answered easily. After a decade without alcohol, it was easier than it used to be to turn down wine. 'Hi, Brodie,' she added to the dark young man. She might not be a pub regular but, in the years they'd all lived in Chapel Road, she'd watched him growing from a gangly teen to a bearded, confident man in his mid-twenties.

'Iron brew?' Josefin queried, brow creasing, while Brodie clinked ice into a tall glass and reached for an orange can.

'I suppose it's just a weird spelling of that – it's I-r-n B-r-u,' Ezz agreed. 'A popular drink in Scotland.'

'I would like to try, I think.' Josefin picked up Ezz's fizzing glass and sniffed it. 'Is it alcohol?'

'No.' Ezz breathed in its barley-sugar sweetness.

From behind the bar, Brodie said helpfully, 'You can have a whisky in it. We call that a Girder.'

Josefin looked baffled. Ezz supposed in Brodie's brogue it had sounded to foreign ears like 'yukun hay a wusky on it', and repeated his words in her English accent.

Josefin nodded enthusiastically, beaming at Brodie. 'I like whisky.' They began an earnest discussion about the relative merits of Talisker or the whisky liqueur Drambuie. Josefin chose Drambuie, and Brodie got busy with ice, Irn-Bru and a double Drambuie, while Ezz made a mental note to offer to drive Josefin home, imagining her falling in the copse, and having to sleep rolled up in her Puffa coat.

Soon the two women were seated near the cheerfully dancing flames of the log fire. The pub was quiet, probably because it was a weekday. The Regular Drinkers switched bewilderingly between English and Gaelic as they drank pints and exchanged banter with Brodie, deadpan until they all roared with laughter. Two middle-aged couples sat at another table, occasionally joining in.

Ezz sipped the ice-cold Irn-Bru that was almost as brightly orange as its can and brought out one of the titbits that working in the local leisure industry had lodged in her memory. 'Drambuie's meant to have originated in the Broadford Hotel in Broadford Bay.'

'Oh?' Josefin took a healthy draught of her spirit-laced version. 'I like it. What did he say my drink is called?'

'A Girder,' Ezz supplied. Then, when Josefin looked uncertain, took out her phone and found an image of an iron girder.

Josefin spluttered into instant laughter, making her face rounder and redder and her eyes merry. The description 'natural' was perfect for her – no make-up, no highlights, a basic haircut and an out-in-all-weather complexion. 'Very good. You don't drink alcohol?'

72

Ezz shook her head. Although she liked Josefin, their relationship wasn't close enough for her to bare that tender part of her soul. She turned the conversation. 'How are you liking Rothach in winter?'

'It's not quite as cold as Sweden, but so beautiful. Tomorrow, I bring the children to the beach here in the village. If we have fine weather the next day, we are all to drive around the island, I think.' Josefin tilted her head consideringly. 'Perhaps not Grete. I don't know.'

Ezzie felt curiosity stir. So far, Grete hadn't pursued the chat about Christmas visitor attractions, despite her apparent enthusiasm during their video call of only a few days ago. 'I haven't seen much of her.'

Josefin crossed her legs, which were clothed in comfy brown corduroy. She frowned. 'No, I have not either. But I have been with Mats and the children.' Her expression softened.

Ezzie tilted her head enquiringly. 'I'm sure you love Astrid and Alvin. They're so cute.'

'Yes, yes.' Josefin beamed. 'They are lovely children, and so lively. I have a very good job.' She took another sip of her drink and lowered her voice confidingly. 'I should not say it, but I like it better now I live in Mats' apartment while Inger is away.' Josefin peered out from a fringe that lay like a slew of quills across her forehead. 'Since the divorce, the children spend half the week with Inger and half with Mats, so I must do the same. But now Inger is with her new partner, Andreas, on a big motor yacht, so we all stay together – Mats, the children and me. Mats, without her, is relaxed.'

Ezz stared. Mats and Inger were divorced? She'd had no idea. And a new partner for Inger? Ezz remembered her as beautiful in a way that invoked thoughts of salons, gyms and expensive boutiques, but had a trick of looking through employees as if they were part of the furniture.

While she waited to see if Josefin would expand on the subject, Ezz remembered Mats playing soldiers in the playground fort, wind-blown and laughing, silvery eyes alight. When he'd blushed beet red at being caught, she'd even felt a stirring of liking that she definitely hadn't felt when he'd sent her to the pub with Josefin. But maybe that wasn't too much to carp about . . . considering she was now in the pub with Josefin again.

Anyway, it seemed that Josefin liked Mats enough for both of them, as she continued extolling his virtues. He was kind and courteous. He never shouted at Astrid and Alvin. He'd taken a break from his job to be with his kids while their mother was away. Ezz listened, knowing that Josefin was being indiscreet about their employers, but too curious about Mats to find a way to shut her up.

Cheeks growing ruddier, Josefin drank two more Girders, which meant she'd downed three double Drambuies, and went on to talk about herself. 'I spent my childhood north-east of Gothenburg. There were farm fields but also forests and rocks. When I was married, we lived in Gothenburg for my husband's job, but then we separated. Our son, Lars, lives in America.' Josefin smiled fondly when she mentioned her son, and then turned the conversation to Ezzie. 'Where in England was your home?'

'I came from Suffolk, a county in the east of England, where it's quite flat and agricultural. We lived in a village in the countryside, a gorgeous place to grow up, about an hour and a half from the sea.' Ezz was beginning to enjoy Josefin's company. She seemed open and friendly and, like Ezz, didn't have the people around her she'd usually hang out with. 'It's very different to rocky, craggy Skye.

And here the sea's only a couple of streets away from my cottage.' Ezz smiled just to think about Rothach. 'My sister Thea and I came here when Rothach Hall had just been restored. Thea applied for a job first, and when I saw the photos, I fell in love with the place. They needed an assistant manager, so I applied. I left an ex behind, but we weren't married.' The explanation tripped from Ezz's tongue. None of it was untrue, but it left out the part about her and Thea having other things to leave behind in Suffolk apart from boyfriends.

By ten o'clock, Ezz, Josefin and the Regular Drinkers were the only ones left in the pub, the couples having pulled on their parkas and left. One of the Regular Drinkers, who habitually ran a hand over his suede-like head of buzzed hair, smiled at Ezz across the room, making Josefin send Ezz a meaningful waggle of her eyebrows. 'You have an admirer.'

'I think he's called Gus – short for Angus,' Ezz murmured. 'And he's a married dad. Not on my radar.'

Josefin pulled a face. 'Oh, no. No married men.'

Then the door opened and Mats Larsson strolled in, pink-cheeked from the cold but wearing a thick blue-grey fleece in place of a coat. Something flared in Ezz's chest at seeing him so unexpectedly, and it took her a second to assume her professional smile.

'*Hej, hej,*' he said to Josefin, grinning, then to Ezz, more formally, 'Good evening. I've come to give Josefin a lift home.' He glanced at their glasses, which were both half-full of orange liquid. 'Do you mind if I grab a quick coffee while you finish your drinks? Mum said she'll listen out for the children.'

Ezz felt she had no choice but to mask her surprise and say, 'Please do.'

'This is called "a Girder".' Josefin picked up her drink to show Mats. 'It's whisky liqueur with Irn-Bru. It's growing on me.'

He answered good-naturedly. 'Don't tempt me when I'm the one who has to drive back.' He ordered black coffee from Rosamund, who'd taken over the bar from Brodie, and then pulled up a stool at their table. He glanced around at the proliferation of twinkle lights and polished brass. 'Nice place,' he said to Rosamund, when she brought his mug of coffee.

Rosamund beamed. 'Thanks. It is.'

As Josefin had trained all her attention on Mats and was chatting about whisky, Ezz pushed away the last of her sugary drink. 'If you have a lift home, Josefin, I'll go.'

Josefin rose to give her a warm hug, but didn't attempt to change her mind. 'Thanks for coming out with me, Ezzie. I enjoyed it.'

'Me, too.' Ezz said general goodnights, pulling on her coat as she shuffled from behind the table.

Mats rose politely. 'I hope I haven't chased you away.'

'Not at all,' she replied equally politely.

Ears burning with the cold as she hurried across the road to the welcoming warmth of home, she wondered about Mats and Josefin. The easy way he'd sat down for coffee and a chat didn't indicate much distance between employee and employer. If they were both divorced, there was nothing to prevent a relationship, though the nanny was a decade older than Mats with his shampoo-commercial-glossy hair and designer jeans and boots. People fell for who they fell for.

She let herself indoors, switching on the light that bathed her hallway in a golden glow. In one way, she considered Mats a better human being for valuing Josefin as a friendly, competent woman.

But also, judgy though it was . . . what a waste.

The phone in reception was ringing. It was Tuesday morning. Orla had returned to work after her time off but didn't answer. Ezz turned away from her computer and reached for her landline phone, intending to take the call from there.

The ringing stopped.

She began to swivel back to her keyboard when she heard a male voice in the lobby say, 'Rothach Hall.'

She froze, grimacing. It sounded like Mats had answered the phone. *Why?* The landline was for business.

'Oh, really?' she heard him say. 'No, I wasn't aware. I'm Mats Larsson. My parents own Rothach Hall so you can speak to me. Mm-hm. Mm-hm. Oh?' Then after a lot of other listening noises he said, 'Certainly we'd be interested. I'll give you my email address so you can send over your proposal. I'll speak to a couple of people at this end . . . yes, do.' A clatter suggested the handset had been replaced.

Ezz scarcely had time to wonder what query he'd felt it necessary to deal with himself when Mats strolled into her office, looking pleased with himself.

Her first reaction was to explain. 'Orla must have left her desk for a moment. I was about to answer the call in here.'

He waved away her words. 'It was very interesting.' He wore running gear, the muscles of his long legs visible beneath tight joggers, and he stuffed his hands into the pocket of his hoodie. His hair was messy. 'I had no idea your sister had been in a gardening TV show. *Garden Gladiators*, was it?'

Horror sizzled through Ezzie like a static shock. She licked suddenly dry lips.

He waited, as if expecting her to launch into an account of the show and Thea's involvement. When she only gazed at him, he continued. 'That was the production company. Apparently, they're resurrecting the show, and they want to talk to us about filming here at Rothach Hall – with your sister front and centre. It sounds like a great opportunity. People love to visit a place that they see on TV, so visitor numbers should shoot up. We might even become a destination on organised tours. Filming will begin in the coming summer, so they want to scout the location and chat to Thea.'

Words seemed to fire themselves from Ezz's lips. 'She won't do it. You shouldn't ask her.' A buzzing began in her ears, and she grasped the reassuringly solid edge of her desk in case she fainted at this awful news arriving out of the blue. Or out of the self-satisfied mouth of Mats Larsson.

His smile vanished. 'Excuse me?' He seemed to draw up his long frame to appear even taller than usual. When Ezz gazed at him mutely he gave her a cold look. 'I think we can safely let her speak for herself, don't you?' Then he spun on his heel and marched from the room. A moment later, the front door opened and then snapped closed.

Ezz unfroze. She grabbed her phone with trembling hands and called Thea. As she waited out the ringing tone, she seethed. Bloody Mats Larsson. His quelling look had said: *Who do you think you are?* Well, she was Thea's sister; that's who she was. 'Come on, Thea, answer,' she whispered. But it was voicemail that picked up. Ezz gabbled a message. 'Ring me the second you get this.' Fingers trembling, she texted the same few words.

Thea didn't reply.

Ezzie jumped to her feet and paced, craning vainly through the window in the hopes of seeing Thea busy in the grounds. What could she do? Grete would never expect Thea to work with a TV crew again, but Ezz had seen her go out with Josefin and the children earlier, the children coming to the office door to chorus their hellos and Grete saying, 'Ezzie, we must talk soon,' before waving and following the others out into a freezing winter day. Erik Larsson would understand too, but Ezz could hardly send him an email: *I don't like your son's way of doing things and your wife's gone out so I'm going to interrupt your busy day with my worry.*

Should she run after Mats and find a way to halt him? But he'd seemed so welcoming of the contact from *Garden Gladiators*, and, frankly, snotty with her, probably because she'd forgotten everything her online course had taught her and challenged him in the panic of the moment. She tried Thea's phone again. Still no reply, though Ezzie knew she was somewhere in these vast gardens, parkland, and woods. After another fruitless glance through her window, she hurried from her office, across reception and up the dogleg stairs, half-running into the public rooms on the top floor. They were, as she'd expected, deserted, though looking festive after she'd repeated the stars and garland treatment up here.

She tried the back window first. From there she could see over to where Manor Road joined the main coast road and beyond to the foothills of the Cuillin Mountains. The bracken and heather in their winter colours of gold, russet and brown made the hills look like enormous tabby cats' backs below a cold blue sky. The only greenery came from swathes of pine and spruce. For once she spared the view only a glance before peering down into the courtyard, then trying to see through the greenhouse glass. No Thea.

Moving swiftly into a front room, ignoring a Christmas swag of pine and berries on the windowsill near a gallery of framed delicate and aged fabrics, her gaze combed the formal gardens and lawns, across the park to the paddock where Mary and Clive grazed, and Scotch and Haggis rested their heads on each other's necks.

And finally, in the entrance to the herb garden, she spotted Thea, foreshortened because Ezz was two storeys above.

A figure faced Thea. It looked like Mats Larsson.

'Shit,' Ezz hissed. And her heart plummeted like rocks tumbling down the Cuillin Mountains.

Chapter Six

Mats stared at Thea. 'What did you say?' he asked slowly. The only competition for their voices came from the wind rattling dead leaves along the ground and mewing seagulls swooping above.

Thea's chin was set and her eyes were defiant. Red ear defenders dangled from her fingers and a leaf blower leant against her because she'd been clearing a pathway. She was perfectly white. 'If the *Garden Gladiators* people come, then I go,' she repeated flatly. But then her eyes filled with tears. 'I left that life behind,' she choked, then turned and blundered away between the hall and the west lawns, the leaf blower swinging wildly in her grip as she rounded the back of the grey-stone building.

He stared after her in disbelief. What was it with these Wynter sisters? Had nobody taught them the value – the common courtesy! – of explaining themselves? Slowly, he became aware of the wind cutting through his running gear, chilling the sweat on his body from his run. He turned towards the hall but headed for the front doors.

He crossed the lobby. Ezzie's office was empty, so he couldn't seek clarification from her.

Entering the family quarters, he jogged up to his room, dumped his sweaty workout clothes and stepped into a hot shower, soaping himself with quick, angry movements. He was hardly out and dressed when he heard a vehicle outside. A glance through one of the enormous windows showed him that his family and Josefin had arrived home, and he ran downstairs to meet them.

'Pappa, Pappa.' Astrid and Alvin raced towards him up the broad downstairs corridor.

He swooped them up, replying in Swedish despite his own best efforts to stick to English in the UK. 'Had a good time?'

'We went to the beach—'

'There's the sea and—'

'Alvin put his foot in a pool—'

'I put my foot in a pool,' Alvin confirmed, and he and Astrid dissolved into giggles, while Josefin and Grete pulled off their coats.

Mats put the warm, breathless children down and turned them gently towards Josefin. 'You go with Josefin for a few minutes. I have to talk to Farmor.'

Grete had been turning away, but now she paused and raised enquiring eyebrows.

While Josefin helped the children with their coats, he ushered his mum along the corridor to the home office at the front of the house, most often used by Erik to keep his finger on the pulse of his empire during visits to Rothach, and where there was a computer and printer.

Mats waited for Grete to take the chair behind the

wooden desk. Between them, the Wynter sisters had rubbed him up the wrong way and he felt better pacing the floor. 'I can't understand some people,' he snapped, barely giving Grete time to seat herself.

'Your father again?' she answered in dismay. 'I had a long talk with him this morning and thought he was beginning to see why we need time away.'

Mats halted. 'Pappa?' he asked blankly. 'No. Not him. Something that's just happened.'

Grete relaxed back in her chair. 'Tell me. If you can stop running around the room long enough,' she added drily.

He took a deep breath. 'We've been approached to use Rothach Hall's gardens as a filming location for a gardening programme – for a fee that would mitigate some of Rothach's running costs and probably increase visitor numbers. Did you know that Thea Wynter was a star of this show in the past?'

'Yes,' Grete answered hollowly.

Mats resumed pacing. 'I mentioned it to Ezzie, and she looked at me as if I'd turned into a snake. She said – rudely – that her sister wouldn't do it. So, I asked Thea myself and she was just as disrespectful, saying that if the filming people come, she'll leave.'

'Oh, *Mats*.' Grete's hands flew to her face. 'You should have spoken to me first. Last summer, Thea was stalked and harassed, *here on our property*, and it was linked with that show. We told you about it. Don't you remember? Tavish was involved, which is why it was considered best if he left.'

Mats halted. He stared at Grete, a sinking feeling in his chest. 'Remind me,' he suggested quietly, and dropped into a chair.

Grete folded her hands. 'Some time ago, Thea appeared on a popular reality gardening show located where she worked then. She crossed swords with a social media influencer, who followed her all the way to Skye. When she refused to co-operate with him on some campaign, he rallied social media against her. Erik threw the man off the estate and threatened him with the police. I know you're impetuous, Mats, but Pappa and I protect our employees,' Grete reproached him.

'Oh. Shit.' He winced as he remembered jumping on his high horse when Ezz and Thea didn't immediately love the news he'd thrust at them. He rubbed his hand through hair, still damp from the shower. 'Like the financial officer I am, I followed the money.'

Grete hesitated. 'True. But employees are people. And . . . Mats? They're not *your* employees. Rothach isn't like Larsson Fiskeri, where you're on the board. Rothach Hall belongs to Pappa and me.'

'Shit,' he groaned again, remembering the horror in Ezz's blue eyes and the tears in Thea's dark ones. 'I overstepped. I'll talk to them.' He rose and rounded the desk to give Grete an apologetic hug.

But she hadn't finished with him yet. 'No,' she said decisively. 'It would be better for me to do it. Not only are they excellent employees of long-standing, deserving our consideration and respect, but, between them, they run this place. If we lose the Wynter sisters, it will be a disaster. I need to talk to Ezzie anyway, so I'll explain that you didn't have the full story, and she and I can speak to Thea together.'

Mats stared at his mother. 'If it's going to be a difficult conversation then I should stay,' he objected, feeling worse by the second. 'You don't trust me?'

For once, Grete's smile was nowhere to be seen. 'I'm the best person for the task.'

Mats was left feeling like a naughty boy as she strode briskly out.

The gardeners' room smelt of compost and chemical fertiliser. It was barely warmer than outdoors, but at least they were out of the freezing rain and blustering wind. Not having grabbed her coat before running out in search of Thea, Ezz huddled into her jacket. 'If Mats insists on talking to the *Garden Gladiators* people, I'll go over his head to Grete or Erik.'

Thea's dark eyes were stormy yet fearful. 'Don't. I've already been rude to him, but there's no reason for you to compromise your job as well. I'm not going on the telly ever again. I'll just leave Rothach Hall.'

Ezzie's stomach turned over. She didn't treat Thea's threat as idle, even knowing that abandoning the gardens she'd worked so hard to establish would break her heart. 'If you go, I go,' she promised grimly. 'I know the family has only been on this winter visit for a couple of days but there's a funny atmosphere. I've hardly seen Grete and, gorgeous or not, Mats seems every bit as entitled as his ex-wife.' She wished now she hadn't let his attractions even enter her mind, because now it felt like a lack of judgement. Bitterly, she added, 'Feeling safe here hasn't lasted long, has it? Bloody Mats Larsson's like Tavish was – grab an idea and sod how anyone else feels.'

Thea nodded, expression bleak. 'Erik might be blunt, but he's caring. He gave me support when I needed it.'

The wind rattled the door latch as if trying to get in. Ezzie sighed. 'We'd better get back to work, or we'll be sacked anyway.' She scooped Thea into a wordless hug, exchanging comfort with the one person who understood absolutely everything about her.

Then Ezz opened the door, careful the wind didn't bash her in the face with it, and dashed across the rear courtyard with her head dipped against needle-like rain. Once indoors, she paused to straighten her jacket and smooth her hair before crossing the lobby. Orla looked up with her customary pleasant smile, her grey cardigan and skirt teamed with a smart white blouse, her light brown hair drawn back in a tight ponytail. Ezzie paused, trying to recover her usual easy interaction with staff members. 'I've not found ten minutes to chat today. Did you and your husband enjoy your time off?'

Orla's eyes brightened. 'Aye, we stayed in Drumnadrochit, where the Loch Ness monster tourist stuff's based. We loved it. It's very pretty.'

'It sounds as if I ought to put it on my list of places to visit.' They chatted for another minute, Orla visibly buzzing after her winter break, then Ezzie returned to her office and tried to concentrate on the Rothach Hall website, intending to discuss updates with the designer. Instead, her attention strayed to the view through the tall, imposing windows, a vision forming of cameras and boom mics stalking Thea over the lawns like cats after a rat. Though it had once been an odd kind of thrill to see her composed, compact little sister on TV, chatting with another presenter or encouraging contestants in the gardening competition, that had been a different Thea, one who wore facial piercings and coloured streaks in a zany hairstyle. The idea of a more mature, natural Thea in the same role felt bizarre.

Never before had her personal loyalties intruded into her professional life, and she was frightened. Was their time on this glorious island to end? Wouldn't Thea be here to see the flowerbeds bloom? Would Ezz soon be clearing her things from this burnished walnut desk? Would they move from Rothach village in search of new positions? The prospect of them finding jobs together again seemed slim. It had only happened here because Rothach had been recruiting hard after refurbishment.

A voice from the doorway made her jump. 'Ezzie?'

Startled, Ezzie leapt to her feet, catching her elbow painfully on the desk. 'Grete. I'm sorry. I didn't hear you come in.'

Grete smiled, though her eyes behind her glasses were serious, her silver fringe sweeping her forehead. Carefully, she closed the door behind her and then pulled up a chair, seating herself before gazing expectantly at Ezzie.

Slowly, Ezzie sat too, her thoughts awhirl. Was Grete here to finally discuss Christmas? Ezzie's pad was already full of suggestions about the Christmas visitor activities Grete had once seemed so keen to try out. Or was it camera crews? Was Ezzie going to have to take a stand against *Garden Gladiators* that would make all her fears come true? A lump lodged in her throat.

'You must not worry,' Grete began softly. 'I will tell the television company that we at Rothach are not interested in their show.'

Keyed up to hear the worst, Ezz could scarcely believe her ears. Hot waves of relief made her dizzy. Her vision blurred with boiling tears.

Grete, clearly understanding the choked silence, reached forward to pat Ezzie's hand. 'Mats did not know the story. Erik sometimes grumbles about the costs of Rothach and the accountant in Mats responded.'

Ezzie nodded, in an agony of embarrassment at being

unable to offer a business-friendly smile and her usual 'Of course.' Instead, she rose unsteadily and crossed to the coffee machine in the corner. Searching through the pods for the cappuccino she knew was Grete's favourite, she managed to grab a handful of the tissues and discreetly mop her eyes, glad of waterproof mascara. She made two cappuccinos and, by the time she returned to her desk, was in command of herself.

Taking her cue, Grete proceeded as if the last few minutes had never been. 'If we are to offer Christmas events this year, we must approach hotels soon.'

Ezz pulled her pad closer. 'I've selected six good hotels on Skye that offer Christmas breaks. And a list of activities that could be arranged in the time available, like a lantern walk with a special café menu to follow.'

They discussed their ideas, but, finally, Grete sat back with a grimace. 'We have left it late to persuade people to travel here for a walk in the dark and haggis.' She twinkled ruefully. 'It is better left for next year. But I would like to see more of Rothach Hall dressed for Christmas. It is our first Scottish Christmas. A tree in the lobby, and another in the family lounge. A lot of lights.' She swept an arc with her arms, as if encompassing a host of bling.

'I'll ask Thea to choose the trees from the grounds,' Ezz agreed, unbalanced by how suddenly the usually rational Grete had dropped her business ideas for this year.

Grete's expression lightened. 'And ask Thea to join us now. Telephone her, please. Perhaps more cappuccino?'

Ezz made the call and in three minutes, Thea was knocking on the door, a polite mask not doing a great job of disguising her apprehension and anxiety.

Grete rose, looked straight into Thea's angry, fearful eyes and apologised simply and sincerely, as she had to Ezz.

'Oh,' said Thea, every muscle in her body visibly relaxing. 'Um, thank you. That's a massive relief.' The look she threw at Ezz was full of astonished delight. In no time, they were sipping cosily and discussing Christmas trees.

'I look forward to a big family gathering in December,' Grete said. 'You have Christmas plans together perhaps?' She motioned between the sisters with her finger.

Aware that her time off over the festive season bore a hovering question mark, Ezz just smiled, but Thea put down her cup and beamed. 'Our sister Valentina will be here, and then we'll go to her home for Hogmanay. We're very excited because she's bought a cottage in the village as a holiday home. She's visiting one weekend soon, isn't she, Ezz?'

Reminded that she hadn't yet talked to Grete about having a weekend off, or to Orla about making herself available to fulfil any family requests, especially as Orla was presently rostered off on Sunday herself, Ezz answered, 'That's right.'

When Thea's role in the tree discussion was over, Ezz was left with Grete. It seemed a good opportunity, though her online course hadn't prepared her for this exact situation. She took a breath. 'I'm hoping to ask your view on something.' Then the planned explanation of the downtime situation tumbled out in an awkward rush.

Grete's silvery eyebrows rose above her glasses in dismay. 'Of course, you must take your time off. I am sorry this was never discussed.' Embarrassed colour stained her cheeks. 'I have been wrapped up in our arrival and did not realise you were here too much. It will be good if Orla could cover your absences, but we will need very little apart from housekeeping.' Grete rose, her usual twinkle back in place. 'A little more money for Orla, I think. Let me know what is appropriate.'

'Of course.' Ezz beamed in relief, rising to walk Grete to the door, grateful that her world felt back on its axis. She waited for the family door to close behind Grete, then, feeling ten times lighter than a couple of hours ago, smiled at Orla, sitting behind the reception desk. 'Can you come into my office a moment, please?'

Orla looked anxious but hurried to follow as Ezz settled herself behind the desk. Ezz began, 'I've been speaking to Mrs Larsson about arrangements while the family's here. As we don't have our new assistant manager yet, I'm hoping you can cover my days off. It will mean a small salary increase—'

But she got no further. Orla clasped her hands and blurted, 'Ezz, I'm sorry. I'm to hand in my notice. We visited Drumnadrochit so my husband could attend a job interview. He's just heard this morning that he was successful. His new boss's husband works at the Loch Ness Centre and thinks there might be a vacancy for me. We're to leave before Christmas.'

Ezz's buoyancy faded into a second of dismayed silence. With an effort, she summoned a smile. 'That's a surprise, but congratulations. I hope you'll both be happy in your new jobs.'

But this news, on a day of seesawing emotions when she'd crashed from anger at Mats Larsson's big ideas, to fear she'd have to leave her job, and then into relief that Grete's calm hand of authority had prevailed.

For once, she just wanted to go home and shut herself away.

Chapter Seven

It had rained for the full ten days since the enquiry from the TV production company, and the weather seemed to have affected everybody's mood – including the aptly named Wynter sisters, who'd accepted Mats' apologies with fixed, but not warm, smiles.

Annoyingly, last night Mats had experienced an incredibly erotic dream about Ezzie Wynter. It had centred around her saying 'of course' a lot, but with a completely different intonation to her usual cool British reserve. It had left him in an unsatisfactory, semi-horny state, half feeling that he knew Ezzie more intimately than he really did and half horrified that his libido didn't know where he wouldn't be welcome. It brought to the surface things he hadn't realised he'd been feeling, like how sexy a beautiful, willowy blonde was in the plainest business suit imaginable. How startling blue eyes could be hard to look away from or a politely smiling mouth difficult to ignore. And how he minded that she didn't like him.

But at long last the weather was cold and beautiful again, and in the morning he took the children and Josefin on a trip to Broadford, where the shops were strewn with fairy lights that got Astrid and Alvin chattering excitedly about *Jultomten*, or Santa Claus. They strolled the main road to the cabins that formed Skye Market, which were as many different colours as the cottages of Rothach village, then stopped at a street vendor for hot chocolate, and shortbread sprinkled with icing sugar that the server pretended was snow. Just as Mats was beginning to feel a stirring of Christmas spirit, he received a call from his father.

'*Hej, hej,* Pappa,' he answered with the hand that wasn't holding the cup of hot chocolate, half anticipating another grumble from Erik that Mats wasn't at work, or perhaps a business matter that he needed to discuss.

But Erik proved to have other things on his mind. 'How is Mamma?' he asked gruffly. 'I've been talking to her, and she doesn't sound herself. Maja and Jonas say the same.'

Mats hadn't spoken to his sister and brother recently, but knew they'd kept in touch with their mother. He hesitated. 'I think you're right,' he said eventually. 'She's spending a lot of time alone, reading or watching TV. I keep trying to involve her with the family, but she seems to have things on her mind.' He didn't want to say in so many words that she was quiet and grumpy, and Erik seemed to be at the heart of the problem. His loyalties lay equally with each parent.

'Oh.' Erik sounded dismayed.

The call left Mats feeling out of sorts. This extended winter holiday wasn't going entirely as he'd hoped. He gazed up at the splendour of Beinn na Caillich looming over the town, the mountain's top third white with snow, and decided that by leaving his mother to her own devices he was letting her miss out on the beauties of Skye. The feeling persisted as they drove home for lunch and the winter sunlight hung hazily over the frozen moor, making the ochres and golds of the rocks and bracken beneath the lilac sky look like a pastel drawing.

After lunch, he caught Grete before she retired to the lounge to curl up once again with a book. In Swedish, he said, 'It's a lovely day to be outdoors, Mamma. Come with us on a walk. The children aren't seeing much of you.'

He saw refusal flicker in her eyes before the mention of her grandchildren made her smile, though her acquiescence was lukewarm. 'I suppose we should make the most of the weather.'

Josefin joined them, wrapped up in her green coat with a toffee-coloured hat, and the children raced around excitedly, their voices ringing on the clear, frosty air, calling on the adults to admire the sea, the boats, the gardens and anything else that caught their eyes. The frost hadn't thawed and flattened the grass with its twinkling coat.

Then, 'Look, Farmor, the café's open,' Astrid yelled, though it was open every day apart from Sunday, dressed for Christmas in a cloak of twinkling white lights, a row of icicles hanging from the roof. A Christmas tree glittered a welcome from the window, as if luring them inside for gingerbread and cinnamon buns.

'OK, we can go in,' Mats said, not feeling equal to the *you can't have cake every day and you had shortbread this morning* argument. But he regretted it when the five of them entered the warmth of the brightly lit café and found a circle of parents with children joining in songs and poems.

'Hello,' a cheery bespectacled woman called from

behind the counter. 'Lovely to have a dad joining us for Friday Rhyme Time. As it's nearly the end of November, we're singing winter and Christmas songs.'

'Hello,' chorused at least eight welcoming voices.

Mats vaguely remembered that the café provided a meeting place for groups. Though he didn't term November 22nd 'nearly the end' of the month, when he saw Josefin, the children and even his mother happily finding chairs in the circle he gave in gracefully, especially as he could smell coffee. Soon he was adding his baritone to songs called '10 Warm Mittens' and 'Do You Hear the Christmas Bells?' which he didn't know but were easy to pick up. He felt an idiot, but the children loved it. Alvin, unable to keep up in English, just made a singing kind of noise. Astrid was the only child of her age, as British five-year-olds – unlike their Swedish counterparts – were at school.

When they paused between songs to give people an opportunity to top up their drinks, a young woman with a mop of ginger curls smiled at Josefin. 'And are you Mum?'

Josefin roared with laughter. 'No! Mats is Dad, and I am Nanny.'

'Oh, the grandmother?' another lady asked, looking embarrassed. She cuddled two children on her lap, who were peppering her with crumbs.

Mats could think of no elegant way of explaining that whilst Josefin could be his children's grandmother age-wise, she was in fact the hired help. And if the Brits didn't have so many names for grandmothers, such as granny, nanny, grandma, nanna or nan the confusion wouldn't have arisen to make him and Josefin feel awkward.

Stiffly, Josefin explained. 'No. I help Mr Larsson look after Astrid and Alvin. *The* nanny.'

Astrid, who was evidently able to follow the exchange, put in helpfully, 'This is Farmor,' as she tugged Grete's sleeve, which meant Mats embarking on the explanation of Swedish grandparents being designated father's mother, mother's mother and so on. He was glad when the scones came round, and even gladder when his phone rang. He checked the screen and saw his sister Maja's name.

Quickly, he asked Josefin and Grete, 'Can you stay with the children?' Then he went outside. '*Hej*,' he said into the phone, switching to their native tongue and smiling to think of the youngest of his siblings, her brown hair flipping over at the ends. At thirty-five, Maja would end her most recent maternity leave in January. Little Ronja would be one year old in February. In Sweden, mother and father shared just over a year and a quarter's parental leave, and Maja had been back to her PR job for three months while Nils took some leave, and then they'd swapped again. Their eldest child Walter had begun school this year and three-year-old Liam was in daycare. Rather than a full-time live-in nanny like Josefin, they also had daily help from Nils' aunt, who covered what other childcare the parents couldn't.

Maja returned his greeting. 'Jonas is here, too, and we're on speaker. Is Mamma OK?' she went on. 'Whenever we talk to her, she seems glum.'

'Glum. The perfect word, though I've persuaded her out with us this afternoon.' Mats explained the activity taking place in the café. 'Pappa sounded glum, too, when I spoke to him earlier.'

'He's as growly as a bear,' Jonas' deep voice confirmed. 'Is Mamma really just taking time out?'

But then parents and children began to file out of the café and Mats stood back nodding goodbyes. When Josefin and Grete emerged holding Astrid and Alvin's hands he said, 'I'll come along later,' so Maja and Jonas would be alerted that he was no longer alone.

Astrid and Alvin craned up to be kissed goodbye, as if they wouldn't see him again for days, then, when the little party had moved far enough away, he resumed the conversation with his siblings. 'Mamma told me she wants to travel, and Pappa wants to stay at work, so she's gone off without him. Maybe it's to see how he likes it.'

Maja snorted. 'He doesn't like it. I met him for lunch yesterday and even cuddles and smiles from Ronja and Liam didn't cheer him up for long.'

'And he came to us on Sunday, and not even pickled herring made him smile.' Jonas sounded injured.

Mats sighed. 'I hope they're going to be OK at Christmas. We haven't all been together in one place for years and I really want Astrid and Alvin to have a fantastic time, especially as they won't see Inger except on video calls.'

Jonas sniffed. 'You'll have had weeks roaming the wilds of Skye on your own by then. You ought to be relaxed enough to cope with anything.'

Behind Mats, the lady who ran the café emerged, locking the door with a friendly wave goodbye. The blue was leaching from the sky, and gold and apricot streaks appeared, the temperature already dropping. Mats began to wander towards the hall past the play park and the shrubbery as the conversation fell to their various children.

By the time they ended the call, he was almost at the hall's rear courtyard. He put away his phone, still thinking of Grete acting out of character. On his previous visits to Rothach, the family had shared the cooking and housekeeper Gwen had been asked to prepare the evening meal only once or twice a week. But this time, Grete had shown no interest in cooking, and Mats and Gwen were sharing preparation of dinner between them. This evening it was his turn, and he'd planned kalops, a mildly spicy Swedish beef stew.

He was just wondering whether he ought to ring Erik again and try and get a better feel for whether there was real cause for concern over his parents' marriage when he heard tense voices. Set into the wall of one of the stone outbuildings was a utilitarian door, and the voices seemed to be floating out of the ventilation holes along the bottom. First came Ezzie's voice. 'Are you still rattled?'

'Worried, I'd say,' declared a voice he swiftly identified as Thea's. 'Since the *Garden Gladiators* people got in touch, I'm scared they'll lie in wait to jump out at me. I know it's unlikely because Skye's too remote for them to travel here without contracts and a schedule, but I'm having nightmares about visitors pouncing for selfies to post on social media.' She pronounced *social media* as if tasted bad in her mouth. 'And what if Fredek comes crawling out of the woodwork?'

Mats should have hurried past. The conversation being held in a chilly, uncomfortable venue told him Ezz and Thea thought themselves safe from listening ears. But who was Fredek? As their conversation concerned Rothach Hall and Mats had been the one to make the mistake of talking to the TV production company, he felt justified in lingering.

Ezz's voice came again. 'I suppose *Garden Gladiators* thought that after the crap on social media in the summer, they could use the buzz to reignite interest in the show. But Grete's told them there's no chance,' she added soothingly. 'I'm sure you can rely on her.'

'Her, yes. But what about Mats?' Thea demanded, and

Mats' stomach shrank at her dubious tone. 'What if Grete returns to Sweden? Would he green-light the show after all?' She gave a mirthless laugh. 'Dev and I are wondering whether to move on now, while we can control things.'

Something cold squirmed in Mats' stomach. Thea was thinking of leaving despite Grete's best efforts? And because of him?

Ezz gasped. 'But your home's Thistledome, and Valentina's just bought a second home in Rothach—'

'Thing is,' Thea ploughed on doggedly. 'Dev can mostly work remotely, but he's getting engagements to lecture to sports business students, and work with Under-21 football teams. Brand awareness is important to young athletes and he's proving a great coach. It would benefit him to live near an airport or a high-speed rail link. Leaving the island would be awful, but it might be for the best to start again.' The words were brave, yet her voice was tight with wretched dismay.

'But that's starting again *again*. It's not fair.' Ezz's voice trembled. 'We got away without criminal records.'

Mats suddenly had trouble breathing. *Got away with?*

Then Ezz's voice sounded much closer to the door, as if she were preparing to exit the uncomfortable rendezvous. 'I'd love to think I'd weather it if the story came out but, realistically, people love to gossip. On Sunday, I could hardly shut Josefin up about Mats and his divorce.'

Mats suffered another jolt to his system. Josefin gossiped about him? He'd never actually asked her to sign a non-disclosure agreement, but not gossiping about employers came with a nanny's territory. Then the door rattled and he woke up to the fact that he was about to be caught eavesdropping, so he back-pedalled smartly around the corner of the stone outbuilding to a nook formed between it and the greenhouse.

He heard the sound of a door opening and Ezz saying, 'See you later,' in a sad, flat voice. To his relief, the brisk tapping of her heels headed in the other direction, back towards the hall, and then faded.

Troubled, Mats eased himself from his cobwebby nook and followed slowly. As he passed the ventilated door again, he heard someone blowing their nose – presumably Thea – but hesitated to intrude. Then he heaved a sigh, realising that as his mother was so low right now, his conscience wouldn't allow him to dump a conversation about criminal records in her lap without first making certain that she had to be involved. Thea didn't feel like his natural starting point, though. Ezzie Wynter was Rothach's manager.

And, apparently, personally involved . . . Heavily, he crossed to the back door of the hall, and then into the lobby.

Orla glanced up from behind the polished wood of the reception desk. 'Good afternoon.' Her smile was wide and bright, freckles decorating her pale skin.

'Good afternoon,' he returned cordially, and took another couple of steps to check through the open office door whether Ezz was seated at her desk. And there she was, neat and composed as if the emotional conversation he'd just heard had never happened, poker-straight hair falling in a natural frame around her face. After a smile in Orla's direction, he strode into Ezz's office, closing the heavy wooden door behind him.

She glanced up and offered him a courteous if puzzled smile.

He waved her back to her seat as she prepared to rise

and slowly took the chair opposite, searching for a way into what could only be a tricky conversation. His dad would have just asked the questions to which he wanted answers. His mum would have tried instead to draw Ezzie gently along the conversational corridor that led to the same destination. Mats was more like his mother.

'Everything OK?' he asked.

'Of course.' The corners of her mouth tilted up, but her eyes didn't smile.

His mind flicked back to that erotic dream, and he had to make an effort to keep his gaze from her lips. 'I just want to assure you,' he began carefully, 'that all thoughts of working with the *Garden Gladiators* are over. I was impulsive when they called – a failing of mine, my parents often tell me – but after Mum explained the backstory, I realised I hadn't thought things through.'

Ezzie's eyes flickered, as if she was unsure of where this conversation was going. 'You were kind enough to say so at the time,' she murmured.

Annoyance prickled up his spine that, like some exaggerated butler character from a period drama, she daren't say the word 'apologise' to him. 'I don't want you to think I'm some entitled asshole.' He made a face. 'Uh, that's US English, isn't it? Should I say entitled arsehole in UK English?'

For an instant she compressed her lips as if trying not to smile. It sparked off a flash of something inside him, brief but powerful, but he no longer followed his lust. That's how he'd ended up married to Inger. Gravely, Ezzie confirmed, 'Arsehole.'

Now it was his turn to want to laugh. Instead, he answered equally gravely. 'Good. We're agreed.' But though she was attractive when her eyes glittered with amusement behind her stilted façade, unfortunately, he was here to voice a serious concern. He shifted in his seat. 'And now I'm going to apologise again,' he said . . . apologetically. 'But I heard you and your sister talking outside and, as my children are on these premises, I'm going to have to ask you why you mentioned getting away without criminal records.'

Ezz turned completely, shockingly white.

Compassion for her obvious distress softened his voice. 'I expect you're going to quote some employment law that says I have no right to ask. But you're not my employees because that honour falls to my parents and when I hear people who interact with my kids talking as if they have shady pasts to hide, my Daddy Bear instincts kick in. I protect my cubs. I hope you'll forgive me for doing things my own way, but now I'm beginning to imagine sinister reasons behind Thea not wanting to be on camera.'

Slowly, so slowly that it was as if she were ageing before his eyes, Ezz sagged. Her hands rose to her face, and covered her eyes.

Mats watched her, his breathing quickening as his heart rate ramped up at the anguish that rolled off her in waves. How serious was it, whatever she was trying to hide? He swallowed. 'You can tell me. You can trust me—'

'Crap,' she said, her voice muffled by her hands.

Astounded at this blunt rudeness, he halted.

She brought her hands down, revealing an expression that managed to be both hard and woebegone. 'I can't trust someone who sends me to a pub without knowing my relationship with alcohol.'

One part of his mind acknowledged that she was trying to deflect the conversation from its original direction, but he was astonished enough to let her. 'When I asked you to take Josefin to the pub that lunchtime? But then you went there with her yourself. Voluntarily.'

'There's a world of difference between being shoved into a situation and approaching it in a planned way.' From the Stepford employee she'd been till now, Ezz had morphed into the picture of truculence. 'I could be an alcoholic. You didn't know that I wouldn't give in to temptation and go on a bender.'

'Are you an alcoholic?' he asked, aware of the conversation careering still further off-piste.

Impatiently, she shook her head. 'No. But I could have been. My point is that you have no basis for saying I can trust you.'

Mats tried to regain control of an unravelling situation. 'If I was insensitive, I'm sorry. But if you have a criminal record, I need to know for my kids and probably for my parents.'

Her face was still translucently pale. 'As you pointed out, your parents are my employers. In Scotland, an employer is allowed to ask me about my convictions – though, to follow the law of the land, they'd first offer me counselling from an appropriate body. For my part, I should disclose any unspent convictions, and certain spent ones, depending on the job I'm expected to perform. But *I don't have any convictions of any kind*, so what I choose to tell you and your parents is *nothing*.'

Slowly, he said, 'I'm not sure that's going to cut it.'

Visibly, she flinched. She turned to her keyboard, typed rapidly, then waited while a shiny black printer nearby clicked and burbled, her hand outstretched to catch the piece of paper it churned out. Then she scribbled on the foot of the sheet, folded it into an envelope and sealed it before picking up her bag and coat and stalking past him.

As he spun on his chair to watch, she approached the white door to his family's quarters, stuffed the envelope underneath, then marched off towards the back of the house.

Stunned, and wondering what the fuck was going on, he stepped out into reception, where Orla was gazing at the white door, wide-eyed at Ezzie's bizarre behaviour. Mats treated Orla to a curt nod, and then stormed through the door. Inside, he picked up the long brown envelope. It was addressed to Grete Larsson. Ignoring that, he ripped it open.

Ezzie's address was at the top, along with *Friday 22nd November*. The body of the letter was brief.

> *Dear Grete,*
> *It's with sadness that I must resign my role at Rothach House with immediate effect.*

And a spiky flourish of a signature. He rubbed his chin. For Ezzie to have thrown in her job rather than answer a question, he'd either entirely mismanaged the interview or she had more to hide than he'd thought. Possibly both.

After searching the downstairs rooms for Grete, he ran upstairs to tap at the door to her suite. She let him in with a frown that suggested she hadn't miraculously returned to her usual tolerant, happy self.

'I'm sorry,' he said. 'But Ezzie Wynter has resigned.'

Grete's jaw dropped and shock registered in her eyes. 'Resigned? *Ezzie?* But why?' She reached for the letter, read it, then flipped it over as if in search of further explanation. Her gaze sharpened. 'Do you know what's happening? Why is she not working her notice? Why is the letter so terse?'

He blew out his lips. 'Let's sit down, and I'll tell you what I know.'

As she listened to his account of overhearing Ezzie and Thea's furtive conversation, Grete's expression switched from bewilderment to dismay. 'None of this is like Ezz, but she has seemed subdued ever since the television company rang here – damn them. She was upset when this person pestered her sister a few months ago.'

'Was his name Fredek?' he guessed. 'Thea mentioned that name and sounded frightened.'

Grimly, Grete nodded. 'Yes, I think that was it. He was the person your father threw off the property for harassing her. But why did Ezzie bring alcohol into the discussion?'

He spread his hands and shrugged. 'An example of why she couldn't confide in me, she said. Or to distract me while she decided what to say about criminal records. I thought if I dealt with it, it would be less official than if I brought the situation to you, but she's left me with no choice.'

'I must talk to her.' Grete rose, still clutching Ezzie's resignation letter.

'She's left,' he said. Then, because his mother looked so despairing, he hugged her, noticing that her bones seemed nearer the surface now. She wore her years so lightly that he sometimes forgot that she was seventy-two.

Slowly, Grete resumed her seat. Loath to leave her with a frown on her forehead and woe in her eyes, he crossed to the windows and shut out the late afternoon darkness. A coffee machine stood on a small wooden unit, but judging that they'd both benefit from something stronger, he left the room and jogged downstairs. From the kitchen he caught the sound of Alvin's bubbling laughter and Josefin's friendly chatter. He turned off the hall to the dining room and the drinks unit, where he mixed two sturdy gin and tonics and added ice from the mini fridge. When he stepped back into the corridor, he caught sight of another thin brown envelope on the doormat.

His heart sank.

He lodged a drink on a convenient lamp table so he could swoop up the envelope. This time 'Grete Larsson' was written on the front in a different, untidier hand.

He carried it upstairs to his mother unopened, handing it over with a sigh, an apologetic look and the gin.

Wordlessly, Grete opened it, scanned the contents, then passed it to him. He read:

> Dear Grete,
> Please accept my resignation as from today.
> With kindest regards,
> Altheadora Wynter

'Shit,' he muttered, feeling as if he'd poked at something and discovered too late that it was a wasps' nest.

Grete took a gulp of gin. 'The sisters were adopted – I don't know if you knew. But I've never known any siblings more loyal to each other.'

He shook his head. 'I didn't know that, but I'm pretty certain that loyalty is not the full story here. They're tied together by something they want to hide.'

He didn't know what, or if it was appropriate for him to know, but he did want to repair any damage he'd done, as well as removing the slump from his mother's shoulders at the loss of the Wynter sisters.

Chapter Eight

Without telling Ezz, Thea or Dev, Valentina had booked dinner at the Broadford Hotel to celebrate her being in Rothach for the weekend. Ezz had never felt less like getting dressed up for an unexpected treat, despite a stunning festive menu and their table being near the most sumptuous Christmas tree she'd ever seen. It looked as if it had been draped in crystals.

Hopefully the surprise element accounted for Thea's air of discombobulation, which Ezz was sure she wore too, though she tried to add a smile for Valentina's sake and say things like, 'This is ace.' Grief at leaving Rothach Hall lay like ice in her stomach and she was sure Thea felt the same.

Dev, freshly shaved and his dark curls tamed, looked as if he'd pinned his smile on with an effort.

But Valentina was busy drinking prosecco that shimmered with glitter, in an off-duty mood as Barnaby and Gary were miles away with Gary's family. 'I'm so excited,' she enthused, easing aside an elegantly Christmassy table decoration of white candles and red-berried holly. 'My goal's to have the refurbishment of the cottage complete by early June, so we can spend the summer holidays here. When our annual leave's used up, we'll just work from home. Do you think there will be a good, local registered childminder for when you can't help with Barnaby?' she asked Ezz.

'Bound to be. We're excited too. It'll be fabulous to have you here for weeks at a time.' Ezz couldn't look at Thea or Dev for fear of seeing their gazes haunted by the knowledge that they might have relocated by the time the summer holidays arrived. She'd already spotted kind, concerned Dev giving Thea quick, consolatory hugs and dropping kisses on her hair. Luckily, there was no longer any trace of the tears Thea cried when Ezz had broken the news that they'd been so disastrously overheard.

Eventually, Valentina looked over her glass of glittery prosecco. 'Is something up? My big-sister senses are pinging.'

Ezz sent Thea a look that she hoped said *leave this to me.* 'Sorry,' she said. 'I had a problem at work this afternoon that involved a frank exchange of views with one of the Larsson sons.' She remembered how jokily he'd begun the interview – getting her defences down, she now realised. 'He's an entitled arsehole.' She was acutely aware that she couldn't tell Valentina she'd resigned without telling her why.

Continuing the fabrication, Thea made a show of patting Ezz's hand. 'It's not just you. I don't like him.' She made an apologetic face at Valentina. 'We didn't mean to bring the party down, but we've been so happy at Rothach Hall and now this knobhead's making life difficult. Let's not talk about him.' She raised her orange juice. 'Let's toast your new second home, Valentina. I'm hoping to join you in the morning to check it out.'

Dev toasted with his pint, his dark curls falling towards his eyes. 'To Valentina's new cottage. *Lang may yer lum reek* – or good luck and good fortune for the future.'

'What Dev said.' Ezzie raised her tonic water, quite impressed that between her and Thea they'd conjured up a reason for their subdued demeanours.

Valentina returned the toast. 'OK. But let me know if you need any help.'

Half-heartedly, Ezz thought about heading off any involvement from Valentina with, *I know my employment law, thanks,* but that seemed like inviting a heated discussion about whether a manager needed advice from a lawyer, instead of dancing lightly over the subject, so she said, 'Are you coming to look at the cottage too, Dev?'

Dev slipped one arm around Thea. It wasn't an unusual display of affection from him, but Ezz thought it particularly protective, and was glad her little sister had such a fantastic partner. 'For at least part of the time, I hope,' he said. 'But I have an online meeting with a client. As a start-up I can't afford to turn even weekend meetings down.'

Seeing an opportunity to create a stepping stone to Thea and Dev having a plausible reason to leave Rothach village if they had to, Ezz asked, 'Have you told Valentina about being approached to lecture to students on sports business courses?'

As she'd known she would, Valentina leapt on this interesting development, and Ezz could relax and eat her steak and chips. When Thea sent her a grateful look, she was able to grin back.

OK, so she and Thea had resigned without notice, but it was a gnarly problem rather than the end of the world. Thea and Dev could sell Thistledome and move somewhere near a city. And Ezz? She'd decide what to do when she'd recovered from the immense blow of losing her position at Rothach Hall. Ezz was a calm, competent person. She could start again somewhere else, even if Grete and Erik wouldn't provide a reference. Her tenancy at her cottage could be ended. Furniture could be sold, transported or stored. She'd always fancied the cruise ships. She could probably get an admin job on one of those. Or she could simply circulate her CV around the hotels on Skye and continue to live on the island.

No, it definitely wasn't the end of the world.

It was just the end of working somewhere outstandingly beautiful in a job she adored.

At just after nine on Saturday morning, they congregated outside Overlook Cottage, the last of the row at Fishermen's Cottages. Skye was living up to its name of the Misty Isle and Ezz, Valentina, Thea and Dev were enclosed in a cloud that allowed them to see no further than the top of the Causeway or the rocks at the end of the Quays. At the edge of the mist, the sea was a shifting sheet of pewter, though its shushing and sighing seemed muffled.

'Ta-dah!' Valentina brandished the key and then tried to use it in the lock, as they all huddled into their coats and pulled their hats over their ears. 'Grr,' she growled, as the key refused to turn.

'Let me try.' Dev was able to turn the key after a struggle, but then had to put his capable shoulder to the door to force it open. 'Oops,' he said ruefully when the woodwork gave an ominous crack.

'No problem,' Valentina laughed. 'Keith the builder's coming at eleven to measure up for a new door and frame. This one wouldn't keep the mice out.'

'It kept us out,' Ezz observed, following her into a dim and musty interior. The wooden stairs rose before them, painted at the edges, as if a carpet runner had covered the rest. They coughed at the dust coating every inch of chipped paintwork and the filthy wallpaper bestrewn with faded pictures of boats.

'Why do empty houses always have screwed-up newspaper on the floor?' Valentina demanded, nudging a ball of it with her toe. 'Apparently, the old guy who lived here wasn't house-proud. After he died, his daughter and son couldn't agree on whether to put money into doing the place up before selling, so it's been just mouldering away while they bickered. Come look at the kitchen.'

Gingerly, they followed, careful of a frayed rug with a curling lino surround as they passed through the living room to a cramped area where ancient cupboards buckled from damp around an cracked pot sink. They paused to peer over each other's shoulders.

'Phew,' Thea complained. 'Stinky.'

But Valentina was smiling. 'Keith thinks I should be able to knock into the bathroom behind this and create a bigger kitchen, with skylights.' She waved grandly at the sagging ceiling above them, then led them through the back door into a patch of jungle.

Deadpan, Thea observed, 'Ezz, this is even wilder than your garden.'

Ezz laughed. She liked her garden untamed for the bees and other wildlife, and Thea's gardener's soul was offended that Ezz's idea of 'doing the lawn' was to sprinkle the grass with wildflower seeds. She huddled into her blue ski jacket. 'Barnaby will have a great time making dens in these bushes.'

'No, he won't,' Valentina responded reprovingly. 'Because it's all going to be dug out and lawned. A very little lawn,' she admitted. 'Let me show you one of the reasons I wanted the house.'

They trooped back through the mouldy kitchen and musty living room, and then cautiously up the creaking stairs. 'Some of the treads could do with replacing,' Valentina allowed. 'But come into the biggest bedroom.'

She led the way into a room where the carpet was filthy with mould and mouse droppings and the wallpaper was no better than downstairs. 'Look.' Valentina had had the foresight to bring up a scrunch of newspaper and now she rubbed fiercely at the largest window to reveal a view of Rothach Bay. The mist shifted just in time for a shaft of light to touch the grey wintry sea. 'Wow,' Ezz breathed. 'This is going to be awesome.'

'It is,' Valentina agreed gleefully. 'And the garden will have a wonderful view of the sea too, when the jungle's chopped down.'

'Fantastic.' Thea gave Valentina a big hug, obviously sharing her sister's excitement. 'Where will the new bathroom be?'

'In here.' Valentina showed them the other bedroom, which would have a fine view of the beach at the front and a less lovely one of the cliff face at the rear. 'The back section will become the bathroom, leaving Barnaby a nice room at the front.'

Then she looked at her watch. 'Keith should be here soon. I think it might be an idea to start collecting the rubbish to bag up— Damn! I bought rubble sacks especially for that, but I've left them in my room at your house, Ezz.' Frowning, she glanced at her watch.

Ezz turned towards the stairs. 'No problem. I'll nip back. You wait for the builder.'

After the fusty interior of the cottage, it was great to be in the fresh air again even when enveloped in the soft mist. As far as Ezz could see, Harbour View was deserted except for gulls bickering loudly over something on the road, threatening each other with hooked beaks and flapping grey wings. Taking deep breaths to clear her lungs of dust and mould, it took only five minutes for Ezz to get home, panting from the steepness of Creag an Lolaire.

When she reached her front path, she was just reflecting that the muffling mist felt like a cocoon, if a damned chilly one, when a man climbed from a nearby car. The likelihood of this being Brodie or some other neighbour made her glance up with a smile and a greeting ready on her lips.

But then the man said, 'Ezzie,' and she froze. It was Mats Larsson. He hovered closer. 'Can we talk?'

Before, her heart had lurched once or twice when she'd seen him, but now it pounded as if she was in one of those videos where a human comes face to face with a bear and doesn't know whether to freeze or run like hell. It took her an instant to remember that she also had words to draw on. 'I'm busy.' She sidled a step up her front path.

Mats took two steps forward, his smile rueful. 'I thought of calling first, but knew you'd ignore me.'

She waggled her head, the universal body language for 'maybe'. Keys in hand, she took the last few steps to her door, the wet, long grass either side of the path stooping as if to wipe her boots.

She could step inside and slam the door in his face.

112

Satisfying as that thought was, she'd need to come out again in a few minutes, so all he'd have to do was wait. There was no way out of the back of her house apart from scrambling over the fence and then risking the steep rock and scree between Chapel Road and Friday Furlong.

That would be idiocy. *Would it, though . . . ?* Yeah, it would.

Reluctantly, she turned to face him. He paused. His golden hair poked from below his black beanie hat and his expression was hard to read.

She tried not to let her voice wobble. 'I'm in the middle of something.'

'Ah, yes.' He nodded. 'Your big sister's visit. You told me about it. But nobody answered my knock at your door, so I presume she's not here. Maybe she's at Thea's?'

Sweat broke out on the back of Ezz's neck. Thea's address was a matter of record at Rothach Hall, just like hers, and she wanted him there even less than she wanted him here. Sooner or later, he'd run across Valentina, who'd demand to know what was going on and treat Mats like the knobhead and entitled arse that Ezz and Thea had dubbed him. Anger made her lips tingle. 'What do you want?'

'Can I come in?' He even took a half-stride, as if certain she'd say 'yes'.

'No. Say what you need to say out here.' She stared him down.

But then he took her by surprise. He said, 'I think you're in trouble and I want to help.'

Trouble. Pain shot through her temples as tension clamped its steely hands on her skull. 'No idea what you're on about.'

He took another half-step. She could see every line in

113

his face now, and the shades of grey and blue in his eyes. Even flecks of green. His voice was husky as he held her gaze. 'People don't resign without notice unless they're staring down the barrel of a gun. You've been a perfect employee for nearly a decade, so I think you're scared. And if you're not scared of getting hurt yourself, you're afraid for someone you love,' he added. 'At first, I was angry when you wouldn't explain what I overheard about a criminal record. Then, of course, my mother was upset when you resigned.' He gave her another rueful half-smile. 'But later, after Astrid and Alvin were asleep, I went down to your office to switch off the computer and the lights. I sat in your chair and saw the email half-written, your pad full of notes and reminders, and I knew that for you to abandon us like that, the gun barrel must be very big.'

Shockingly, Ezz's throat began to ache with unshed tears.

When she didn't – couldn't – answer him, he added, 'Mum's sad and baffled. She'd only told me a couple of days earlier that the Wynter sisters ran Rothach Hall and it's obvious that she's fond of you both. I explained yesterday's conversation as best I could, but I hardly understood it myself – except that I defended my family blindly and was accusatory, demanding explanations instead of inviting confidences.' Grimacing, he added, 'I haven't told Dad yet. I wanted to talk to you first.'

Ezz could no longer see him, not because the mist had swallowed him up but because of a veil of tears.

A sigh came from deep in his chest. 'Any HR department at Larsson Fiskeri would be horrified at me. But I'm not your employer, Ezz. My parents are. Can you confide in me as a friend?'

She swallowed what felt like a golf ball. 'When did we

become friends?' Refusing to let him see her wipe the tears from her eyes, she blinked and hoped the moisture would evaporate.

'I'd *like* to be your friend. I'm concerned about you.' Then, when she didn't reply he asked softly, 'Is it Thea? Mum reminded me that she had trouble with a man. Is he threatening her? Has she done something he can blackmail her with? As long as my family won't be hurt by whatever she's done—'

The reflex to protect Thea sprang to life. 'It was me,' she snapped. Then she clapped a hand to her mouth, appalled the words had escaped, after all the years of pretending, bending the law, hiding the truth. She tried to retract. 'Thea was protecting me, but it's nothing to you. It won't harm you, your kids or other family.' Again, she swallowed. 'I'd like you to leave. I'm sorry if our resignations are inconvenient.'

She might as well not have asked him to go. He carried on doggedly. 'If it's *you*, why's Thea so petrified of being on camera? If she'd just said, "Thanks, but I'm not interested in *Garden Gladiators*" I'd have let the approach drop. But she was hostile to the point of rudeness. As were you.'

He paused and shifted his gaze, as if the mist didn't exist and he could look along Chapel Road at the cottages climbing up the bowl in which the village stood, up to the copse hiding the footpath to Rothach Hall. 'I feel like crap,' he continued quietly. 'Because I acted – no, *reacted* – like a jerk, only concerned for me and mine.' He smiled faintly, disarmingly. 'But we have agreed that I'm an entitled asshole.'

'Arsehole,' she corrected, feeling the tiniest drop of tension ease away. She found a tissue in her pocket and blew her nose. She thought of Thea, Dev and Valentina

115

waiting in the dirty little cottage that was soon to be transformed into Valentina's gorgeous retreat and that she and her family would be here so much more often than presently, when she lived full-time in Inverness, miles away.

And she thought about Thea on the brink of leaving Skye. With bone-deep certainty she knew that despite it being convenient for Dev to work from somewhere more central, he loved Thea too much to ask her to leave Thistledome if it could be avoided, because it was going to rip out her heart. The name of the cottage was a play on words meaning 'This'll do me' and Thea hadn't changed it when she bought the little home. Ezzie sighed. If she took the risk of trusting Mats Larsson with the truth, then there was a chance that Thea – and Ezzie – could keep their jobs. All that would happen was that one more person would be in on the secret.

Except . . . 'It's possible that if I explain, even if you accept my explanation, that then you'd run off and tell Grete and Erik and all your family. No doubt they'd tell others, and it would be common knowledge. That's not an option.'

He rocked on his heels while he considered. 'In your opinion, do they need to know? Will it hurt them not to?'

Her turn to consider, the mist chilling her face. 'I don't think so. But then I don't think you need to know either. If I'm the trusted employee of long standing that you suggest, you should accept my word that I'm not a danger.'

A frown puckered his brow. 'This is just swordplay. I'd prefer you to accept *my* word that if I agree with you that Mum and Dad don't *need* to know, I'll keep your secret.'

Ezz wavered and wondered. If they ran again, she and Thea wouldn't just be leaving behind their lives on this

116

wonderful island, they'd be leaving without a fight. And if Mats felt compelled not to keep her confidence . . . well, then running away would still be an option. But there was a chance. She felt as if he wanted her to take it.

She turned to her front door. 'You'd better come in.'

In silence, he removed his coat and hat to hang in the hall. His coat was cherry red and expensive-looking. She took him into the kitchen. 'Mind the step,' she said automatically as she stepped down from the hall, all too familiar with unwary guests entering the kitchen in an ungainly sprawl.

Her small kitchen table stood against a wall, so the two black shiny chairs faced each other. Without offering a coffee or other hospitality she took one seat and indicated that he take the other. Her home was bigger than Thea's, but not by much. They'd shared the house when they'd first come to Rothach, before Thea had felt settled and stable enough to move into Thistledome, so that they each had a place of their own. The memory of their cautious optimism that they'd found forever homes prompted fresh tears to prickle in her eyes.

'I'll just text Thea to say I've been delayed.' Quickly she stabbed out on her phone screen, *Mats has turned up. Stay there. Tell Valentina I'm on a work call.* The terse message would cause a jolt in Thea's heart, but Ezz knew she'd do exactly as asked, trusting her sister to know what she was doing, just as Ezz would have trusted her if their roles were reversed. Silencing her phone, she stuffed it into her pocket and lifted her gaze to Mats' eyes, as silvery as the wintry sea.

Heart thudding, she felt as if she was about to put all her money on one number on the roulette wheel. 'About ten years ago, in England, I was driving Thea's car and hit

117

a cyclist,' she said tersely. 'He'd stopped around a blind bend and had been impossible to avoid, but I panicked. I'd been partying the night before and thought I'd still be over the legal drink-drive limit. I . . . I'd served a ban for drink-driving before. Though the cyclist accepted the blame, I would have gone to prison because he received life-changing injuries – that's the law. As it happened in an isolated spot, it was possible for Thea to say she was the driver and pass the breathalyser test. Later, the cyclist kept involving Thea in his life because she was on *Garden Gladiators* and had a following, which he wanted to tap into. At first it was just a road safety campaign, which Thea was happy to help with, but then he reinvented himself as a social media influencer and became a nuisance. We were nervous about the attention, so left our old jobs and relationships and started again up here.'

Her hands had curled into fists as she talked but she tried to relax them, concentrating on Mats' face.

His fair brows knitted above his eyes, causing furrows on his forehead. 'That's everything?' he asked unemotionally.

She tried to be objective and factual. 'That's the crime – covering up a crime is a crime. But then in the summer, the cyclist discovered where Thea was and when she wouldn't join him in a fresh social media campaign, he claimed to have remembered that it wasn't Thea driving. When someone discredited him, he gave up.' The someone had been Dev, who'd put a lot on the line to create the illusion that the truth was a lie, but there was no way she'd expose him when he'd done it for Thea. 'So, we thought it was finally behind us, until the production company for *Garden Gladiators* contacted you.'

His brows lifted a fraction. 'I see why you reacted so

negatively to my enthusiasm over them filming Thea at Rothach Hall.'

She nodded.

He sighed, sinking back in his chair and rubbing his forehead. 'Who's the Fredek I heard you mention?'

'The cyclist.' Fatigue swept her, not just from the tumultuous day yesterday but from living with a decade of fear and regret. 'Just to be clear, if you feel compelled to share this information with the police and they can prove the case, Thea and I will be in deep shit, because the punishment for perverting the course of justice can be stiff. You might think that's what we deserve, of course.' Ice formed around her heart at the thought.

'I see.' He gazed at her contemplatively. 'And your remarks about having an unhealthy relationship with alcohol . . . ?'

She understood that he was asking for full disclosure. 'After my parents died, I drank too much and became dependent. I told you the truth that I'm not an alcoholic, because I was never diagnosed. As far as I know, I was just a heavy drinker. After the accident, I stopped. What if I *had* been over the limit? What if it *had* been my fault? What if I'd killed someone?' She took a steadying breath. 'But sobriety's hard. Unfortunately, alcohol's all too bound up with celebrations, with gifting, with unwinding. What works for me is to try to be in control of when I'll encounter it. I'm always scared I'll slip back into letting drink affect my life.'

'And I ambushed you when I asked you to take Josefin into a pub.' Understanding shone in his eyes.

'That's right.' Wearily, she leant her forehead on her hand. 'But in view of everything else, it doesn't really matter.'

While he sat silently, looking too large for the chair, brow furrowed, her gaze roved aimlessly around her kitchen. The units and worktop were tired but serviceable. It had been her home all through the years of half-expecting the past to catch up with her and spoil the peace she'd found here on Skye. Despite Thea buying Thistledome, Ezz had clung to the reassurance that a rented home made it easy to move on. But once Fredek had been vanquished, and even before Valentina had dropped her bombshell about buying a cottage here, Ezzie had entertained thoughts about giving up her status as tenant. There was a cottage for sale on Friday Furlong, which would have a stonking view of the bay. She'd even conjured up a cute name for it – Heaven's Haven. Pipe dreams now, probably, to plan a kitchen and decide on palest sage green for the outside walls.

She closed her eyes, dreading that Mats Larsson would call the police and inform them what she'd confessed to. No matter how much it was her word against his, she and Thea could be called for interview. Fredek would almost certainly get a chance to renew his accusations. Any attempt to make the police think the evidence was circumstantial and anecdotal would entail repeated denials and lies. Lies. Her life had been filled with them for a decade.

When would it ever end?

Chapter Nine

Mats stared at this complex and tortured woman, her pink oversized jumper swathing her upper body in soft folds. It didn't seem the same Ezzie of the severe black suit, the perfectly efficient, self-effacing employee. And the Ezzie who'd once made the monumental mistake she'd just outlined? That was someone he didn't know at all. Her confession painted her as a criminal and a liar, and he'd only her word for it that Fredek-the-cyclist had been at fault for the accident. Yet all he felt for the frightened, strained woman was pity, as she waited bleakly for his next words. That was yet another Ezz – vulnerable Ezzie beneath her façade.

'If everything you say is true,' he found himself saying, 'I have no need to share the information with anyone.'

Her eyes popped open, twin blue pools of apprehension. '*If* it's true? How will you decide?'

He shrugged. 'Facts can be corroborated, can't they? The accident would have been reported.' He made his voice firm but non-threatening. If he'd learnt one thing over the past two days, it was that when it came to this one aspect of her life, Ezzie Wynter could go off like a firework.

Almost imperceptibly, her shoulders relaxed. 'Oh, of course. The village is Wordwell. Google it. It was in our local paper. If you can be bothered to wade through years of Fredek Kowski's social media accounts, you'll find images of Thea working with him on his road safety campaign.'

He held up a hand, a smile forming. 'The paper will be enough.' She'd been so willing, even eager to supply the information that he felt he barely needed to perform the internet search. But he did, and sure enough, up popped articles in the online version of a Suffolk newspaper. Nowhere did he find an account of Thea going to court. 'Thea was never charged?' he asked, just to be sure.

Ezzie shook her head. She looked tired and defenceless, her eyes enormous with hoping-for-the-best-but-fearing-the-worst. 'She wasn't at fault . . . I mean *I* wasn't . . .' She almost quivered with tension.

To give himself a last opportunity to think things through, he rose, filled two glasses with water and returned to the table, setting one before her and taking a couple of gulps from the other. 'As what you've told me seems true, I'll keep your secret.'

Ezz blew out a breath as if someone had punched her in the stomach. 'You're keeping your word?' With trembling hands, she picked up her glass. Her gaze remained on his.

Her relief caused him an inner glow. 'Do you think you and Thea will rescind your resignations? I'd score a lot of son-points if I could tell Mum that you'll both be at work on Monday.'

122

A flicker of a smile crossed her lips. 'You need son-points?'

'Every son does,' he said solemnly, though he was thinking mostly of alleviating the extra lines that had appeared on Grete's face at the shock resignations of the Wynter sisters.

Ezzie looked thoughtful. Colour even began to seep back into her cheeks. Tiredly, she rose and filled the kettle before switching it on. 'I need coffee. Want one?'

He wasn't a fan of instant coffee but didn't feel like breaching the tenuous peace between them by asking if she had a machine or percolator. 'Thanks. Black without sugar.'

She nodded, staring out of the window while she waited for the water to boil. Following her gaze, he saw a garden like a mini meadow, and the ground rising steeply above it, the colours muted by the mist. The kettle clicked off and she made the coffee in red mugs, adding milk to hers before carrying them back to the table. Looking more like her usual self, she fixed him with her gaze. 'I do like your mum.'

'You don't like me?' The words were out before he could consider them, so he chose to add a boyish smile, as if he were teasing.

Her eyebrows arched in surprise. Then she uttered a colourless 'Of course.'

He groaned. 'Oh, no, you're of-coursing me again. That means you've mentally returned to the status of employee of Rothach Hall. I don't know whether to be relieved, or disappointed that you're hiding yourself behind your bland façade.'

'Bland?' Her eyes sparked. 'I would have said "professional".'

He snorted. 'You can be professional and still have a personality.'

She glared at him. 'I have a personality.' But then she bit her lip, as if suddenly unsure of herself.

'Of course.' He winked.

Now her lips curled in an unwilling smile. 'You're not supposed to ridicule employees.'

'You're not my employee,' he reminded her. 'But you're sometimes a bit "Stepford".' He smiled, to show it was a gentle tease rather than a criticism.

Ruefully, she wrinkled her nose. 'Am I? I had no proper training concerning interaction with your family. Tavish Macbetha guarded that aspect of the manager's job jealously. I've done an online course and I tried to pick up where he left off but often feel as if I'm acting on guesswork.'

Glad she'd let her guard down, he said, 'Tavish was slimy and obsequious, and I didn't like him. You're personable, efficient and polite, and I think that's all Mum and Dad require.' Seeing that she still looked uncertain, he added, 'Dad was glad to get rid of Tavish so I don't think you have to hold him up as the gold standard.'

She even managed a laugh before looking thoughtful again. 'I can't speak for Thea, but I'm happy to forget my resignation. Delirious, in fact. Would you like to speak to her yourself? Or should I?' A hint of mischief entered her smile. 'If I'm the manager again, and we don't have an assistant manager, it's actually my job.'

He slouched down into his chair and lifted his coffee mug. 'Then you do it.' He was rewarded by a smile so bright and radiant that it took his breath away.

Within twenty minutes, coffee drunk, he was braving the mist lurking in the narrow, roller-coaster lanes back towards Rothach Hall, happy he'd be able to assure his mother that it had all been a misunderstanding stemming from his original rubbish handling of the TV company approach.

His tally of son-points would climb while his promise to Ezzie would be intact.

Ezzie floated back down the hill to Fishermen's Cottages as if weights had rolled from her shoulders. Perhaps she ought to be anxious about finally telling someone the truth but, despite his self-confessed impetuosity, the pragmatic yet sympathetic way Mats had dealt with her story made her confident that he'd keep her secret. Even the weather joined in her good mood as the sunlight burned through the mist, creating a golden glow that repainted the colours on the cottages around her.

As she neared Overlook, she saw a heap of dirty carpet outside and then Thea rushed out, her arms full of desiccated lino. Skin dusty, dark hair tied in a tight bun, she'd shed her coat despite the freezing temperatures and her green knitted jumper had developed a hole in its sleeve. With a furtive glance back through the open cottage door, she hissed, 'What happened?'

Briefly, Ezz recapped, stressing how she'd come to make the decision to confide in Mats after keeping their secret for so long, then held up crossed fingers. 'I think it comes down to take it or leave it. And if we leave it, we're unemployed and will probably have to leave Skye.'

Thea's eyes shone with tears. 'Do you think we can trust him? *Shh*, here comes Valentina.'

Valentina arrived in the doorway, hands on hips in mock irritation. 'You're a fine one, Esmerelda Wynter, leaving us to the dirty work and then swanning up looking relaxed.

Thea said you were on a work call. Were you sorting out what happened yesterday?'

Ezz found herself beaming. 'Yes, I hope it'll be OK now. I've brought the bin bags.'

'Good,' Valentina said. 'The builder's been and gone, but he's returning with his truck at four to collect the rubbish, so we need to get a move on.'

'Yes, ma'am.' Ezz gave Valentina a salute, then hurried indoors to heave out the damp old kitchen units that Dev was ripping off the wall, grabbing a few seconds to pass on the gist of the good news to him, causing a huge smile to blaze across his face.

They could all stay on the Isle of Skye.

Chapter Ten

Having waved Valentina off to Inverness the evening before, Ezzie entered her office on Monday morning with the sensation of everything being the same but different. The office was the same . . . but she was different. Lighter. Happier. Cautiously optimistic. Her heart felt funny and fizzy, as if it knew how close she'd come to losing her life in Rothach Hall. She started her computer and thought about Mats sitting in her chair to switch it off after she'd stormed out on Friday. The email she'd been drafting was waiting in her outbox. Her pen and pad lay neatly on her desk.

Gwen bustled in, unaware of the tumult since they'd last seen each other, her neat bun almost exactly the colour of the grey stripes on her dress. 'It's a month to Christmas Day. My great-niece Caitriona says she's filled in the online application for temp staff, as you asked.'

Ezzie found Caitriona's application and read it quickly. 'She sounds great, especially as Peony and Georgia have asked for three days over Christmas and two over New Year. I'll email her and say yes please.'

Gwen beamed. 'It'll be grand if Caitriona joins me in the kitchen. She's a bright and willing lass.'

Ezz was about to answer when she caught the sound of the large front door opening and voices on the air.

Gwen whispered, 'Those bairns surely love their fresh air. They're out in their boots and coats every day.'

Then 'those bairns' – Astrid and Alvin – bounced in through the office door. 'It snowed,' Alvin yelled, his cheeks pink and eyes shining. 'On my yacket.'

'It's *jacket* in English,' Astrid reminded him witheringly. 'But it did snow a bit. Tiny flakes blowing around.' She beamed at Ezz, who beamed right back. They were such beautiful children. In their snowsuits and woolly hats, blond curls peeking out, they looked like models from a magazine.

Grete and Mats crowded in, propelling the children further into the room. Grete looked more relaxed than lately and even wore her usual twinkly smile. 'Ezzie,' she began.

'It's *Christmas*!' Alvin burst in, bouncing on his boots, leaving damp spots on the carpet. He bounded up to Ezz's desk. 'Scottish Christmas, and pudding.'

Smiling, Ezz leant over the desk. 'Gwen and I were just talking about Christmas, and I was wondering what your family would like.'

'Christmas with presents,' Astrid said helpfully.

'Definitely with presents,' Mats agreed, grinning. 'But they're Santa's department, not Ezzie's. And when we said we'd need to discuss Christmas with Ezzie, we meant Farmor and me. And not necessarily the instant we reached home.'

'But it's only a month to Christmas,' Astrid pointed out. 'You said. And that Emil, Filip, Walter, Liam and Ronja are coming in less than three weeks, straight after Lucia Day.' To Ezzie she added, 'Lucia Day is when the light comes. We couldn't be in the procession this year, because we're here.'

Grete patted Astrid's head. 'It's a Swedish tradition, is it not? The children carry candles and we go to church.'

'That sounds wonderful.' Ezzie shifted her gaze to encompass Mats and Grete. 'Whenever you'd like to—'

'We have *julbord*,' Alvin interrupted, clambering onto the only empty chair.

'We'd accomplish more if you children went indoors to Josefin instead of interrupting.' Grete raised her brows.

Astrid and Alvin immediately quieted. Grete's words seemed to signal that a meeting had been declared, because she stripped the children of their snowsuits while Mats carried in extra chairs.

'Would anybody like a drink?' Gwen offered, taking control of the pod machine. The adults chose coffee and the children hot chocolate, which Gwen topped up with cold water for safety's sake.

Mats threw his coat over the back of his chair. 'This is a special Christmas for us in Scotland, so we'd like to choose the best of everything. In Sweden, our main day is Christmas Eve and here it's Christmas Day – so let's have both.'

'We've arranged it with *Jultomten* – that's Santa – to bring half the presents on Christmas Eve and half on Christmas Day,' Grete added solemnly. 'On Christmas Eve we'll prepare a *julbord* of herring, meatballs, saffron buns, and all our traditional treats. As I'm Norwegian, we usually have cloudberry cream, too. Do you know cloudberries? They look like your blackberries but are golden. Apparently, they grow in Scotland too.' She looked enquiringly from Ezzie to Gwen.

'We can look into getting some,' Ezz returned, writing it on her pad, trying not to betray that she'd never heard of cloudberries.

Gwen sounded dubious. 'Perhaps we'll get them online, frozen or dried if not fresh.'

Grete looked horrified. 'Then I will ask my daughter Maja to bring some. On Christmas Day, we will like a traditional Scottish Christmas dinner. Please remind me what it is.'

'Like anywhere else in the UK, really,' Gwen began. 'Turkey, roast potatoes, pigs in blankets—'

Astrid and Alvin burst into giggles. 'Pigs in *blankets*?' Astrid spluttered. 'I want my pig in a duvet. Or a sleeping bag.' She almost fell off her chair with laughter.

'In . . . a car,' Alvin suggested, bouncing in his seat.

'No, the cars are for the ponies.' Astrid was obviously enjoying the flight of fancy.

Ezz grinned at their giggles. 'Pigs in blankets are just small sausages wrapped in bacon.'

'Aw.' Alvin looked deeply disappointed and climbed onto his grandmother's lap to suck his thumb.

When the food had been discussed, Ezz said, 'The Christmas trees are coming soon and we'll need extra decorations for them. I wondered whether you'd be choosing them or—'

'Yes,' Astrid said with alacrity. 'Farmor just said we didn't bring any *tomtar* with us, but that's OK because we're in Scotland.'

Ezz glanced at Mats for enlightenment. 'Part of our folklore,' he explained. '*Tomtar* are what you might think of as trolls. They live under our houses. They're a bit mischievous, but they keep us safe. At Christmas, they form part of the decorations.'

While Ezz was trying to imagine this, Gwen went back to work and Grete said she'd leave the choosing to the others and go upstairs to rest. Ezz somehow found Astrid climbing on her knee, asking, 'Can we see decorations on your computer?' Then Mats plonked his chair beside hers and scooped up Alvin, and they made a happy group raiding online stockists for angels, lights, baubles, tinsel, balloons and a small artificial tree for the children's playroom. Only one supplier said they didn't deliver to the Scottish Highlands – not that Skye was technically part of the Highlands – and the rest promised delivery by the weekend.

The only tricky moment was when Alvin corkscrewed round on Mats' lap to say, 'Will Mamma come for Christmas?'

Mats held him tightly. 'She's with Andreas this year, *lillen*, and you and Astrid are at Rothach Hall with me. But we can FaceTime Mummy after lunch.'

'Yeah,' said Astrid instantly.

Alvin just shrugged and rested his head tiredly against Mats' shoulder. Ezz's heart melted when she saw Mats drop a consoling kiss on his son's blond hair. Although she'd never reached a place in her life where a child of her own seemed a great idea, she sometimes felt she was missing out and wished that her nephew Barnaby lived closer. She was looking forward to having him at her place over Christmas, though.

'I wonder what Josefin's making you for lunch?' Mats said, probably as a distraction.

'Pepparkaka.' Alvin perked up.

Mats laughed and gave the tiny body an extra hug. 'Gingerbread? She's making that for Sunday. You and Astrid will help, I think.'

Astrid slid from Ezzie's lap and rubbed her tummy. 'I'm hungry.'

Mats gathered up their outdoor things. 'It is lunchtime, so that's good. Thanks for all your help, Ezz.' He dropped his voice. 'Everything OK? I think Mum's decided to act as if she never saw the resignation letters.'

She found herself smiling into his eyes, seeing only kindness there. When she'd found him strange and distant at first, he'd probably been uptight and anxious about his children – and his ex-wife, of course. Catching herself wondering what closeness remained between Mats and Inger, she accompanied him to the door. 'That sounds comfortable. Thank you.'

She watched him follow his children, nodding pleasantly to a middle-aged couple who were hovering by the reception desk, which Orla had strung with twinkling fairy lights. A bowl of cones lent their piny scent to the air. The woman was short and rounded, her brown hair streaked with grey. The man had lost his hair altogether and was taller but stooped, with blue eyes and weather-roughened cheeks. Ezz turned to them. 'Hello, can I help you? Sorry, the receptionist must have gone to lunch. We don't get many visitors in winter.' The couple stared at her.

'Are you looking for the public rooms?' Ezz asked pleasantly. Then her attention flew back to the man. 'Oh, you were here a few weeks ago . . . ? You must have enjoyed your visit.' She smiled, remembering how he'd hovered on the drive and needed encouraging indoors.

The man beamed. 'I enjoyed it very much. It's nice you remember me.'

The woman took a tiny tentative step. 'You're Esmerelda Wynter. We've come to see you.'

'Me?' Ezz was puzzled by the way the woman's knuckles had whitened around her bag strap. Then misgivings struck as she remembered someone had once threatened to sue the hall after they'd tripped on the stairs. It had been during Tavish's time as manager. Mindful of Grete and Mats on the other side of the door to the family side, she took a step back. 'Would you like to come into my office?'

'Thank you.' The woman sounded faint, as if being arrested or something, but trying her best to be brave.

The man rested a reassuring hand on her back, and they entered, glancing about the polished, comfortable room. The additional seats were still ranged around, and they selected two.

After Ezz had seated herself on her own side of the desk, she covered a rising sense of apprehension with a smile. 'What brought you here today?'

They exchanged glances. Then the woman said waveringly, 'This is my husband, Rick Colville, and I'm Kay Colville. But I used to be called Kay Loveless.' She sucked in a deep breath. 'And you used to be called Lindy Loveless.'

A buzzing began in Ezz's ears. She stared at the frightened-looking woman, trying to rehear the words and check whether there could be any interpretation other than the one that had blazed into her mind. She, Ezzie, *used to be called* . . . ? The room seemed to shimmer. A sudden noise at the window startled her and she glanced up to see hailstones bouncing from the glass like handfuls of white pearls. She'd become so cold that she could have been standing out there.

But then came a strange feeling in her chest, as if her heart recognised the small, uncertain woman in the room. 'You're . . .'

The woman's voice shook harder. 'I'm your birth mother.' She gulped. 'Oh, dear. Could I have a glass of water?'

Ezz had to force her legs to carry her to the water cooler and fill three glasses. Rather than pass the drinks into waiting hands and risk skin touching skin, she placed their glasses on their side of the desk. Resuming her seat on legs like cooked spaghetti, she lifted her own glass to her lips and sipped, the rim chattering against her teeth.

Though she'd heard people say, *I had to pinch myself to make sure I wasn't dreaming,* she'd never really believed it . . . until now, when disbelief was making her feel disconnected and distant. The woman – Kay – had dark, shy eyes, which seemed to drink Ezzie in. An attractive sixty-something, despite requesting the water, she hadn't reached for it, but kept her hands fisted in the lap of her navy-blue skirt.

Ezz dragged her gaze away from Kay to study Rick, his pale skin the type that went pink at the least thing, like hers. He sent her a tentative flicker of a smile. Her voice emerged as a croak. 'And are you . . . ?'

The light that leapt into his blue eyes made them look suddenly familiar. 'I'm your birth father,' he said huskily, and his eyes rimmed pink, to match his cheeks.

A million questions crowded Ezz's brain. Her tongue stuck to the roof of her mouth. Her birth father was *with* her mother? Had they been in touch all this time? Her eyelids fluttered, as if she were about to faint.

Kay shifted nervously. 'Sorry we've surprised you. Rick came before, as you realised, but I couldn't come then. We looked you up online.' Her hands twisted in her lap. 'They tell you not to do it this way, don't they? They tell you to go through an intermediary and get counselling. Sorry that I couldn't wait.' She looked at Rick and gave him a wan smile.

Rick returned it with the kind of affection that spoke of years of love. 'I think we should tell her our story.' He turned to Ezz, his frown suddenly anxious. 'But we don't want to get you in trouble with your boss.'

Automatically, Ezz glanced at the clock and managed to unstick her tongue. 'This can be my lunch hour.'

Rick rose and made to close the office door.

Ezz stopped him. 'It's not that kind of job. If anyone comes to talk to me, I'll need to deal with it.'

He exchanged looks with Kay but resumed his seat. He was tall and loose-limbed. Involuntarily, Ezz glanced down at her own willowy frame.

Unsteadily, Kay reached for the water and sipped. Then she fixed her brown eyes on Ezz again and began. 'Rick and I went out together at school. I was fifteen and Rick was seventeen when we realised you were on the way. I was about sixteen weeks pregnant by the time I confessed. Mum and Dad went crazy. My mum . . .' Anxiety puckered her forehead and she had to sip more water. 'She was old-fashioned. She tutted at girls in revealing clothes or boys who wore earrings. My parents called our lovemaking "misbehaving" that "reflected badly on them".' Her lip wobbled. Rick took her hand. Ezz was incapable of doing more than listen in stunned silence.

'They turned into jailers, walking either side of me if I went out,' she went on in a shaky voice. 'Friends who saw me in town shied away. School excluded me – but I wasn't sorry because everybody made me feel dirty and ashamed. I had lessons with other pregnant schoolgirls in a small room at a place we called "the unit".' She barked a short laugh. 'Any school*boys* involved in our pregnancies remained at their usual schools, of course.'

'That wasn't fun either,' Rick put in morosely, colour suffusing his entire head. 'There was a lot of talk. And Kay's parents wouldn't let me near her. Literally slammed the door in my face. My mum and dad were a bit more understanding. But when the social services asked if they'd like the baby – you – to live with them, they still said no.'

A strange feeling snaked through Ezz at the idea of all the grandparents involved rejecting a helpless baby.

'You were seventeen, Rick,' Kay said patiently, as if this was an old argument. 'I was underage. Everyone blamed you.'

'I was to blame. But we could have got married as soon as you were sixteen,' Rick said obstinately. 'If your parents would have allowed it.'

Kay wiped her eyes and blew her nose. Her nose and eyes were red, and she wore the weary air of someone used to tears. 'I didn't stand up to my parents. If you read the timeline of adoption in England and Wales, it will tell you that forced adoptions had stopped by 1980, when you were born, but that means "forced" by social workers and courts. But also there's "forced by circumstance". My parents worked on terrifying me. My life would be ruined. *That boy* had ruined it. Having sex under sixteen was *illegal*. I could protect you from being called a bastard by giving you up for adoption, whereas keeping you would be selfish and make Mum and Dad live with the shame. They owned a house in a nice street and said we weren't the kind of family to have illegitimate kids running around.' Her eyes burned into Ezz, and Ezz felt immobile in their tractor beam. 'They said I couldn't keep you if I lived with them,' Kay choked. 'So, I'd be out on the streets. The social worker did say that she'd do what she could to help if I wanted to keep you. She was never clear about how or when, and I used to think that I might end up trying to look after you while we both lived under a hedge. No defined alternative was actually offered. I was . . . a silenced voice.'

Slowly, Rick took an old photograph from his pocket and placed it on the desk.

Ezz's gaze fell to its burred corners and faded colours. A curly-haired teenage girl smiled bashfully in the shelter of the embracing arm of a gangly youth with hair that fell forward over his forehead, the rest brushed back behind his ears. It was blond, straight hair, like Ezz's and his smile was sharp at the corners and his nose very straight, also like Ezz's.

The hail rattled against the window again. The room grew dimmer as big, bruised clouds sank lower over Rothach Hall. Normally, Ezz would have switched on the lights, but she felt unable to move. This was what she'd both dreamed of and feared since she was old enough to consider what it meant not to have been born to Maxie and Vince, the wonderful couple who'd loved her and protected her and earned the right to be called 'Mum and Dad'.

In the face of Ezz's unyielding silence, Kay sighed. 'I gave birth to you in hospital. You were so beautiful and looked just like Rick. I had you with me for a day, then you were gone.'

'As Kay wasn't allowed to contact me, I found out from the social worker that you'd been born,' Rick supplemented. 'It was a weird feeling. I was angry. I got in fights. I left school without finishing my A levels and got an apprenticeship as a bricklayer. I've got a building company, now.'

Ezz just listened. She felt heavy and stiff, as if made from new leather.

'I did my O and A levels at a different school,' said Kay, who seemed caught up on conveying details. 'Mum and Dad still treated me like a naughty kid, but the social worker told me something important – that education is the key to a better life and—' she leant forward '— *independence*. She used to say it emphatically like that. I think she realised my mum cowed me and I needed to get out from under her thumb.'

'Worked, didn't it?' said Rick. He smiled into her eyes.

Surprise made Ezz find her voice. 'You're together now?'

Kay smiled, looking relieved that Ezz had broken her silence. 'Yes. We're married.' Pleasure rang in her voice.

Ezz fought to straighten this out in her head. 'Like . . . you met each other again later? Recently?'

Both Rick and Kay's smiles faded. 'We got married when I was eighteen,' Kay explained. 'The day I was dropped off at uni, I wrote to Rick and told him where I was.'

'I drove straight there.' Rick's blue eyes shone. 'She was eighteen and away from her parents. I'd finished my apprenticeship. We went to the register office and made the arrangements. By the time the notices had gone up and all that, I'd changed jobs to one near her uni and found us a rented flat. We got married.' Triumph rang in his voice, and maybe an echo of disbelief, as if marvelling at their own actions.

'I didn't tell Mum and Dad for ages,' Kay admitted, looking at Ezz apologetically. 'I studied hard. Rick worked hard, to keep us both. I'd finished my entire first year at university before we went back to my parents' house together and told them.'

'I thought your mum was going to lay into me,' Rick said sombrely. 'Especially when it became obvious that there was nothing they could do, and my parents had known for months. Your mum was *wild*.'

Kay winced. 'She could be a difficult person,' she explained to Ezz. 'Hard to ignore but hard to get along with. Excellent at emotional blackmail.'

A rumble of thunder sounded in the distance. A flash of lightning lit the room.

Rick leant forward, as if to make certain that Ezz could hear him. 'I wanted Kay to stay away from her parents. Her mum was domineering, and her dad didn't try to intervene. They hadn't earned her love, but she felt duty to them. Those months before we admitted we were married were lovely.' He folded his arms, and then his legs. 'It took her parents about five years to thaw enough towards me to be civil, but we never forgave each other.'

Ezz stared at him, fascinated by the colour of his eyes, so like her own.

He took out his phone, fiddled with it for a moment, then laid it on the desk facing Ezz. This time the image was the pin-sharp phone-camera display she was used to. Two women grinned out of the camera, both with mousy, wavy hair, one flowing and the other bobbed. They were curvy, wearing ribbed T-shirt dresses and flip-flops. The one with bobbed hair rested an arm affectionately on the shoulder of the other.

Rick's voice seemed to come from a long way off. 'Julia and Iona. They're your sisters.'

She gazed into the screen, something rising like bile in her throat. Thea and Valentina were her sisters . . . not these strangers. 'You didn't give them away then?' she asked bluntly.

The awkward pause felt as if it could shatter, like glass. Kay stammered, 'W-we were married by then. It wasn't the same.'

Ezz sat back without touching the phone, which she imagined would be warm from Rick's pocket. Her father.

Rick's face crumpled. 'When a child's adopted, you can't ask for them back. You were gone. You had a new name and a new family, but you weren't forgotten. We always went out on your birthday, just us two, and we drank your health. And cried.'

Ezz sucked in air, and it felt like the first proper breath for ages. 'And every year, on my birthday, I feel sad that it's the anniversary of the worst day of someone's life.'

Kay's eyes widened. Passionately, she cried, 'That wasn't the worst day. The worst day was when they took you away!' Tears had begun to ease from her eyes, and her top lip squared off as if she were fighting a sob. 'No warning and hardly a goodbye. Just pills to stop my milk and an assurance that I'd have other kids. I was sent home the same day, and Mum told me to put it behind me.'

'It?' Ezz whispered, shaken by the sordid account. Valentina's jokes about them being mistakes that had been swept under the carpet didn't seem so funny now she knew it was true. She fought for composure, to quell her rising rage and think clearly about the present. 'Why have you come looking for me now? If you got married in late 1983, that's decades ago.'

Her sharp gaze caught an exchange of uneasy glances. 'It was difficult,' Kay muttered at last. 'I was ill when Julia was born. My mum was the only one who could help. There was this "at last you've got it right" vibe.'

'Where is your mother now?' Ezz asked, already knowing what she'd hear.

'She passed away,' Kay whispered.

Outside, the wind flung fresh hail at the windows. Thunder rolled. Lightning flashed. Ezz usually loved storms, but this one seemed to be clamped around her head. 'You couldn't defy her to check I was OK?' She looked between the two of them and pictured instead of their shocked and miserable countenances the warm, laughing faces of her parents Maxie and Vince Wynter. She fought for composure. 'Your mum was right,' she said to Kay. Words began tumbling from her. 'I was never called a bastard. I was called "sweetheart" and "darling", and I was loved every day until Mum and Dad died. They were wonderful people, who made music that made people dance.'

She lifted her voice over the rattling of hail. 'All my memories are with Maxie and Vince and the wonderful sisters they gave me. You say you had no choice? No voice? Well, neither did I – just like you didn't give me a choice about you disrupting my life today. I've lived without you, and you've lived without me, yet suddenly, decades after you married and began part two of your family, you want to crash in here to see me?'

Kay began to sob. Rick sat in stunned silence, gazing at Ezz. Maybe it was seeing those blue eyes, so similar to her own, that made her pause. With an effort, she softened her voice. 'I didn't know my birth name – Lindy Loveless.' She didn't point out the irony of the surname. 'So how did you know my adoptive name? The TV show I watched about adoptions kept saying how hard it is for birth parents from my birth era to get that information. Did an agency get it? I thought they had to contact me first, and not just go blabbing my details to you.'

Rick rubbed his face. His voice was hoarse, as he was trying not to join Kay in tears. 'Like Kay said, she had a social worker when she was pregnant and after. She accidentally left a piece of paper behind at Kay's house once. Your adoptive name was on it. And like Kay said, recently we googled you.'

Ezz felt as if her forehead would split because her heart, unable to cope with the mass of emotions, was directing the overflow to her brain. 'You've known my name since *then*?' She jumped up. 'I don't even know why you're here. I'm obviously still a dirty secret, a source of shame, or you wouldn't have waited until my grandmother died to find me.' Shaking, she drained the last of her water, having to fight to keep it down.

Kay's tears eased from her eyes. 'It's not really that,' she protested.

In the face of Kay's distress, Ezz summoned her few remaining manners. 'I'm sorry to be angry. It was human error that created me, human error that allowed you to know my adoptive name, human frailty that kept you away. But we're strangers. You have your family and I have mine – the family that chose me. Lindy Loveless, she's not me. I'm Ezzie Wynter. Do you . . .' She drew in a long, strangled breath that hurt her throat. 'Do you think you could leave?'

After a long silence, during which Ezz stared blindly from the window, they rose and left. She listened to their dragging footsteps.

It wasn't until Ezz heard the front door close and turned back that she saw a white business card on her desk. In a no-nonsense blue font, it read: *Rick Colville, general builder. The best around.* Then there was a phone number, email, and a street address in Coventry, England. Scrawled hastily in a white space were the words: *We were kids*.

Ezzy began to cry in enormous coughing sobs.

After a few minutes Thea flew in through the door and flung her arms around her. 'What?' she demanded. 'What is it? Oh, Ezz, what *is* it?'

Ezz lost all control, clinging to her sister as she sobbed and gasped out the story of the birth parents who'd turned up out of the blue. Thea rocked and comforted and didn't argue with what Ezz had done in sending those out-of-the-blue parents away.

That was what sisters did. They gave you unconditional love.

Chapter Eleven

As was usual in the winter, Ezz arrived home in the dark, to an unlit, empty cottage. Her garden light picked out pebbles of ice on the path left by the hailstorm. An iron frost had clamped down on the island and, despite her scarf, coat and boots, she shivered.

Diagonally across the road stood the Jolly Abbot, windows cosily ablaze. Brodie was out the front, rolling a metal beer barrel, hair and beard dark against the light streaming through the door. He waved, then hugged himself to mime how cold it was. She waved back imagining strolling across and into the bar, ordering a large glass of chardonnay and perching on a bar stool to peruse the food menu. The dance of cold wine in her mouth, the smoothness on her throat. The softening of her muscles as the weight of the bad day rolled from her shoulders. Another glass while she ate. And then the slow burn of whisky to round off the meal. Maybe the Regular Drinkers would be in, and they'd chat. She'd have company without the effort of unpausing her dating apps and going through the palaver of arranging a date.

With an effort, she turned away from what would surely be a horrible back-sliding into destructive behaviour, drunken mistakes and hangovers. Her door opened with a small sucking sound, as if to warn her that it had been thinking of freezing shut.

Exhausted by this afternoon's emotional hurricane, she stepped indoors. The door closed behind her with a click and she paused in the dark, listening to the quiet whirr of the boiler that was all that welcomed her home. Abruptly, she missed the company of Thea's fluffy little dog Daisy, who she'd often looked after on her days off. Now Thea's lovely boyfriend Dev worked from home, Daisy stayed with him.

When Ezz had finally stopped crying earlier, it had been all she could do to persuade Thea that she'd survive being home alone tonight, knowing Thea and Dev had already booked dinner at a favourite restaurant. 'You can come with us,' Thea had gabbled anxiously. 'Or we'll eat at home. Or at the Jolly Abbot. Or we can get Rosamund to make it up as a takeaway and eat at yours . . .' Thea had so obviously wanted to ease Ezz's pain, and Ezz had rarely loved her sister more, even while firmly vetoing each and every suggestion. She'd blown her nose and asked, 'How did you know I was upset?'

Thea rubbed her arm. 'Mats Larsson heard you crying and Grete called me.'

'Oh, crap.' Ezz sniffed. So, Mats had heard her bawling like a baby.

Later in the afternoon, he'd stuck his head into her office. 'All right?'

She'd pressed her lips together to hold back fresh sobs

and tried simultaneously to turn her mouth up at the corners in a smile and nod. She'd probably looked like a deranged puppet.

An hour later, it had been Grete's turn to pop in. 'Here are some pepparkakor for you to try. Gingerbread,' she added, though Ezz would recognise most Christmas-related sweet treats at fifty paces.

Then Josefin brought in hot chocolate. 'I made one too many by mistake.' Her gaze had radiated sympathy. 'And this was on the reception desk.' She put down a white, square envelope. On the front was written neatly *Esmerelda Wynter*.

Ezz had smiled and taken the letter without comment and without opening it. She appreciated every little gesture meant to make her feel better but had longed to be alone in her own place. And now she was.

And it didn't feel that great. Her head ached like hell.

Wearily, she fumbled for the light switch and then the yellow walls and red carpet became real. Slowly, she hung up her coat, changed her shoes for the purple slipper boots that had been a birthday gift from Thea, and headed for the kitchen. While she made coffee, she filled the silence by playing music from her phone through the small speaker on the windowsill, then seated herself at the table. That her birth parents and a hand-delivered letter in unfamiliar handwriting had turned up on the same day seemed too much of a coincidence not to be connected, so it was no shock when she finally slit the envelope and found the letter inside had been signed 'Kay'.

The note was on the headed paper of the Scalpay View Hotel, the kind hotels put in rooms and visitors took away as souvenirs.

146

Dear Esmerelda,

I'm so sorry we made you angry. I don't deal well with rage and find it hard to keep my end up in arguments, but there are a few things I wish I'd felt able to say to you. Here they are:

A birth mother is a mother for life, regardless of whether she was able to parent her child.

I envy your adoptive parents because I had the grief and anguish of giving you up and they had the joy of loving you. Still, I'm grateful to them for giving you everything I couldn't – a good life, a nice home, a family, and others to love you.

I've loved you since your conception, and so has Rick. Your not loving us won't stop us loving you.

Love,

Kay

Ezzie sipped her coffee and read the letter again. *Rage.* Had she been guilty of rage? If so, it shamed her. Now, she wished she'd been able to keep the meeting polite and light, asked enough questions to assuage her curiosity, exchanged handshakes or awkward hugs, and said goodbye. Instead, she'd lost control so badly that she couldn't remember her own words.

Her doorbell rang, a fruity *ding-dong* like a distant relative of a church bell. Her heart tumbled. Was it Kay and Rick? Not knowing her address, had they followed her home from work?

Apprehensively, she padded to the door. The Isle of Skye wasn't the kind of locale where doors had spyholes, and the view from the windows was blocked by the porch, so she opened the door a crack and peeped around it.

Then she opened it wider. 'Mats.' She heard relief with top notes of welcome in her voice.

He looked pleased at this reception. His beanie hat was blue today and it brought out the streaks of blue in his eyes, even in the scant light spilling from the hall. Behind him, the frost was beginning to look like a silver-white wolf pelt thickening for winter. He held an insulated bag horizontally between his hands. 'Mum's certain that you won't cook tonight, so has despatched me with a meal and hopes you won't feel awkward about accepting it.'

His eyes crinkled, and her heart gave a giant thump. She stepped back to allow him in, as if there was nothing strange in the son of the bosses driving into the village to deliver her supper. 'That's so kind.'

He brought a rush of the outdoors with him, fresh and chilly. 'Kitchen?' he suggested, though already halfway down the short hall.

'Lovely.' She closed the door and followed him.

He turned, and his smile became winsome. 'I've brought my meal, too, in case you don't want to eat alone. But I can take mine away again. I just hope you like meatballs with mashed potato and lingonberry sauce. I made it.' He unzipped the bag to let her peek in. Each plate had another inverted over it to protect the meal. Heated pads sat above and below. It smelt delicious, and she realised she'd had no food since breakfasting on a cereal bar.

Touched by this unexpected kindness, she summoned a smile. 'It'll be nice to have company. I'll set the table.'

It was a novelty to take plates from a bag and, *hey presto!* dinner was served, the heated pads becoming heated placemats. The meatballs sat in a brown sauce next to glossy green broccoli and clouds of white mashed potato. The lingonberry sauce, ruby red, occupied a small bowl of its own.

Ezz's appetite stirred at the meaty, roasty aroma of goodness, and she helped herself to the lingonberry sauce, which wasn't quite cranberry, but wasn't miles away from it. Her first bite of meatball, sauce and mash widened her eyes. 'Mm. This is special. And you cooked it? Did you bring the sauces with you from Sweden?'

Mats made a faux-hurt face. 'I did not. The meat sauce is made like a roux and the lingonberry is created like a fruit jus, boiled with a little water and sugar until the berries burst. I had to buy frozen lingonberries online, but this meal is my party piece.'

She began to eat with real enjoyment. 'Then I must invite you if I have a party. You can help with catering.'

It was said lightly, but he nodded as if she were perfectly serious. 'I'd accept that invitation. I enjoy cooking. It's relaxing and I like fresh, quality meals.' He twirled half a meatball in the meat sauce, then added a dab of lingonberry. 'In Skye, I have time to cook. Poor Josefin told me today that I'm doing her out of a job, because when she bakes with the children, I join in.'

Ezz didn't think Josefin would mind at all, but just smiled. She wondered whether Mats felt anything in response to Josefin's crush and found herself hoping hard that he didn't. Did that mean she was developing a crush on him herself . . . ? 'I'm glad you're finding Skye so relaxing,' she said, to divert her mind from that surprising path.

As Mats ate, he chatted easily about Christmas presents, conversation between them coming more naturally since he'd asked her to be herself and not worry how Tavish would have phrased everything. 'Astrid wants a Lego princess palace, and a hard hat and toolbelt to wear while building it. Alvin's asked for an aeroplane, and I suspect he means a real one.' His eyes smiled. 'I'd like to buy a few things to remind them of Skye, too.'

'Maybe you'd like a day in Portree?' she suggested, noting this reference to the family's visit having a time limit. Once she would have been delighted to see Mats go. But now . . . she realised she really was in no rush. Her feelings for him had been subtly altered by trusting him with hers and Thea's secret. 'You could buy traditional tweeds, kilts or hand-made soap. The town's pretty. Some of the buildings around the harbour are even more colourful than Rothach village and it's a lovely journey from here, though I'm always shocked how fast the locals drive on the winding roads. I guess they know every curve.' She watched him devour the final meatball with a smack of his lips.

After they'd enjoyed the meal, it seemed only polite to offer coffee in the lounge. Sharing a sofa with him didn't seem a concern after so much had happened, and she placed the two steaming mugs on the small table, then lit a match to the woodstove. She took her seat on the squashy, turquoise sofa and looked at him.

Disarmingly, he smiled, his fair hair gleaming in the overhead light. 'I expect you're wondering if making sure you ate is the only reason I'm here.'

Her own smile became fixed as her heart sank. 'To have a quiet word about professional conduct?' She picked up her coffee and blow across the surface to cool it.

His fair brows swooped together. 'Whose?' He sounded perplexed.

She raised a brow. Her brows were naturally arched, ideal for a 'do you take me for a fool?' expression. 'I was unprofessional getting upset today and I—'

'I'm here because I'm concerned,' he butted in, with a hint of exasperation. More gently, he continued. 'That's what friends do. They assume that someone crying herself sick has a genuine issue, and they get your sister. And they keep everyone else away. If they bring you dinner, it's meant to be a nice gesture, not an excuse to tell you off.' He picked up his coffee and it slopped over his hand. He had to lick it off rather than let it drip. 'I don't know why I have to keep reminding you that I'm not your employer.'

Half her mind was on watching his tongue, but her cheeks still burned. 'Thank you for being so thoughtful. I didn't mean to be ungracious. It's been emotional.' A sip of her coffee, then she replaced the mug on the table with a sigh.

A gleam of a smile softened his eyes. 'Are you OK, Ezzie? I'm not sure what happened except you had visitors and they upset you. Is it anything Mum should know about? You know Dad threw out the guy who bothered Thea. My parents would take a dim view if something like that happened to you, too.'

A tiny warm feeling sparked in her heart. Mats might be impetuous, but that didn't stop him being empathetic. 'It wasn't anything like that. I've never known who my birth parents are but they turned up out of the blue, today. It went badly.' She paused, realising that she was once again sharing something deeply personal with this man. When he just waited, she went on. 'I never realised before what people meant when they said they were in an emotional washing machine, but I certainly felt tossed around and in danger of drowning. I got close to crossing to the pub to drown my sorrows.'

As soon as the words were out, she felt embarrassed

and ashamed. 'I didn't do that,' she added hastily, and perhaps unnecessarily, as here she was, sober.

'Well done.' He sounded as if he might even understand how hard it could be to leave alcohol to those who could handle it. His gaze rested on her, a crease between his eyes. 'Your birth parents arriving like that . . . it must have been a massive shock.'

'They've always known my adoptive name, apparently, and googled me. It came up on the Rothach Hall website.' A band of tension formed around her head, and she massaged her temples. 'I guess scenes like today's are part of the reason not every adoptee has the urge to find their birth family. I might have been happier to see them if I had even half a memory of being someone else, somewhere else. But I was adopted as a tiny baby and had a wonderful life with Maxie and Vince. We sisters all adopted each other, too.' She closed her eyes. 'I yearned for Mum and Dad today. Dad would have hugged me and insisted everything would be OK. Mum would have been wise, making me see all sides of the story. Whereas Kay – I can't even feel gratitude that she didn't abort me, because it's obvious she just left it too late. Kay's mother certainly would have wanted that, otherwise. She sounds a horrible bitch.'

Exhausted, she let her head tip back on the sofa. 'My birth parents have been together all this time, having other children who they didn't give away. Julia and Iona.' Just saying their names felt like a betrayal to Thea and Valentina. 'Two more sisters . . . except they're not. They're strangers. And I'm the eldest, not the middle child, which I've been since Thea joined our family. It all feels . . . *wrong*. I don't want it. I don't want them. I don't want it to have happened.'

He rose to tend the woodstove, opening the squeaking

door and adding sticks and a small log as Ezzie hadn't made the effort to build the flames after lighting the kindling.

'My name was Lindy Loveless,' she said, watching him tend the flames. 'Ironic surname, in the circumstances. I have no connection to it. I'm Ezzie Wynter.' She watched the flames leap and catch.

He returned to sit beside her, his eyes on her, as if waiting for her to go on. She murmured, 'I get my hair and eyes from my birth father. I don't look like my birth mother, so if I have anything of her, it's not immediately visible. But I have my values from Maxie and Vince. They would never have tidied a baby away as a dirty secret. Their love seemed to grow with every child they adopted, and they were kind and wonderful. My birth parents were just . . . careless. Young. They let themselves be shoved around.' Unwillingly, she remembered the scribbled words on Rick's business card. *We were kids*. 'I know I'm being unfair,' she admitted. 'My maternal grandmother was obviously bossy and hard, and it sounds as if my grandfather just went along with her. I understand it must have been difficult for Kay. But they've been together all these years, my first family. Kay and Rick, Julia and Iona.' Her throat burned and she had to pause to swallow. 'Without me.'

Then a warm arm came around her; a friendly, comforting arm that allowed a small distance to remain between their bodies. 'I'm sorry.' His voice was deep and sweet, as soothing as warm water and honey on a sore throat.

She didn't push him off. It felt too friendly and comforting for her to pause to examine what else it might mean. 'How do you think you'd feel, if strangers came along saying they were your parents and they loved you?'

153

He paused. 'They said they loved you? That's a big thing.'

'Kay couldn't say it to my face. I was too angry,' she admitted. She rose and went to the kitchen to fetch Kay's note, collecting Rick's business card from her coat pocket on the way back. She gave him both and waited while he read.

When he looked up, his eyes were moist. This time he took her hand while he said quietly, 'It's not too late for counselling.'

She rested her cheek on his arm and closed her eyes. 'I think it probably is. My heart's too disconnected from them.' It would have been easy to nestle closer and take comfort from this unusual new friend, who was also part of the family she worked for, a wealthy person, a parent, different from her in almost every regard. But so kind.

With a giant blink, she made herself sit up. 'I'm sorry, I'm blethering. Are you familiar with "blethering"? You hear it quite a bit in Scotland. It means talking too much and with too little thought and, in this case, talking too much about myself. How's everything with you?'

A flicker of his eyelids, but he seemed to understand that she wanted a change of subject. 'Everything with me is much as it was. My children are angelic devils. We're all enjoying the fresh air and wide-open space of Skye. Astrid and Alvin love Broadford and the tiny market full of hand carvings and woven or knitted things. They don't seem to notice that every view includes a snowy mountain or the sea, but I suppose they see both in Sweden. The air's so sweet here, without the traffic of a city, and we have the enormous grounds of Rothach Hall rather than the communal garden attached to my apartment. And I love having so much time to spend with my kids.' His eyes

154

crinkled at the corners. 'Mum's preparing for the arrival of the rest of the family, especially her other grandchildren. My sister Maja's been on FaceTime. Ronja has two new teeth, Walter has proposed to one of his little female friends, Liam has swum fifty metres.'

Though she would have been hard put to remember which was Walter and which was Liam, she smiled. 'Children change so fast. My nephew Barnaby will be in bed, but I must talk to Valentina, because she doesn't know what happened today.'

Immediately, he glanced at his watch. 'I'd better go.' But he paused, concern lurking in his eyes. 'You'll be OK?'

'Of course. Thanks for coming and for the lovely Swedish meatballs.' Sometime this evening, perhaps through having someone to spill her heart to, the worst of the anger had seeped away.

Neither of them had finished their coffee but still he rose and stretched. 'The children were excited about the Christmas decorations being delivered soon. Alvin thought *Jultomten* was going to bring them on his sleigh.'

She laughed. 'More likely a delivery person in a white van.'

At the front door, he paused to pull on his coat and hat before opening the door. A gentle touch to her arm, then he was gone, striding down the frosty path under a dark sky pricked with a million points of starry light. She remembered standing further up Chapel Road only a couple of weeks ago and gazing up at the stars, imagining the constellation Birth Family of which she was part. Her heart hurt with the knowledge that though major stars had become visible today, they had so disappointed her with her birth story of mistakes and fear.

She wondered whether her maternal grandmother

had ever acknowledged that she'd failed fifteen-year-old Kay. Ezzie might have squirmed at Maxie sitting her down for mother-daughter talks about human appetites and condoms, but they'd been vital, as was the larger conversation about wise choices. Maxie's counsel had armed Ezzie to deal with life. Her school had provided knowledge of where to go for protection from pregnancy and sexually transmitted diseases.

Fifteen-year-old Kay had sounded clueless and, objectively, it was hard to blame her for that.

The sound of Mats scraping the ice from his car came sharp upon the freezing air, and she gave him one last wave before closing the door and preparing to FaceTime Valentina, who she knew would be just as comforting and empathetic as Thea had been.

She did love those sisters of hers.

Chapter Twelve

Ezz had taken Wednesday and Thursday off this week, as Orla could be on duty to cover the phone and fulfil the needs of the Larssons, and had enjoyed driving up to Trotternish in the north of the island. Hiking the coastal path had soothed away some of the angst of the days before, sandwiches and a flask in her backpack, the snowy peak of the Storr on one hand and the rocky Rona and Raasay across the sea on the other. She wondered whether she could allow herself time off for similar outings once the rest of the Larssons arrived on December 15th, as Orla's last day was the 13th. Grete had told Ezz she should continue to take her days off as usual, but it still felt wrong.

On Friday morning, the last-but-one day of November, Thea strolled into Ezz's office with a cheerful smile. She wore a balaclava with a hat over it and gauntlet gloves that made her look as if she'd swapped hands with a lobster. Her cheeks were pink with cold. 'Christmas trees at the bottom of the steps,' she announced. 'Dev's here to help me and Sheena, and he's made stands.'

'Fantastic. I'll come out.' Ezz pushed back her chair and pulled her coat off the hook behind the office door, before scrambling into it. Anticipating that an extra pair of hands might be appreciated in manhandling the trees today, she'd dressed in trousers and flat boots. Orla had left the reception desk, where she'd recently added red-berried holly to the twinkle lights, and was at the open front door, huddling into her cardigan while she made admiring noises about the two luxurious spruces lying at the foot of the stairs. 'They're handsome trees, are they not?'

'They're gorgeous.' Ezz squeezed past and then beamed at a grinning Thea, Dev and Sheena. A stepladder and tools waited nearby. 'Thea, do you not mind cutting down your beautiful trees?'

Thea chuckled. 'Trees need thinning out to let others grow. And they're not actually my trees,' she added as an afterthought.

A nearby sash window slid up and Mats called out, 'Hang on and I'll give you a hand getting them into the house.' The window slid down again with a clunk.

By the time he appeared in a hat and fleece, Ezz was at the foot of the steps, inspecting the stands Dev had created from split saplings and inhaling the wintry perfume of freshly sawn spruce. She glanced up. 'Mats, this is Deveron Dowie. He's Thea's partner and has kindly helped out with the trees.'

'Thea's a bit wee for this job,' Dev observed, and winked at Thea.

Mats shook Dev's hand and then Astrid and Alvin pelted out of the door, dressed like Mats in fleeces that looked suitable for a polar exhibition and shouting, 'The Christmas trees!' Grete and Josefin lurked more sedately in the doorway with Orla, very sensibly waiting for the trees to come to them.

'Can we have the tallest in reception?' Grete called. 'The ceiling is higher there than the lounge.'

With many hands making light work, the stands and then the trees made it indoors with the minimum of huffing and puffing, and then outdoor clothes were shed in a colourful pile on Orla's chair. Ezz had stored the decorations the children had chosen in her office and now she and Orla carried out box after cellophane-wrapped box, while Grete decided which decorations should be taken into the lounge ready for the second tree.

Mats, Dev and Sheena soon had the first tree in its stand. Alvin swirled the long string of lights around his hands when no one was looking and Ezz's nimble fingers proved adept at untangling them, grinning at the little boy's sudden Christmas joy as he chattered to Grete about the presents he hoped *Jultomten* would bring. Soon she found herself up the stepladder, threading the lights through prickly branches that smelt of winter and outdoors while the children danced around the ladder and laughed excitedly. 'Look! There are so many colours.'

'Can I turn them on?'

Mats chimed in. 'Astrid can switch on the lights, and Alvin open the first box of decorations. But wait—'

Astrid didn't wait. The galaxy of lights burst into life, half-blinding Ezz, who laughed and, blinking, stumbled back down the ladder. 'I think they'll have to go off again until the rest of the decorations have been hung.'

While Astrid did that, Alvin fell on the boxes and removed their lids to reveal a glittering rainbow of baubles. Mats and Dev hauled the other tree through to the lounge and Alvin promptly abandoned the Aladdin's cave of decorations in favour of bouncing along behind them, squeaking and skipping with joy at the excitement.

Astrid remained in reception, enchanted by the baubles. 'Here's a star, Farmor. Josefin, look at the tiny reindeer! Ezzie, I chose these crystals for the tree, didn't I?'

Gwen arrived and immediately called Peony and Georgia away from ironing bedding to bring vacuum cleaners. As they cleared spruce needles and sawdust, the two young women didn't look much more than children themselves with ponytails and make-up-free faces, and let themselves be encouraged into admiring the shining baubles. Then Alvin ran back to investigate the noise made by the vacuum cleaners and immediately struck up a relationship with one of the machines – the kind with a face and a bowler hat.

Soon Ezz, Orla, Josefin and Astrid were hooking the dazzling, glittery ornaments onto the beautifully scented tree, the spruce needles brushing their fingers, while Thea and Grete moved on to the tree in the lounge. Candy canes hooked over branches, tinsel twirled madly up the trunk, and everybody chattered, buoyed by the simple act of bringing Christmas to the hall.

Finally, Ezz climbed the stepladder again, this time to top off the tree with the large silver star studded with tiny white lights.

Astrid was allowed to switch on the rest again and every coloured light sprang to life. Astrid jigged on the spot. 'It's Christmas, it's Christmas, it's *Christmaaas*!'

'Christmas!' Orla and Ezzie repeated, clapping.

Josefin laughed, cheeks ruddy. 'We are early. It is not even December until Sunday. Then we will light candles and make *Lussekatter* – saffron buns – for first advent. Even though we should really wait for St Lucia Day, *Lussekatter* are always good.'

Not sure what first advent was, Ezz admired the finished tree, twinkling and shimmering between the connecting door to the family side and the staircase to the upper storeys. It was a jolly hotchpotch of colour.

Astrid arrived before her with a little jump. 'We have our own tree in the playroom as well. Do you want to see? Alvin and I decorated it. Josefin helped.'

Ezz paused uncertainly. She'd spent all morning helping with Christmas decorations. Did Astrid's invitation come before her waiting office work?

Josefin added her voice to Astrid's. 'Some of the ornaments are made of salt dough that the children made. Come up with us.'

Warmed by the fun of joining in, Ezz answered, 'That would be lovely,' and found her hand in Astrid's as she was led into the family side, up the stairs and along the corridor to the playroom.

There, Astrid flung the door open with a triumphant 'Look!'

A small artificial tree stood near the window – the kind with its own twinkle lights. Two long strings of tinsel, one red and one blue, threaded through the branches. Shapes made from baked salt dough had been inexpertly painted and liberally daubed with glitter. Others were cut from shiny red, blue or silver card. 'Beautiful,' Ezz said, charmed by the home-made decorations that twirled in the draught.

161

'And now let's go see the other tree,' Astrid demanded, tugging Ezz's hand once more.

Ezz wasn't sure Grete expected her to turn up to inspect the tree in the lounge, but when she arrived Mats had joined his mother and was festooning the branches with a string of pretty silver bells. Peony, Georgia and Gwen were vacuuming up the last of the needles – carefully, as Alvin was riding the vacuum cleaner with the bowler hat.

'Astrid wanted me to see the tree in the playroom,' Ezz explained, in case anyone wondered why she wasn't back at her desk.

Mats grinned. 'Impressed?'

Ezz nodded firmly. 'Very.'

'I think Ezzie should be our guest for advent on Sunday,' Astrid announced. 'We have guests for *fika* on advent, and she's the only friend we have here.' Persuasively, she swung Ezzie's hand. 'Will you come? We're going to make saffron buns. Farmor, Daddy and Josefin will drink glögg.' She pulled a face. 'In Sweden, Alvin and I like Julmust but the Co-op in Broadford hasn't got any, so Josefin says we'll have Irn-Bru. That's Scottish,' she added helpfully.

Flustered, though feeling a glow that the little girl saw her as a friend, Ezz said, 'I'm not sure—'

But Mats chimed in. 'That's a lovely idea, Astrid. I'm proud of you for thinking of it. Would you come, Ezz? The Swedish often gather with family and friends on the Sundays of advent to welcome the season. *Fika* just means an afternoon treat such as coffee and cake.'

With so many pairs of eyes on her, Ezz didn't think she could say more than, 'Of course. That's so kind of you.' Incredibly touched that Astrid wanted her at advent, Ezzie squeezed her hand before saying it was time to return to her office. An extortionate quote for public liability insurance for next summer season awaited her negotiating skills.

Josefin followed her out. 'How about the pub tonight?' she asked tentatively. 'But not if you don't want to, of course.'

Ezz, halfway across the polished tile floor of reception, paused, wondering whether Mats had hinted to Josefin that Ezz had had problems with alcohol. 'Sorry. Thea's invited me for supper and to FaceTime our other sister.' Although she'd discussed her disappointing meeting with Kay and Rick with each sister individually, she was looking forward to discussing it again with them both together now that her emotions were settling. What would they feel she should do next – if anything? What did they think of her having two stranger-sisters? It wouldn't change how she felt about Thea and Valentina – that was for damned sure. They were her growing-up-together sisters. Loved-you-all-my-life sisters. More-important-than-anyone-else sisters.

Josefin's face fell. 'Sure.'

But having had a taste of loneliness recently and having enjoyed Josefin's company and appreciated the occasional gift of hot chocolate or gingerbread, Ezz added, 'How about tomorrow evening? We could eat at the pub—'

Instantly, Josefin was all smiles. 'Fish and chips?'

'Definitely.' And Ezz found herself looking forward to it.

She'd barely settled down to wrestle with the insurance quote when her mobile phone rang. When she answered, she was surprised to hear Erik's bluff tones. 'Do you know is Grete home?' he asked, the second that greetings were over.

163

For an instant, Ezz hesitated. Never before had Erik made such a call. 'She was a few minutes ago.'

'No answer from her phone,' Erik grumbled.

Swiftly, Ezz explained about the tree decorating and the vacuum cleaner. 'Perhaps she couldn't hear her phone. Would you like me to—'

'I call Mats, I suppose.' Erik sighed, as if this was an enormous imposition, and politely said goodbye.

At about one, Ezz caught sight of Josefin and the children in reception, and Astrid called, 'We're going for a walk through the trees.'

'Sounds great.' Ezz waved back. She quite fancied a walk herself. Maybe after she'd eaten her salad sandwich. She'd just opened her desk drawer in search of it when Mats appeared through the connecting door and made a beeline for her office.

He presented her with a white-napkin-wrapped parcel. 'Gwen made chocolate cake. I'm bringing you some to have an excuse to check you don't mind about advent Sunday. Astrid's not enjoying the solitude as much as Mum and me. She misses having more people around her – especially her mother, of course – but I don't want you to feel obliged.' He plumped down in the chair opposite.

To give herself a moment, Ezz peeped within the napkin. 'Looks delicious.' Now she was being offered a way out of what was plainly a family occasion of which she possessed only the sketchiest of understanding, she realised she wanted to be there. Tentatively she said, 'I should mention that Orla's off at the weekend, so I'm supposed to be working.'

Mats' fair brows sank deep over his eyes. 'Don't start the "should I take my days off" thing again. I'm certain you work more hours than you're paid for, and you'll be our guest.'

'Oh.' She hoped she hadn't gone too pink at his swift reassurance. 'Then, thank you. I'd love to.'

'Three o'clock.' He jumped up. 'Just come through the connecting door. It will only be family. Unless Alvin decides he wants to invite the vacuum cleaner,' he added.

Ezz laughed. 'Gwen, Peony and Georgia want to get in for a good clean. Gwen's waiting to talk to Grete about it. Alvin can continue his friendship with the vacuum cleaner then.'

His eyes danced, but then he looked thoughtful. 'Tell Gwen to clean on Monday. I'll take the family out for the day.'

And then he was gone, leaving her watching the big white door shut behind him.

That evening, Ezz left her car behind and set off on foot for Thistledome, Thea's cottage, toiling up the steep lanes to the top of the village. An overcast night meant no stars to twinkle down, and apart from exchanging greetings with a couple of the Regular Drinkers near the pub, she saw no more evidence of Rothach residents than lights at cottage windows.

Fraser's dog Scotty barked as she puffed past his gate in Balgown, the roses in his garden bare but for their thorns. When she finally made Loch View, she paused to look over the cottage roofs marching down to the beach between trees that grew in the direction the wind blew. A sense of peace descended. If it meant that she and Thea could stay in this beautiful spot she'd done the right thing confiding the truth about the accident in Mats Larsson.

Then she rapped the bee-shaped door-knocker of

Thistledome. Daisy barked indignantly. Since Dev had moved in, Ezz no longer felt free to knock and enter. Delighted though she was that her little sis had found her soulmate, she had no wish to stumble into the sizzling sex life Thea was so smug about.

The door opened to reveal Dev and Thea grinning, and Daisy exhibiting the springs in her paws. 'Hiya,' sang Thea.

'Arf, arf!' shouted Daisy.

'Thought you'd never come. I'm hungry,' said Dev.

Ezz stepped into their welcome. 'Hiya. So am I. Shush, Daisy.' Everybody talked across one another as Ezz hung up her coat then turned and caught Thea stealing a quick kiss from Dev. 'You two are sickening,' Ezz mock-grumbled.

'We know.' Thea laughed and swished her ponytail as Dev smiled at her, his heart in his eyes. Ezz smothered a pang of envy. It wasn't as if she'd planned to be single after coming to Skye. It was just that small rural communities had no nightclubs or anonymous bars for casual meetings – which was where the dating apps had come in. She'd chosen to date mainly off-island to avoid running into erstwhile casual dates, but the flipside was a thirty-to-forty-minute journey from home, even before Henry the auctioneer and Major Magic had unnerved her.

'We have stew and herby dumplings.' Thea steered Ezz down the hall towards the kitchen table, which was laid for three. 'Dev, can you carry the dish to the table? I'll strain the green beans.'

Ezz watched the easy way they moved around each other while Dev used a towel to lift the dish out of a multi-cooker, and Thea lifted a pan from the hob. Finally, they were ladling stew onto plates, Daisy flopping into her dog bed with a sigh. Thistledome was strict in its no-dogs-fed-at-the-table policy.

'Mm. This is gorgeous.' Ezz cut into a dumpling with the side of her fork. 'I wonder whether Valentina's builder's begun work. When I'm at the hall during daylight hours, it's hard to spot what's going on in the village.'

'I saw his pick-up a couple of times.' Dev lifted his cutlery. 'But Valentina and Gary have to approve his plans before he can order materials. She's only owned the cottage about three weeks. If she has to gain permission to change the windows, she might not achieve her goal of being here this summer.'

'She will,' Ezz and Thea chorused. Ezz added, 'Big sis will organise the builder.'

'She'll find a way to get him to prioritise her job,' Thea added with a wicked grin. 'I'll bet when we speak to her tonight, she's made progress.'

It was only an hour later that they gathered around Dev's laptop; Ezz squashing in with Thea and Dev on the sofa in Rothach, whilst Valentina sat in her elegant primrose-yellow dining room in Rosemarkie, Barnaby at her elbow. It was unusual for Dev to join one of these FaceTime chats, but Ezz thought maybe he wanted to hear who'd been right about Valentina's builder.

Barnaby greeted them first, ready for bed in his pyjamas. 'Yo,' he said, standing beside Valentina's chair.

Ezz burst out laughing, while Valentina's jaw dropped. 'Where on earth did you get "yo" from, Barnaby?'

'Balbir at school.' Barnaby's brown hair fell in his eyes, and he flicked it out again with a cherubic smile. 'Hello, Auntie Ezzie; hello, Auntie Thea and Uncle Dev. Dev, have you been watching footie?' His eyes shone, having recently developed a love of football that his mum and aunts didn't share. 'Me and Dad watched Hibernian play Dundee. We support Hibs. It was two-two until Hibs scored in extra time.'

Valentina broke in. 'Tell Auntie Ezzie and Auntie Thea what you're looking forward to.'

Barnaby frowned. 'Livingston being at home to Dundee?'

Valentina rolled her eyes. 'Not football. We're looking forward to visiting Rothach to see our new cottage, aren't we?'

'Yes!' Barnaby's eyes lit up. 'We're coming to stay, Auntie Ezzie.'

Valentina laughed. 'It's: Auntie Ezzie, *may we* stay with you?'

'Oh, yeah.' Jiggling impatiently, Barnaby repeated the question in its polite form.

'Of course,' Ezzie agreed, before the little boy had finished. 'Separate to your Christmas visit, do you mean? When?'

Valentina answered for him. 'Separate, please – the weekend after next. I know you might be working, Ezz, but the builder wants to talk to me. He's getting the partition wall up, and he's ordered the new windows, but he needs to get the drains inspected and first we need to finalise options for the new bathroom.'

'Is Gary coming?' Ezz turned to smirk at Dev, because she and Thea had been correct about Valentina having the builder working already, but Thea and Dev were whispering together. Dev murmured something about waiting but Thea made outraged eyes and hissed, 'No, now.' Ezz turned back to the screen.

'I think Gary will come,' Valentina answered. 'Thanks, Ezz. I hope it's not too much trouble.'

'Never. I haven't got round to changing the bed you slept in a week ago,' Ezz said with cheerful pragmatism. 'Barnaby can have the camp bed as usual.'

They chatted until Barnaby's bedtime, and Ezz prepared to ask her sisters' views on her suddenly reappearing birth parents now five days had elapsed. But, after exchanging goodnights with Barnaby, Thea spoke before Ezz could order her thoughts. 'Actually, Valentina, you, Barnaby and Gary could come and stay at Thistledome that weekend, because we're going "doon hame" to Dumfries to see Dev's family. We have to tell them . . .' With a pause as if for a drum roll, Thea finished, '. . . that we're having a baby!'

After a moment's thunderstruck silence, Ezz launched herself at the small, beaming woman at her side, and scooped her into a big hug. '*Thea!* Oh, that's amazing! How long have you known? Are you OK? *Congratulations*, Dev.' She kissed Thea soundly on her cheek, then hugged Dev, too, aware of Valentina squealing from the computer screen, and everyone laughing and exclaiming.

Finally, they quietened enough for Thea to enlarge on her announcement, her brown eyes glowing like the polished bronzite sold in Skye Market. She leant into Dev's embrace as if they were sharing their excitement through their skin. 'I wanted you two to know first. I'm twelve weeks along, and we've had a scan, which shows things progressing as hoped. The due date's June 12th.' Thea pulled a face. 'I'll be the grand old age of forty-two by the time the baby's born, so I'm a "geriatric" mum. I've met my midwife at Sleat Medical Centre at what's called the booking appointment where the midwife checks how I am and takes my blood pressure and everything. Valentina,

I'm sorry not to have told you in person but I couldn't wait.'

Valentina waved the apology away. 'Unimportant, except that I can't hug you. How exciting.' Her bottom lip wobbled. 'And emotional. Wow, you'll be such awesome parents.'

Thea wiped her eyes on her sleeve. She laughed. 'The midwife gave me a list of things pregnant women shouldn't eat and do you know what's on there?' She paused for dramatic effect. 'Haggis!'

Dev joked, 'Good job it's just the mum. The Scottish assembly might make me turn in my kilt and sporran if I couldn't eat haggis.'

Thea turned serious. 'I must also avoid heavy lifting, and contact with certain chemicals, including herbicides and insecticides. And I should wear gloves rather than come into direct contact with the soil.'

'We'll work around it,' Ezz assured her. 'But now I see why Dev came with you to lift the Christmas trees. What about the ponies and the donkey? Are there areas for caution there?'

'Blimey. I don't know.' Thea's eyebrows curled in thought.

'Well, Thea's health and that of the baby is the most important thing,' Ezz said hastily, not wanting to introduce negativity. 'It might mean asking Sheena to work more hours or get the seasonal gardeners in early in the spring. Hopefully, Sheena can cover your maternity leave.' She gave Thea another hug. 'Honestly, I'll be the only member of staff left at Rothach Hall soon. I'll have to read up on the latest guidance for your maternity benefits and everything. I think you get a maternity certificate at twenty weeks.'

170

Thea clutched her rosy cheeks. 'I can't believe it's happening. We knew our chances were reduced because of a woman's eggs being poor quality after forty, and were prepared for disappointment really. Will you speak to Erik and Grete for me?'

'Leave that to me.' Ezz couldn't stop hugging her little sister. 'Just make me a new niece or nephew to love. Have you told Ynez?'

Thea beamed. 'We've arranged to FaceTime her and Jean-Jacques later, after Ynez's restaurant is closed. She's working tonight because, though she's semi-retired, she still covers her manager's nights off. I'm sure she's going to be thrilled, though.' Thea's relationship with her mercurial birth mum had got off to a rocky start, but now they were in touch regularly they'd developed a fond relationship.

Because of Thea's wonderful, joyful, unexpected news, Ezzie didn't mention her own birth parents at all.

Later, when the excitement was over and she was strolling home, boats' mooring lights flickering in the darkness of the bay, Ezz's mind circled back to her joking words about soon being the only staff member left at Rothach. The housekeeping crew of Gwen, Georgia and Peony were stalwart, but when Orla left, they'd be down to six, one of whom was Thea, whose role would have to be adapted to her maternity needs. Ezz never remembered staff numbers being so low. If the family hadn't been in residence, it wouldn't have been a problem. The answering machine would have picked up any calls Ezz missed and otherwise things would have gone on at the slow pace of previous winters until spring saw more visitors enjoying Rothach again.

She paused to watch the burn rush down the hillside and under the bridge, glinting in the sparse street lighting.

But if the family wasn't in residence, Ezz wouldn't have Alvin and Astrid popping into her office to explain their dietary preferences, or Josefin inviting her to the pub.

And she would have continued to think Mats as entitled as his ex-wife Inger rather than unexpectedly kind and insightful, despite his tendency to rush into things.

A pair of headlights swooped up Bridge Road towards her, and she stepped aside, making sure she didn't slip down the grassy bank in the process. The burn might not actually be frozen, but it would certainly feel like ice, if she slipped in. The headlights flashed, so she waved, assuming she knew the driver.

When it had growled up Glen Road, she resumed her walk, pulling her scarf higher. Her mind strayed back to Kay and Rick Colville. Presumably they'd left the island after she'd asked them to go. *Told* them to go. Demanded. Shouted . . . ? She wasn't even sure. Perhaps they were home in Coventry, near Julia and Iona. She tried to summon the image she'd seen on Rick's phone. They'd looked like Kay: rounded and with wavy hair.

Only Ezz seemed to have inherited Rick's height. His straight blond hair might be long gone, but the blue eyes and sharp features he'd passed to her had been almost unnerving in their familiarity. Did he look like his parents? He hadn't said much about them, except they'd supported him more than Kay's family. But not enough to agree to take Ezz.

Were Kay and Rick hoping she'd contact them? Answer Kay's letter? She supposed they might be, or Rick wouldn't have left his card. They must have wanted to meet her to travel all the way up to Skye and pay for a nice hotel. But hadn't the time for them to want her been forty-four years ago?

172

'I don't know why I feel so screwed up over this, because I'd always known I'd come from some angsty situation,' she murmured to herself, as she turned into Chapel Road and saw the welcome sight of the lamp in her garden. 'I couldn't have had a happier childhood than Mum and Dad gave me, with music in the house, and cuddles every day.' She turned up her path, fishing for her keys. Maxie, Vince, Thea and Valentina were her family even if they didn't share the blood in her veins.

Kay, Rick, Julia and Iona did – but that only made them connected by DNA. Not by love.

Chapter Thirteen

Saturday evening with Josefin proved quieter than Ezz had anticipated, because Josefin drove to the pub and therefore drank pink lemonade instead of wine or whisky.

'The children spoke to their mother today and Astrid was upset, which meant Alvin got tearful too,' she said in explanation. 'If I get a call saying they wake crying tonight, then I go home.'

A group of older people in a corner burst out laughing and Ezz noticed Thea's neighbours Fraser and Masie among them and gave them a wave. 'Wouldn't Mats go to them?' she asked curiously.

Josefin nodded vigorously, smiling when Brodie brought a steaming plate of golden fish and chips from behind the bar. 'Whoever gets there first comforts the child, I suppose. But when they've been upset . . . I prefer to be near.'

Cutting into a crisp chip, Ezz conjured up an image of Mats and Josefin blundering around in their pyjamas if one of the kids cried during the night. It seemed . . .

intimate. 'You get on very well with Mats,' she couldn't help saying, before popping the chip into her mouth.

Josefin nodded. 'He is a nice man.' Her attention settled on her plate, and she seemed to sink into her thoughts. After a minute of working through golden batter and crispy chips she said quietly, 'He likes you, I think.'

Shock flashed through Ezz and she flushed over her suspicions that Josefin herself had feelings for Mats. Not wanting to upset the balance of the friendly atmosphere by saying she liked him too, she answered wryly. 'Really? If so, he hides it well sometimes.' Then, because she assumed everyone within a mile's radius could have heard her big boo-hooing session after Kay and Rick's visit, she added, 'Though he was kind after I had an emotional meeting on Monday. Did he tell you?'

Josefin's gaze slid her way. 'A little. He said you were adopted as a child and then these people turned up saying they are your parents.'

Ezz nodded, stopping to sip her orange juice. 'I don't doubt they are.' Over the rest of the delicious meal, she shared the story Kay and Rick had told her.

Josefin shook her head sadly. 'There is no winner, in this. Just acceptance or not.'

It was an astute point and Ezz glanced at Josefin with respect. All her life, she, Valentina and Thea had discussed what being adopted meant, and she'd thought herself realistic as to why a first family might have been unable to look after her. Unwanted pregnancy had been high on the list. She'd just never thought that the rest of her birth family would have been going on intact, leaving her behind. Four people were related to her – and she hadn't even asked how many others, like living grandparents, aunts, uncles, cousins – and she felt like the only one not invited to a party.

Rather than spend further time on uncomfortable thoughts, she turned the conversation to Josefin, laying down her cutlery on her empty plate and deciding she'd have a big cappuccino in place of dessert. 'You're staying here with the family for Christmas, aren't you?'

Josefin smiled, her friendly eyes alight. 'I agreed to stay. My son lives in America. I will see him in the summer.' Then she looked wistful. 'He has a new boyfriend, who looks very nice. I look forward to meeting him.'

'That sounds great. It's a shame when family's far away, isn't it? I keep in touch with my other sister and my nephew Barnaby by FaceTime. And my brother-in-law,' Ezz added, realising she'd left Gary out.

Josefin ate a dessert and drank coffee, then took out a card to pay her share of the bill. 'I will see you tomorrow for advent?'

Ezz was surprised by a small flutter in her stomach. Was that a butterfly because the first thing that had come into her mind about the advent gathering was that Mats would be there? She thought of Josefin's remark that Mats *liked* Ezz. 'That's right,' she said. 'I look forward to it.'

After Josefin had left, instead of going home, Ezzie bought another orange juice and joined Maisie and Fraser's table. It was an unusual move for her, but it was an opportunity for company. And she didn't want to give butterflies over Mats too much room to roost.

Much better to let herself be distracted by Fraser teasing Maisie, or their friends sharing their Christmas plans.

Mats stared at his phone screen, and the pretty, perfectly made-up face of Inger on the FaceTime call. Astrid had been so upset when speaking to her mum earlier that Inger had called Mats once it was late enough for the children to be in bed. 'Where's the boat now?' he asked. Behind Inger he could see the kind of stateroom that wouldn't have looked out of place in a Bond movie, with a huge bed, acres of polished wood and fields of glass.

'At Marina Bizerte, North Tunisia,' Inger answered breezily. 'Are Astrid and Alvin OK? I hated them crying for me earlier.'

So had he, but it was a bit late for Inger to start worrying about that. 'I'm looking after them.' Earlier, he'd found the children asleep together in a puppy-like huddle in Alvin's bed, obviously seeking comfort, and his heart had tugged.

'I don't suppose you'd like to bring them south for a lovely hot Christmas?' she asked so sheepishly that he suspected not even she thought this a reasonable request.

He snorted. 'What would I do while you all celebrated Christmas on the yacht?' At her suddenly woebegone expression, he softened. Although she wasn't the most selfless of mothers, she did love her children. Next year, Astrid and Alvin might fly off somewhere for Christmas with Inger and Andreas. He'd be the one missing them and seeing them only on video calls. That's how divorced couples managed things. *My turn to have them for Christmas. My turn to take them on holiday.* At least Astrid would be in compulsory education by Christmas next year, which made it unlikely that they'd ask to take the children on a three-month cruise around North Africa and the islands. He couldn't bear to be away from them that long.

'Inger, when a couple split up, there's an adjustment,' he said gently. 'We agreed that I'd have the children this Christmas while you went off on your cruise with Andreas.'

'Are you still returning to Sweden in January?' she

asked, inspecting her nails. They were a perfect dusky pink.

'That's the plan,' he answered.

Inger heaved a huge sigh and seemed about to speak again when Andreas hove into view in linen trousers and a pale green shirt. He'd grown a beard, and the dark shape gave his face more character. 'We're waiting for you, darling. The tender's here to take us ashore.' As a clear afterthought, he nodded. 'Mats. Good evening.'

Mats imagined himself on Inger's laptop or tablet, a talking head propped up on her dressing table. 'Hi,' he said offhandedly.

Inger nodded at Andreas. To Mats, she said, 'I'd better go. I'll call the children again tomorrow.'

Irritated that their conversation about their children was apparently no longer important once Andreas wanted to go somewhere, Mats said shortly, 'How about we leave it a day or two, unless the kids ask to speak to you? Let them settle down a bit.'

Inger emitted a piteous, 'Oh!' as if Mats was forcing her from their children's lives. Then Andreas grumbled something too quietly for Mats to make out, and she murmured, 'OK,' said goodnight to Mats and ended the call.

Mats flung his phone on his bed and strode to his window. He rarely bothered shutting his curtains on these long nights and he stared over the gardens and the park towards the sea, fancying he could see it glinting in the moonlight. Inger had put on such an air of tragedy, as if she were outside, pressing her face against the gates of Rothach as he cruelly kept her kids from her.

He waited for his heartbeat to slow. Then he moved along to another window. If it wasn't for the copse and the way the land fell steeply away, he'd be able to see Rothach village. Josefin had gone out to eat at the village pub with Ezz tonight and he'd actually felt a twinge of jealousy on hearing their plans.

Somehow, the thought lifted his spirits, because he liked Ezzie Wynter more each time he met her. Tomorrow, she'd be the family's sole guest for *fika* on the first advent Sunday, in the lounge, before the big Christmas tree heavily laden with twinkle lights and shiny ornaments. It was small-scale compared to the gatherings they'd had at his mum and dad's house in Gothenburg, when most of the family and local friends would turn up to kick off the traditional run-up to Christmas. But whatever the number of people, *Lussekatter* or saffron buns would be served, and pepparkakor. They'd light the first advent candle and burn a bit of it. Next week, they'd light it again, plus a second candle, and burn some of both. On the third Sunday they'd relight those two and one more. On the last Sunday before Christmas when all four were lit, this process would have created a sort of staircase of candles, bringing in light to the darkest part of the year.

But only one guest for *fika* was fine. If it was the right guest.

Chapter Fourteen

Sunday morning saw Ezzie sitting in her office, working. The agency hadn't yet offered any suitable candidates to replace Orla. They'd advertise again along with the seasonal positions in the New Year, she decided, and made a list of three grounds staff, two part-timers to share the ticket office, and another on housekeeping because the public rooms needed more attention with increased visitor traffic. Intending to pass a copy to Gwen in case she knew any locals who might be interested, instead of stretching to catch the paper as it churned from the printer, she rose to her feet. Her eyes were irresistibly drawn to the view. Morning mist lay over the park like gauze scarves and she could only see halfway down the drive. But her gaze snapped to a familiar figure at the top of the drive, a man wrapped in a dark overcoat, gazing at the hall. A shred of mist wafted over him, making him look faded, like an old photograph.

Her stomach somersaulted. Rick Colville. Her birth father.

Ezz watched for a long minute. He didn't move. Why was he here? Something to do with her, obviously. Where was Kay?

After another moment, Ezz realised she needed answers to those questions. She turned away and took down her long black coat and went out, tapping slowly down the stone steps in her heels.

He smiled a greeting. 'Lovely place,' he observed, returning his gaze to the hall's façade. 'Most of Skye's stately homes and castles seem to be ruins.'

'They are,' she answered cautiously, feeling the mist's chill slide across her skin. 'Armadale. Knock. Dunvegan. Mr and Mrs Larsson restored Rothach.'

'Done a good job.' He cast her a fleeting glance, then returned his gaze to the hall with its tall windows set in grey stone. 'Love that turret. I've been lucky enough to work on a couple of restoration projects in Warwickshire. I think I'd have liked to be a draughtsman or an architect, if I'd stayed on at school. Missed out on university, as I told you.'

After their last, emotional meeting, it seemed surreal to be standing here with him in gentle conversation. 'I went to uni, but I partied more than studied.' Deliberately she added, 'My parents died when I was twenty. It was my second year at uni, as I'd taken a gap.'

That got his attention. He swung his eyes to hers, sucking in his breath. 'I had no idea your parents died so young. I'm so sorry, pet. Were they good people? Tell me about them.' Tears gathered in his eyes.

As she'd thought he might be stiff or offended, his sympathy wrong-footed her. She mumbled a few sentences about how wonderful Maxie and Vince had been, about Maxie's long auburn hair and Vince's wild curls, and

Maxie having a good business head and Vince being the emotional one. 'I always went to him when I was sad, and he'd play his guitar and sing,' she said, not sure whether she was letting Rick know that she hadn't needed him and Kay . . . or that she'd been loved.

Gently, he smiled. 'They sound great. I'm glad.'

Confused at the mixture of feelings this generated, she turned away to gaze down the drive to where the stone bridge was just about in sight. She knew birth parents often wondered what had become of the child they'd given up and remembered Kay's letter saying she was relieved to know Ezzie had grown up in a warm, loving family, even if she and Rick hadn't been able to provide that. For *her*. They'd provided it not long afterwards for Juliet and Iona. 'I thought you'd left the island,' she said abruptly.

'We stayed for a bit, in case you reached out.' His tone was conversational, and not accusing. 'We wanted to feel near you for a while. We're leaving today. We'll drive for five or six hours then get a motel and do the rest on Monday. Kay doesn't know I'm here, because I said I was going out to get fuel while she packed. I wasn't sure about bothering you at work – or whether you'd even be here on a Sunday – but I wanted to explain something.' Finally, he removed his gaze from the marching windows of the hall and faced her, his gaze as blue-eyed and direct as her own. 'Kay's mum. She was more than a difficult woman. Her rages . . . well she was an alcoholic, and Kay was frightened of her. Kay's so sweet and shy—' His voice wavered, and he paused to swallow.

A feeling crept over Ezz, as cold as the mist. She had to swallow hard. 'I used to be a heavy drinker, after I lost Mum and Dad. But I was over-affectionate when I drank.'

A wistful smile touched his mouth, his blue eyes watery.

182

'I wish Kay's mother had been. Still. Try not to judge Kay too harshly.'

Was that a note of reproof? Fresh anger bubbled up inside her. Tightly, she said, 'Tell me about your daughters.'

If he caught her intention to nettle him by not acknowledging that she was one of his daughters herself, he didn't show it, but continued in the same even, gentle way. 'Iona's an art teacher. Julia's a beauty therapist. Iona's got a little girl. Edina. She's four.'

He spoke so fondly that Ezzie felt unexpected tears crowding behind her eyes. Rather than try and make sense of her tangled emotions, she went on, 'And your parents?'

A grin lifted his pink cheeks. 'A bit creaky now, but alive. And my two brothers—'

Brothers? She had uncles too, and probably aunts and cousins. 'Do they know you're here, all this family?' she broke in, watching his face carefully. 'Julia? Iona? Your parents?'

His face fell. After a pause, he gave a tiny shake of his head.

'So, you're still ashamed of the teen pregnancy you caused.' She took a step away, reluctant to let him see her pain. 'Thanks for coming. Safe journey.'

'Esmerelda. Ezz!' he called after her.

'Got to get back to work,' she flung back, and took the curving stone steps so fast that she almost pitched onto her face and had to fling out a hand for balance.

By the time she'd regained her desk and checked out of the window, he was trudging back down the drive, head down. Then he merged with the mist and disappeared. Stupefied, she attempted to gather her scattered thoughts. Her grandmother had had alcohol problems? Ezz had known there could be a hereditary

183

factor with alcohol abuse, but it was hard to feel sympathy for anyone but Esmerelda Wynter right now. She dropped her head to her hand and covered her eyes, trying to think.

If there had been the first stirring, the tiniest thread of connection to Rick, it had faded when he admitted he and Kay hadn't told her sisters or grandparents that they'd tracked her down. *They must be ashamed of her.* Then she thought of Rick's obvious relief to know she'd been loved. *Or they were just clearing their consciences.*

Even whirled around by emotions, she knew she might be being unfair, but all she could do was *feel*.

Sucking in a huge breath, she removed her hands and wiped mascara from beneath her lashes with her fingers. The *Ghost Kingdom* TV show constantly advocated counselling, so feelings at a range of outcomes could be talked through and examined before meetings like the one she'd just been through. What it didn't advocate was birth parents throwing themselves into your life like flames into a box of emotional fireworks.

She longed to talk it over with Thea and Valentina, but they were both so wrapped up in their own happiness – Thea with her baby and Valentina with her second home in Fishermen's Cottages. She hadn't wanted to interrupt their joyful chatter with, 'And, about me . . .' That wasn't Ezzie. Ezz was strong and organised and self-sufficient. Ezzie had known all her life that she was adopted, so she could deal with Rick and Kay's appearance. Even with the knowledge of having been poor unwanted Lindy Loveless.

Any moment now, she'd gather her cartwheeling emotions and work out how.

* * *

Astrid and Alvin's upset of the previous day had been put to the backs of their minds in the excitement of baking saffron buns and, under Gwen's expert tuition, Scottish tablet – a traditional sweet that was made in trays and cut into cubes, a bit like fudge though less yielding. Astrid yodelled, 'Next week Gwen's going to show me how to make Scottish macaroons. And guess what they're made of, Dad?'

Mats glanced at Gwen's secretive smile and realised he wasn't meant to guess correctly. 'Dinosaurs?' he asked solemnly.

Astrid planted her sugary little fists on her hips. 'Silly, Daddy. Potato.'

'Potato?' He was genuinely surprised.

Gwen twinkled. 'Aye. The centre's made of potato and icing sugar, rolled in chocolate and coconut. Macaroons are grand.'

'Can't wait,' he said, thinking that actually, he probably could.

Alvin, who'd been kneeling on a stool, scrambled down and ran to Mats. 'We going in the lounge with the Christmas tree for advent, amember, Daddy?'

'*Re*member,' he corrected gently, swinging his little boy in the air. 'But first I have to ask Gwen to throw you in the washing machine with the tablecloths, because you're covered in sugar.'

Astrid pointed to the utility room where the washing machine stood. 'Yes, do it.'

'*Nej*, nooooo!' Alvin squealed before dissolving into a gale of giggles.

Mats turned for the stairs, Alvin on his shoulder like a sack of coal. 'OK, I'll take you for a quick wash and change instead.'

Josefin fell in behind with Astrid, who was still jokily advocating for her brother to be put in the washing machine.

By the time the children were clean, Grete was waiting in the lounge where the twinkling Christmas tree dripped with baubles and tinsel and smelt of the woods. She'd taken trouble with her hair and applied make-up, which Mats took as signs she was feeling more herself. As nobody had thought to make the glögg ahead of time, Gwen had bought mulled wine from the supermarket, and it waited in a warming bowl over a tealight beside the fire.

At precisely three o'clock, a light knock sounded on the apartment door, and then Ezz appeared, stepping self-consciously down the hall. With her willowy frame, she reminded Mats of a beautiful stork, lifting her slender legs and carefully placing each foot.

'Ezzie!' Astrid shrieked like a whistle. 'Do you want saffron buns or Scottish tablet? We helped Josefin and Gwen make them. And look how beautiful the Christmas tree is. We've lit the advent candle over here.' She appropriated Ezz's hand and towed her towards the window ledge beside the French doors that led into the private garden, where every twig dripped with moisture from the day's mist and the swing and treehouse looked damp and unloved.

Ezz smiled and wished Mats and Grete, 'Good afternoon,' as she let Astrid drag her along, with Alvin bouncing like a ball beside them. The light from the Christmas tree haloed her head as she passed by. On the sill, four white candles stood on a wooden box decorated with artificial pine fronds, which Grete had found at Skye Market because no one had thought to bring one from Sweden. 'It's up high so Alvin can't get it,' the girl explained solemnly.

Mats and Grete joined them and, ushering the children back a step, Mats struck a match to light the first candle. 'We'll only let it burn for a little while. Next week we'll light two, then three, and four on the final Sunday.'

'Then the candles go up like this.' Astrid drew a zigzag in the air.

Ezzie duly admired the candles and their stand. 'What a lovely tradition.'

Hospitably, Grete said, 'What would you like to drink, Ezzie? Mulled wine, soft drinks or coffee?'

'Coffee, please,' Ezzie said, but she looked unusually unsure of herself.

Mats put down his mulled wine and took a lemonade instead. Why did Ezzie look so weird? She was pale and distracted, her smiles for the kids wide but unconvincing. Surely she wasn't thrown off-balance by her employer making her coffee? At this moment, Ezzie was a guest.

Grete passed Ezz a cup, asking conversationally, 'Do we often get a white Christmas on Skye?'

Ezz gave that wide but unconvincing smile again. 'I'm afraid the weather at Christmas is no more predictable than any other time of the year. I like it when it's frosty or misty, but it looks even more amazing when we get snow – a real winter wonderland. When the mountains are white all over rather than just at the tops, they seem to be made from icing.'

'That sounds fantastic.' He kept an eye on the plate Astrid was now carrying. It bore two S-shaped saffron buns, their whorls studded by raisins, and two cubes of caramel-coloured Scottish tablet. Proudly, she presented the plate to Ezz.

'Ooh, is that for me?' Ezz was still smiling. 'Thank you, Astrid.'

Alvin had settled on the floor near the table, his legs bracketing an empty plate. Scottish tablet was clutched in each of his chubby hands, and he smiled beatifically as he munched. '*Tack så mycket.*'

'That's "thanks so much",' Astrid told Ezzie. 'Farmor, Farmor, you haven't eaten any tablet.' Astrid pulled her grandmother over to the table.

Momentarily, Mats was left with Ezz. He dropped his voice. 'Are you OK?'

'Fine, thanks.' She nodded enthusiastically, took a bite of the saffron bun and added, 'Mmm,' but even her murmur of pleasure didn't totally distract him from studying the look in her eyes. It reminded him unpleasantly of how she'd looked when he'd sprung his news about the *Garden Gladiators* team wanting to film at Rothach.

They watched Astrid supervise Grete's choice of Scottish tablet. 'Astrid's like Inger and loves a party,' he said.

'She's lovely,' Ezz murmured. 'Both your children are.'

'They're very fond of you, especially Astrid.' When she didn't answer, he murmured, 'Is something upsetting you?'

She could have shrugged it off, but instead she met his gaze, her blue eyes filled with shadows. 'My birth father came again earlier. He and Kay have left the island today. I – I would have liked to talk things over with Thea or Valentina but they're both busy.'

'I can see why his visit would rock you,' he murmured. Impulsively, he added, 'How do you feel about meeting for dinner? I make a good listener. And I hadn't realised I'd miss people my own age so much on Skye.' When her blonde eyebrows lifted in surprise, he felt he should add, 'Or is there a boyfriend to object?'

'No,' she said slowly. She studied him, then said suddenly, 'How about the Jolly Abbot? It would save travelling miles as a lot of Skye restaurants are closed in winter.' Then looked surprised, as if she hadn't meant to say it.

Though he'd been envisaging one of the nice hotel restaurants on the island and would have been perfectly happy with a drive of five or ten miles, he accepted before she took it back. 'Great. Eightish? I like to put the children to bed.'

'I'll meet you there.' She still looked startled that the conversation was taking place.

'Ezzie, Ezzie!' Suddenly Astrid was there, tugging impatiently at Ezz's black jacket and smearing it with crumbs. 'Would you like another saffron bun?'

Ezz answered, 'Thank you. I *would*,' as if she'd never heard a better suggestion and they went together to the food table, where Josefin was gently discouraging Alvin from eating more tablet.

Mats felt a hand on his arm and realised Grete was beside him, her glasses reflecting the lights of the tree. 'You're going out with Ezzie?' she asked in Swedish.

Irritated to have been overheard, he bristled. 'Any reason I shouldn't?' He raised his eyebrows, wondering if they arched as much as Ezz's did.

'Yes,' she said calmly. 'Soon you'll be based in Sweden while her life's here.'

He bit back a sharp retort about being too old to allow his mother to manage his life. 'I do realise that, Mamma. We're just going out for a meal in the village pub, as friends. Last night she did the same with Josefin.'

Grete furrowed her forehead in the 'don't take me for a fool' expression that he remembered so well from his teenage years. But then, a little up the hall, the white door from reception opened noisily and they both turned.

189

A familiar burly figure stepped into view, with windblown brown hair and cheeks ruddy with the cold. Mats blinked at the unexpected vision. *Pappa?*

Astrid erupted with glad cries of 'Farfar, Farfar! Why are you here?'

Erik stooped to let Astrid race into his arms and planted two loud kisses on her forehead. 'Because this is my house,' he rumbled reasonably, putting out another arm to receive Alvin.

'But you're coming later, with the others,' Astrid cried.

Erik made huge, surprised eyes. 'How can that be when I am here with you? Am I not a nice surprise?'

'Yes, yes!' Astrid gave him another hug. But over her head, Erik's gaze sought out Grete.

Aware of his mother's frozen silence, Mats stepped forward to hug his father, bulky in his coat. 'You're a very nice surprise. You're just in time for *fika*.' In his peripheral vision, he watched Ezzie and Gwen diplomatically melt away in the direction of the kitchen, carrying empty coffee mugs and plates.

Erik approached Grete and lifted his bushy eyebrows. 'Are you well?' he asked in Swedish.

She stepped forward and gave him both her hands, and a peck on the lips. 'Of course.'

Apparently satisfied for now, Erik began chatting to Astrid and Alvin in a mixture of English and Swedish. Ezz and Gwen returned, greeting Erik as friendly employees would, offering drinks and saffron buns. Mats made sure Ezz had fresh coffee too, not seeing why she should slip from guest to employee just because his dad had turned up without warning.

When he had a moment to speak quietly to Grete, he murmured, 'Would it be better if I stayed in tonight?'

190

'No. Probably better if you went,' she returned, then edged over to join Ezzie and Erik, as Erik – unfortunately – had turned to business.

'Does all go well in my absence?' he asked, before devouring a saffron bun in two bites, chewing while he awaited Ezzie's answer.

Instantly, Ezz put down her coffee, assuming employee status. She turned awkwardly to include Grete, probably feeling that reporting to Erik while Grete stood there might look like going over her head. 'This morning, I've worked on an email regarding the Christmas activities you talked about for next year, ready to reach out to six reputable hotels on the island in the hopes of partnering.'

'What Christmas activities?' Erik asked, regarding a chunk of tablet quizzically before popping it into his mouth.

Ezz hesitated, her gaze flicking towards Grete. Calmly, Grete stepped in. 'I asked Ezzie to explore winter visitor attractions. We talked of partnering with hotels by offering events for their guests and a festive menu at the café.'

Erik looked blank. 'Here? Why?'

Ezz's eyes widened as her glance at Grete plainly said, *Have I spoken out of turn?*

Grete gave a wintry smile. 'I looked for ways to make Rothach Hall more self-supporting . . . as you are talking of selling.' She lifted her chin.

Ezz's gaze swung to Erik, horrified. Mats shared her reaction. *Selling?*

Erik looked uncomfortable. He switched to Swedish to rap out a tense: 'We should discuss this privately.'

Grete shrugged and nodded.

Ezz's eyes shot to Mats, as if hoping he could transmit a translation. Then clearly feeling her role in the conversation to be over, she drew on her employee status to excuse herself. 'I'll help Gwen clear up.'

Soon she'd vanished into the kitchen. Ten seconds later, she glided past the lounge with a smile and bustled out through the connecting door. A guest no more.

The room fell quiet in her wake. Josefin distracted Astrid and Alvin by helping them switch baubles around on the glittering, multi-coloured Christmas tree with its swathes of silver bells. Mats watched his parents silently sipping coffee. In Swedish he said, 'I had no idea you were thinking of selling, Dad.'

Erik made a scoffing noise. 'Your mother and I had one conversation, that's all.'

Grete rapped out a reply, low and angry. 'When I asked if we could visit Rothach for longer each year, instead of working, working, working, you said you'd rather sell the damned place. That was your answer – not to ease up so we could spend some of the money we've earnt, but simply remove what you saw as the cause of the argument, regardless of how much I love Skye.' Hurt and accusation rang in her voice.

Erik beetled his thick eyebrows but adopted a pacifying tone. 'You're half owner, Grete. You know I couldn't sell without your agreement.'

Grete took a step closer to her husband, eyes glinting. 'What I know is that you could make it very difficult to keep Rothach Hall, because you retain the major control of everything. When it comes to Larsson Fiskeri I have worked by your side for decades, but *I* don't hold a title of CEO or chairman. I am executive officer, second-in-command, responsible for formulating policy for the board's approval, but with no vote of my own. You decide what our joint income will be and how much we can afford to funnel towards Rothach Hall. So, I looked for ways to bring in more money.'

Mats rocked on his heels, unsure whether to say, *You need to discuss this alone,* or to stay and listen. He'd assumed that Rothach Hall would one day pass to himself, Jonas and Maja so they and their children would be able to enjoy the gracious old house for years to come. It hadn't occurred to him that his dad would consider cutting the family connection with Skye. After overseeing the restoration of Rothach Hall, he'd thought Erik loved the place too. His parents had both wanted the hall, after all.

Grete bit out, 'You didn't want to take your hands off the reins of the company to take prolonged breaks with me, so you rattled your weapons to make me see things your way. But it didn't work, because here I am at Rothach.' Her voice tightened. 'And here I may stay.' With one last scorching glare, she turned and swept from the room. Diplomatically, Josefin kept the children occupied debating which baubles were the shiniest.

Erik, ruddier than ever, glanced at Mats, looking shaken. 'Do we have any snaps?'

He shook his head. 'We're being Scottish. We have whisky. But if I were you, Dad, I'd keep a clear head. I don't think your discussion with Mum's over yet.' Annoyance at his father for trying to bluster his way through every problem made him add, 'Now I know why she's been so unlike herself.'

About to turn away he was halted when Erik murmured, 'I love her. I can't lose her.'

All Mats' anger seeped away. Had he ever felt one half of the love for Inger that he heard ringing in Erik's voice? He softened his voice. 'She's tired. She doesn't want to work so much. Would it be so bad to take time off with her sometimes? The business really isn't everything, Dad. I've found that. This time enjoying life with the children . . . it's made me realise that I used to work too much. Life's for enjoying, too, and time away from loved ones is time we never get back.'

Erik passed his hand across his mouth – not quite hiding the trembling of his lips.

Mats was dismayed, but before he could find a way to help his growly but loveable bear of a father, Grete returned softly to the room. Her eyes, even behind her glasses, were pink-rimmed. When Erik turned towards her, she laid a tentative hand on his arm. 'I'm sorry,' she said. 'You came a long way to speak to me, so I shouldn't have stormed out. Come upstairs and tell me what you came to say.'

Mats had to swallow at the way his parents gazed at each other, each reading the face of the other with the familiarity of decades of shared love. Newly aware of Grete's silver hair and Erik's round-shouldered stoop, Mats cleared his throat. 'Sounds like a good offer, Pappa.'

Erik nodded, though his attention remained on his wife. 'Yes. We need to talk,' he told Grete. He took her hand, and together they left the room.

Mats didn't mind that their attention had been too much on each other to say goodbye to him. Optimistic that his brief heart-to-heart with his dad might have made Erik think hard about exactly *what* he should say to Grete to return them to sharing life's path, Mats crossed the room to enjoy the company of his children.

Ezz readied herself to meet Mats at the Jolly Abbot, half-expecting a text or call crying off after Erik's surprise arrival.

Why had he suggested they go out this evening? Was that in the friend zone? Or edging into the dating zone? Which did she want it to be?

She regarded her reflection in her mirror, applying the Law of Opposites. *If I bother with make-up he won't turn up. If I go over there looking like Plain Jane, then he will.*

Better look good, even if she ended up alone, she decided, and reached for her make-up bag.

The Law of Opposites could not have applied because when she reached the beery warmth of the Jolly Abbot, she found Mats waiting at a table laid for two. Rosamund grinned from behind the bar while she pulled a pint and cocked her head towards Mats. 'Says he's waiting for you, Ezzie. I have my beady eye on the two of yous.' As the table where Mats waited was in the middle of the room, Ezz suspected that she and Mats had been set up as the entertainment.

He rose with a welcoming smile, and then dropped a tiny kiss on her cheek. The kissing was new. Evidently, he'd decided on evening manners. Or out-of-hours manners. Or dating manners . . . ? Or all three, because he took her black coat and hung it up for her, too.

She felt almost shy when she murmured, 'Hi.'

Then Brodie emerged behind the bar with a towel over his arm and a wiggly walk, as if the Jolly Abbot had been transformed into an upscale restaurant. He spoilt the effect slightly with a strident: 'Mum says, do you want a drink, hen? Yer man there has one of those alcohol-free numbers.'

A couple of titters sounded from the other patrons. Hoping it would calm her hot cheeks, Ezz said, 'Tonic water, please.' Brodie bowed and reversed obsequiously away, plainly enjoying his caricature of a posh waiter.

A grinning Mats hissed, 'Don't you ever bring men here?'

'No. And you can see why. Also, they're seeing a lot more of me in here than usual,' she whispered back, picking up her menu but feeling more like fanning her face than reading it. Brodie reappeared, still with the towel draped over his arm, bearing a tray aloft, and slid Ezz's drink before her with another bow, then tapped the menu. 'Mum says we've no Cullen skink, but there's crab soup instead.'

As Brodie waltzed off again, Mats' eyes were dancing. 'What the hell is a skink?'

She produced a deadpan expression. 'I thought your family dealt in fish products. Can't you catch skinks? I have heard that they're fast and canny.'

Someone nearby laughed and turned it into a cough. Mats, glancing at her suspiciously, took out his phone and consulted it before reading out, 'Cullen skink is a soup made of smoked haddock, potatoes and onion.'

'Oh, yeah. Silly me,' Ezz replied solemnly.

This time half the bar laughed and when Mats asked Brodie what the catch of the day was, they all roared, 'Skink!' and howled again.

Mats laughed back and ordered Atlantic salmon, while Ezz chose goat's cheese and beetroot salad.

'I'm glad you came,' Mats said simply. 'And I'm sorry if Mum and Dad worried you by talking about selling Rothach Hall.' He rolled his eyes. 'I don't think Dad ever meant it. He didn't want Mum to come to Skye without him, and he growled it in the heat of the moment.'

'That's a relief.' But Ezz hadn't been unduly worried once she'd witnessed Erik's discomfiture at being called on it. If Grete had taken it to heart, it was no wonder she'd retired into her shell.

'So, you're keen on staying at Rothach Hall now? It's not long since you were hurling your resignation around,' he teased.

'True. But I didn't want to leave – I felt I had to.' She could look him in the eye over that one, because he knew why she'd reacted as she had. 'I love Skye, even when the mist's in or the burns are freezing.'

The teasing note left his voice. 'I'm glad you stayed too. Otherwise, it's unlikely we'd be together this evening.'

A tickle ran up her spine. 'Oh?' she said neutrally.

He eyed her for several long seconds. Then he leant closer, excluding the rest of the bar. 'That sounded . . . unenthusiastic. Are you worried because I'm divorced? I'm a year into my "life after wife", you know. She was the one who found someone else, someone I don't happen to admire, but she left because the marriage wasn't great.' His silver-grey eyes were serious. 'I've got the two best children in the world out of it, though.'

At his last words, and the sincerity of his expression, Ezz had to ease her throat with a sip of her drink. 'People our age have generally had past commitments. And your children are gorgeous.'

He smiled, grey eyes silvery in the soft lighting. 'Have you been married?'

'No, just a living-with. Ramsay – in Suffolk.' He seemed a long way in the past.

'He didn't want to come up here with you?' Mats tilted his head enquiringly.

She fiddled with her glass, wiping the condensation from its cool, slippery sides. 'He didn't,' she said slowly. 'But more honestly, we didn't have much in common once I stopped drinking. He thought alcohol-free Ezz boring, and I found drunk Ramsay obnoxious. I've just dated

197

casually since I was up here.' And she told him about Henry the auctioneer and Major Magic, making the story as funny as she could.

Instead of laughing, he frowned. 'Has it left you dubious about men?'

She shook her head. 'Do I seem it?'

'You seem uncertain tonight.' A cleft still hovered between his eyes. 'And I don't think it's because your fellow villagers are watching you. If I've done anything—'

'No,' she cut in. Realising she was fiddling with her napkin instead of her glass now, she put it down, sucked in her breath and let it out again. 'I'm a bit nervous.'

A long, slow smile dawned on his handsome face. 'Nervous in a good way? Because we're having dinner together?'

She shrugged. 'And because . . . I'm not sure if we're having dinner together "in a good way" or in a friends way.'

Laughter jumped into his eyes. 'I'm hoping for the good way.'

She relaxed into her chair. 'Then so am I.' After that, everything felt more comfortable. Ezz was conscious of a sweet, humming tension inside her, something she hadn't felt recently – but all, as he termed it, in the good way. It didn't matter that he was only on the Isle of Skye for a couple of months because that was how she usually played things. Nothing serious. Nothing heavy.

Brodie arrived with their meals, though without the pantomime waiter performance this time, just a friendly, 'Enjoy your meals.'

But as she picked up her cutlery, she froze, a thought crashing into her mind. One reason she'd avoided anything serious or heavy was that she'd known she'd feel honour-bound to divulge her secret about the accident that had changed the lives of her and Thea. But, to save Thea from fleeing the village, she'd already confided in Mats. He hadn't reported her or been disgusted by her fall from grace. She *could* get serious with him. Except she couldn't because soon he'd leave. Sheesh, they'd had just one date! How long he'd be on Skye shouldn't even be entering her head. A growing attraction to Mats Larsson was confusing her, that was all. Dates – and sometimes sex – without a future was exactly what she did.

A deep voice broke into her reverie. 'Is there something wrong?'

Mats was staring at her, and she realised she'd been sitting motionless before her salad, cutlery poised. With a tiny headshake, she laughed. 'I was miles away.' When his frown didn't shift and his mouth opened again as if he was about to probe more deeply, she decided on distraction. Leaning forward confidingly, she made her voice the merest whisper so no big-eared fellow patron would overhear. 'I'm soon to inform your parents formally, so I can share it with you now. I'm going to be an auntie again. Thea's expecting a baby.'

Instantly, his frown was vanquished by a great, beaming smile. Eyes alight, he copied her thready whisper. 'That's fantastic! How exciting for her and the rest of your family. Mum and Dad will be thrilled. I know she's high in their estimation.' Clearly confident that Thea's news had been the reason for her reverie he began to tuck into his meal.

Shoving to the back of her mind the fact that Mats wouldn't be in Skye very long, she showed interest in him, in time-honoured date etiquette. The evening began to whiz by. They covered favourite sports – he liked cross-country skiing, ice skating, running and padel, which explained why he was spare and rangy; she liked to walk in winter and swim in summer. On music: she liked singer-songwriters, often female; he liked retro rock like Meatloaf and Black Sabbath.

Eventually, she found herself talking about Rick Colville's latest visit and the news of her maternal grandmother's alcohol-fuelled rages.

His eyes widened. 'No wonder your birth mother let your grandmother make decisions about you. She was too young to withstand anger.'

Something tingled through her. She wasn't certain whether it was surprise at his instant insight, or remorse that she'd shown anger towards Kay herself. Again, she remembered Rick's handwritten, *We were kids*. 'Sounds that way,' she murmured, wishing that she'd been even slightly more understanding of Kay's situation. They were on coffee now and were the last customers in the bar, whilst Brodie and Rosamund crated empty bottles and collected glasses. Ezz gazed into her coffee cup, wishing its froth could foretell the future, as tea leaves were supposed to. She had to swallow. 'Does it seem wrong to you that I'm so hurt they only felt they could look for me once the grandmonster had died? Meanwhile, they made a cosy nest with my birth sisters, and they didn't tell anyone they were coming to look for me. It makes me feel that they needed to check I was acceptable before introducing me to everyone else.'

He laid a warm hand gently on her arm. 'I'm not in your situation, but I suspect it's more complicated than that. Have they told your birth sisters that you exist?'

She thought back. Slowly, she answered, 'I don't think I asked in so many words, but I doubt it, or they'd have told them they were coming here looking for me. Or for

Lindy Loveless, anyway.' With an effort, she lightened the conversation. 'I'm glad Astrid invited me to join you for advent. It's fun to see the kids get excited about Christmas, isn't it?'

Immediately accepting the change of subject, he laughed. 'Astrid's really taken to you. She's already asked if you can come next Sunday as well.'

'At least somebody wants me,' she quipped, though Astrid seeking her company again caused a blooming warmth around her heart.

'She's not the only one who wants you,' he answered lightly.

'Then all her cousins will turn up and she'll forget I exist,' she continued, wondering exactly how he meant that last remark, and trying to subdue a blush.

He grimaced. 'I'd love to contradict you, but she adores Filip and Emil and gets up to all kinds of tricks with Walter – he's what's politely known as a livewire. Mum's half-wishing she hadn't brought Haggis and Scotch to live with Mary and Clive now. Walter will be clamouring to ride them.'

'All sorted,' Ezzie said smugly. 'One of Sheena's friends has her own ponies and, if requested, she'll help the children ride Haggis and Scotch. They brought their tack with them when they came to live with us. Mary's too elderly and dignified, of course, and Clive's too unpredictable.'

Then Rosamund called from behind the bar. 'Ezzie, I hate to break up your date, but you'll cost me my licence if I don't chuck you out now.'

'Blimey.' Ezz checked her watch and saw it was well past eleven. 'Sorry, Rosamund.' To make up, she carried their empty coffee cups to the bar.

Rosamund grabbed the opportunity to murmur, 'He's a hottie, eh?' turning Ezz crimson once again.

201

Then Mats displayed his gentleman credentials by holding her coat so she could slip her arms into the sleeves. Or maybe it was an excuse to have his arms around her for a moment, his hands not quite brushing her body as he brought the two halves of the coat around in front of her.

'Night,' called Rosamund and Brodie, grinning.

'Night.' At least the freezing air cooled Ezzie's cheeks as they stepped outside. 'Brr. The mist's lifted to leave a frosty night.' She pulled her coat tightly around her. Then, perceiving that Mats meant to walk her home, laughed. 'I can walk across the road on my own.'

His smile sounded in his voice. 'But the rule is, if you walk a date home, you get a goodnight kiss.'

An answering smile took charge of her mouth. 'Since when?'

'Since I made the rule up,' he said equably. In approximately forty strides, they reached her garden path. He surveyed her garden. 'Have you lost your lawnmower?'

'It's a wildflower garden,' she said with great dignity. 'In summer, it's a mass of colour and the bees love it. Being kind to the bees is very important . . . especially to people who, like me, don't like gardening.'

He laughed, a rich sound. Then, gently, he turned to face her and dipped his head towards hers. And despite his joke 'rule' about earning a goodnight kiss, he waited.

Ezz liked men who didn't pounce, assuming kisses and more would automatically be part of the date. She raised up on her toes and brushed her lips across his. Instantly, he closed the small space between them, and dotted kisses on the corners of her mouth and then down the side of her neck. A wave of desire made her grip his shoulders. His soft lips settled on hers, extra gentle, and though that felt like exactly what she needed, heat rushed through her, and her lips parted. In an instant he deepened the kiss, his tongue stroking hers, his arms encompassing her. Despite the thick coats between them, she felt aware of the shape of his body and heard the 'Mm' deep in his throat. It felt as if she didn't hold his shoulders, she'd float up among the stars. Normally, she'd consider that a good place to be, but not while Mats was here on Earth kissing her.

When he drew back, his breathing was noticeably uneven. 'Can we go out again? Maybe not to the village pub though.' There was a laugh in his voice. 'Maybe at the weekend?'

'Valentina's coming,' she said regretfully. 'Thea and Dev are going to Dumfries to spread the baby news and Valentina, Gary and Barnaby will borrow her cottage.'

He touched his lips to hers once more, as if he needed to check it had really felt so velvety and tingling between them. 'Before the weekend, then. Come to Portree with us tomorrow. You can show us around. I've stayed too long in the Rothach environs and could do with getting out and about, entertaining the kids. And before you ask, it's fine for it to be on work time, because Mum's coming.' He hesitated. 'At least she was before Dad arrived.'

'I'm off tomorrow anyway as your mum said to catch up what time I'm owed,' she said.

And she melted against him for more kisses.

Chapter Fifteen

Monday in Portree was lovely. On the journey there, Josefin sat between the noisy children in the centre row while Erik and Grete claimed the very back seats of the Volvo. Mats smiled when he saw them and murmured so only Ezz could hear, 'I believe they had a heart-to-heart yesterday. They've been all smiles since they came down to breakfast together this morning.' He indicated that Ezzie should take the front passenger seat while he slid behind the wheel.

She risked a quick glance over her shoulder under the guise of fastening her seatbelt and saw Grete and Erik apparently chatting amicably. 'It's great to see your mum smile. What did you tell your parents to explain my presence at a family outing?'

Grinning, he swung the car around and set off down the drive. 'No explanations necessary,' he said, which could have meant anything.

They crossed from the Sleat Peninsula over the frozen

moorland, where ice glittered in the roadside ditches like mercury. They stopped to tumble from the car and photograph the pink and yellow-streaked sky above the snowy peak of Beinn na Caillich, which towered behind Broadford. 'Beinn na Caillich means "mountain of the old woman",' Ezz told them as Astrid and Alvin posed for photos with the mountain in the background, their breath hanging in clouds in the frosty air. 'Confusingly, there's another Beinn na Caillich on Skye, not far east of here at Kyle Rhea, and also one at Knoydart on the mainland.'

When they'd admired the wildness of the moor, they piled back into the Volvo and followed the coast road in and out as if following the edges of jigsaw pieces, the road undulating past frozen beaches, upturned boats and a lone ferry chugging over the glassy inner sea.

It took them about an hour to reach Portree, which was built around a sloping bay, like Rothach but bigger. The grey-tiled buildings rose up in tiers as if to get the best view of the snowy mountains on the Isle of Raasay across the water, and the boats chugging slowly in and out of the harbour. Leaving the Volvo in a small car park, they found their way down to the harbour via a curving flight of stone steps, which Alvin insisted on conquering on his own, one step at a time.

Every form of boat bobbed on the corrugated grey sea from rowing boats to quite large fishing boats. Astrid loved the piles of creels and nets. Alvin was fascinated by an orange fishing boat with its own crane. Grete admired the pink, yellow and blue buildings that appeared on so many pictures of the town, brighter than the pastel cottages of Rothach village.

Back up the steps, they found the town itself twinkling with fairy lights as if a swarm of fireflies had decided to come to Portree for Christmas. The town was a favourite with tourists, and the shops were dressed to attract them, with lights reflecting from shiny red baubles, and model Santas beaming behind their reindeer. 'Do you have reindeer in Sweden?' Ezz asked Mats, standing outside a shop with a bountiful number of reindeer pulling Santa's sleigh.

He nodded, his blue woollen hat pulled snugly over his ears. 'In the north. And moose, of course, and lynx – though they're not common.'

Absently, she straightened Astrid's hat, which was slipping over one eye. 'Maybe Santa should have had moose to pull his sleigh. They have longer legs.'

Laughing, he adjusted her hat, just as she'd adjusted Astrid's.

As they wandered the quaint high street, Ezz was able to stock up on her favourite handmade soap for herself, and as stocking fillers for Thea and Valentina. Josefin bought matching kilts for her son and his boyfriend, sheepskin mittens, knitted jumpers, shortbread and whisky.

'I must remember Irn-Bru from the supermarket, to make Girders,' she told Ezz, with a grin.

Ezz grinned back. 'Better get some Drambuie too, then.'

Erik and Grete bought Astrid and Alvin toy Highland Cattle, which were advertised as 'coos' – 'cows' in a Hebridean accent.

Showing their kindness, they also bought a 'coo' for Thea's baby, Ezz having told them the happy news as soon as they met that morning. Ezz, not to be outdone, bought the baby a cream-coloured hat and bootees knitted from Skye sheep's wool. The hat had rabbit ears and the bootees white pom-pom bobtails. Her heart gave an excited skip at the thought that she'd be an auntie again soon, and *this time* her nephew or niece would live close enough for Ezz to know and love them in real life, rather than mostly via FaceTime.

Mats' hand brushed Ezzie's a couple of times, while Alvin rode on his shoulders, but otherwise last night's kisses might never have happened. Ezz liked his discretion, especially in front of his kids – and, of course, Erik and Grete, her employers.

It was a lovely, happy day, with two visits to cafés, one for lunch – the one nearest the Christmas tree ablaze with coloured lights in the centre of Somerled Square, by Astrid's demand – and one for afternoon scones before they left for home. Everyone was full of smiles, and Josefin's ruddy cheeks were almost orange in the chilly air.

Both children fell asleep on the journey back. The early darkness had fallen by the time the car drew up outside the hall; the twinkle lights twirled around the bases of the flagpoles bright in the darkness. It was past five, so Orla would have closed it to visitors before going home.

As they got out, Alvin rubbed his eyes and blinked as specks of white landed on his face. 'Little snow,' he cried happily.

'Little flakes,' Astrid amended. 'I want to stay outdoors and wait for it to be enough to make a snowman.'

The adults laughed. Diplomatically, Ezz said, 'I think you should wait indoors though, in case that takes a while.'

'There was snow on the mountains today though,' Astrid argued. 'They looked like cakes with icing.' Then she dragged off her pink hat and began to tug the zip of her coat, declaring contrarily, 'I'm hot.'

'Let's go in before we take off our coats,' Josefin suggested, extending an encouraging hand. 'Then we can have hot chocolate.' Her eyes twinkled beneath her beige woolly hat. Astrid and Alvin ran to join her, and the trio disappeared indoors and through the white door to the family side, closely followed by Erik and Grete.

Ezz went to her office. It was her day off, but as she was here she might as well check Orla hadn't left any notes on her desk. Quietly, Mats followed her. 'Can you join me for dinner tonight? Maybe at one of the hotels, rather than the village pub. I could pick you up at eight. I like to be there for the children's bedtime when I can. I'll be back to full-time work in January, so I want to make the most of them now.'

'That sounds great, and eight's fine.' Ezz hadn't enjoyed being the centre of attention at the Jolly Abbot any more than he had, but the warmth in her cheeks was mainly due to Mats moving into her space, his gaze on her mouth. And forgetting that she was at her place of work, she found her eyes on his mouth too. He hovered nearer, as if preparing to kiss her.

Then Josefin's voice came sharply, from behind him. 'Would you like hot chocolate, Mats?'

He turned away from Ezz and strolled out of her office. 'No thanks, I'll make coffee.' He went through the door she held with a smile over his shoulder for Ezz and mouthed, 'Tonight.'

Josefin's expression was very different when her eyes met Ezz's. Shadowed. Taken aback. Dismayed.

Ezz flushed guiltily. Dammit. Why had her professionalism deserted her? She might have been advised to be less formal than Tavish, but holding up her face to be kissed by the son of the household was taking liberties. And Josefin had looked *so* unhappy. She might have once said that Mats liked Ezz, but Ezz had shrugged it off. Now there was betrayal in that light brown gaze before Josefin turned away.

Ezzie hovered at her desk, wondering whether she could say something to smooth things over with Josefin, and if so what.

Then the door to the family area reopened and Josefin reappeared carrying a steaming blue mug, Astrid in tow. 'We brought you hot chocolate,' sang Astrid, skipping on her toes.

'Wow, thank you.' Ezz took the cup from Josefin with an appreciative smile.

Josefin did *not* smile back. 'Would you like to go to the pub again tonight?' she asked instead. Her tone was carefully neutral, but her eyes bored into Ezz.

Ezz understood. Josefin had caught the breath of the word 'tonight' as Mats had mouthed it and was just trying to confirm her suspicions. Steadily, she answered, 'I'm afraid I'm busy already, but tomorrow . . .'

But Josefin was already turning away. 'Tomorrow I am busy. Come, Astrid. Ezzie needs to go home.'

Astrid looked from Josefin to Ezzie as if she'd expected to stay for a chat, but then sang, 'Bye, Ezzie,' and skipped after Josefin.

'Thanks very much for the lovely hot chocolate,' Ezz called after them. But she knew that thanks hadn't been what Josefin had wanted to hear.

As arranged, Mats picked Ezz up at eight and drove her to a hotel further down the peninsula. Good headlights were essential in the dark and winding lanes, and more of what Alvin had dubbed 'small snow' danced across the road like glittering white midges. Mats didn't mention Josefin being miffed and Ezz didn't enquire. It would be mean to bring to his attention that Josefin seemed to be feeling snubbed and jealous, and Ezz felt bad enough already at hurting the feelings of the woman she'd begun to consider a friend.

The meal was delicious, but service was leisurely and so when they returned to the village it was nearly midnight. Rothach sat in a frost pocket and every inch glittered as the tyres crunched gently down the slope of Low Road before it flattened into Chapel Road. Even the lights of the Jolly Abbot were off. Mats killed the engine and turned to her in the warm confines of the car, his face all angles and planes in the shadows. 'Sorry it's so late.'

She touched one finger to his lips to stem his apologies. 'It's fine. But I won't invite you in for coffee, as I have to be up in the morning.'

He looked rueful, lifting her hand to his mouth and kissing her fingertips. 'Mum's making plans for the next couple of evenings now Dad's here and they seem to be getting over their bump in the road. Are you free on Friday? I could take the children to the beach and tire them out, so they go to bed earlier.'

She raised her eyebrows consideringly. 'That might be possible, if you don't mind a short evening. My sister and family are coming to stay at Thea's for the weekend, but they're leaving Inverness after Valentina and Gary finish work so won't arrive till latish. Why don't I cook dinner here? Then I'll be free to join them whenever they arrive.' She hadn't offered a man dinner at her house since coming to Skye, but she knew that if she asked him to leave, he would. He was Mats, someone she knew real things about rather than what he said in his dating profile.

He nibbled her fingers and her stomach curled at the shaft of desire that shot through her. 'Fantastic,' he murmured.

It was quite a few minutes before she got out of the car and made for her front door, once more floating, as if Mats' kisses unspooled her string so she floated like a kite over Rothach Bay.

Mats arrived at Ezz's cottage just before seven-thirty on Friday evening. She opened the door to find him huddled in his coat, a few white flakes on top of his blue woollen hat. Drily, he said, 'The small snow has turned to big snow.'

Ezz welcomed him in, gazing at the flakes' swirl and flurry in surprise. 'I didn't even notice it had begun. I've been on the phone with Valentina in the lounge and the curtains are closed.'

Mats halted in the middle of wiping his feet on the doormat. 'Is Valentina in Rothach already? Do you need to leave?' Although his words were considerate, disappointment tinged his voice.

She shut the door on the snow veering and swirling about the streetlamps like white confetti. 'No, poor Valentina, Gary and Barnaby are making slow progress. There's snow on the A87 and a couple of cars have slipped off the road near Loch Cluanie. They'll go straight to bed when they finally get here and see me tomorrow. Luckily, Thea and Dev set out for Dev's family in Dumfries early this morning and got there without seeing a flake.'

His lips curved as he made short work of removing his coat and hat. 'I'm sorry for their difficulty, but happy to have you to myself for longer.' He moved in to drop gentle kisses on her lips. A *zing* shot down to her toes, taking in all the good places in between. He looked dazed, as if he'd felt it too, and it seemed to take him a moment to collect his thoughts. 'What do we have for dinner?'

She turned towards the kitchen. 'Fried herring with a

211

lime and pepper crust, boiled potatoes, broccoli and red cabbage. Then chocolate ganache with figs if you have room.'

'I'll have room,' he answered promptly. 'What can I do?' He surveyed the table, already set, the oily frying pan awaiting the fish, and the potatoes resting in a saucepan of water. As she was expecting not only Mats this evening, but that Valentina and family might visit during the weekend, she'd hung up strings of Christmas lights. A pink set twinkled along the top of the window, and a gold string along the mantelpiece in the lounge.

'How about choosing drinks? I'll have a fruit cocktail.' She indicated the fridge. If he wanted alcohol, he'd have to cross the road to the pub.

But he took out a zero beer for himself, and a mocktail for her, then he propped his nice behind against the cupboards and watched her cook, asking how she'd made the pepper crust she pressed the fish into and exactly how much lime would be enough. He was a big, warm presence. And she was ultra-aware of him.

'My parents are spending a lot of time together in their suite,' he said, as he watched her take out another pan to make herb butter sauce. 'What herbs are they?' He nodded towards her chopping board.

'Parsley and thyme, with a smidgeon of dill.' A month ago, she'd have answered his comment about his parents with a polite, neutral smile, but a month ago she wouldn't have had Mats Larsson to dinner and he wouldn't have discussed his family life with her. It was a nice, cosy feeling to be chatting while she cooked their meal. 'Do you think Erik will stay right up till Christmas?'

He made a musing noise. 'To be decided, I think. Mum's clear that she wants to spend more time here or travelling.

Dad may be left with a choice between being semi-retired or semi-married.'

The first hint of frying herbs hit the air as the butter liquified in the pan. 'How do you feel about that? Can you get the cream from the fridge, please?'

He located the cream and handed her the tub, cold in her hand. 'I hope he chooses semi-retirement, of course.'

'I hope so, too.' She measured out hot water and added stock cubes. The potatoes had boiled so she turned down the heat and then gave the fish a last toss in the crushed pepper and flour mixture before adding it to the frying pan.

The hot oil hissed a fierce welcome and he retreated a step. 'I can see why Mum wants to be here. It's beautiful and restful. I could live here myself. Tell Larsson Fiskeri to appoint a new finance officer and open a restaurant selling dishes made from the local catch.' He nodded at her frying pan, now sizzling gently, its aromas swirling around the room. Her heart skipped at the idea of him living on Skye.

But it was only a second before he added, 'It's an impractical plan, of course. Inger and I must share Astrid and Alvin. The children love both their parents and need that love to be returned.'

She nodded, put a steamer full of broccoli on top of the potato pan, flipped the fish and then turned the heat up to thicken the sauce while she stirred, snatching a moment to check his expression. The corners of his mouth had turned down and, his gaze distant, sadness and regret lingered in the lines around his eyes. 'Do you wish you hadn't needed to get divorced?' she asked softly.

Instantly, his gaze snapped back into focus. 'Hell, no.' He rubbed his jaw. 'Andreas is much more Inger's type – rich. I just want to make everything as easy as I can on the children.' He gave a short laugh. 'I was uncharacteristically dazzled by her. By the time my sanity returned, we were married. It was a big lesson in "don't follow lust – follow logic". We were married for five years. She was young, gorgeous and vivacious, and hated me working so much. I should have seen trouble coming. She didn't respect my parents for having made their own money, though that's exactly why I admire them. She wanted me to be "more aspirational" but I never knew to what I was meant to aspire. Sitting on a yacht with nothing to do isn't my idea of fun.' He grinned ruefully. 'Apart from this year, I generally get four or five weeks' holiday a year. Her ideal is four or five weeks a month.'

Ezz nodded to show she was listening, lowering the heat beneath the sauce and warming the plates while she deftly slid the fish onto kitchen towel to blot the excess oil.

He stepped out of her way while she plated their meals then, as if they were used to sharing a kitchen, reached around her to stir the sauce while her hands were busy. She paused to remove her red apron from over a dark green jersey dress before placing the steaming plates on the table while he took their drinks. 'This food looks fantastic. Let's not mention Inger or divorce again tonight. Esmerelda Wynter, a beautiful, intelligent woman, has just cooked me a restaurant-worthy meal, and I want to enjoy every crumb. *Tack för maten*. That means thank you for the meal.' His eyes smiled.

She took her seat and picked up her cutlery, happy at the change of subject. 'What do you say before a meal? Like *bon appetit*, but Swedish.'

'*Smaklig måltid*.' He raised his zero beer in a toast, and she clinked with her mocktail.

They ate slowly while the snow whispered at the

windowpanes. 'Do you know the Norwegians came to Skye?' he asked, cutting through the crispy coating of the fish, his knees touching hers beneath the table.

She paused to look at him askance. 'Did they?'

He nodded. 'Mum told me. In the thirteenth century, King Haakon moored his fleet in Loch Alsh. He had a dust-up with Scotland's King Alexander and then died. Under a treaty I don't remember the name of, Scotland was given the Hebrides and Isle of Man, and Norway got Shetland and Orkney. Kyleakin was named after King Haakon. At some other time, there was a Norwegian princess who stretched a chain across the Kyle Akin strait to extract a toll from boats.'

That rang a bell in Ezz's mind. 'Is that the legend of Saucy Mary? I have heard about that. Her castle's a ruin now – Caisteal Maol – and she's supposed to be buried on top of Beinn na Caillich near Broadford. And surely the Vikings came earlier than that from what later became Norway. There was a huge Viking presence on all these islands and the west coast.'

'I hadn't thought about that.' Unexpectedly, he added, 'You're so relaxing to be with, Ezzie.'

She laughed as she cut up her potato. 'Now you're trying to make me blush. Tell me about Gothenburg.'

Eagerly, he began. 'It's close to the Norwegian border, which is why Mum was in Gothenburg with her friends, visiting the market, and fell in love with the boy with the fish stall.' His fair hair shone under the kitchen light, and his silver eyes looked stunning. 'It's a seaport, of course, with big canals. Some of the buildings are colourful. Copper roofs have turned green, others are bright red. It's a good city, with parks and cafés, bridges and museums. My apartment is in Stampen, which is a regenerated area

215

and a bit trendy. I rented it when . . .' He paused, and Ezzie remembered him saying he didn't want to talk further about Inger or the divorce. He changed tack. 'But soon I'll find a house with a garden for the kids.'

She listened as she enjoyed the silky sauce that contrasted with the crunchy coating of the fish, trying to absorb the sound of Swedish place names that fell from his lips. Johanneberg. Götaplatsen. Näckros Park. Lorensbergs Villastad. He took out his phone and showed her images of gothic churches and boatyards filled with cranes and gantries. Consulting Google, they discovered that Gothenburg covered just less than one-third of the area of the Isle of Skye.

'So, Gothenburg's bigger than Rothach,' she commented, straight-faced. They'd finished their meal and he'd stacked their plates and taken both of her hands across the table. She enjoyed the feeling of his big hands warming hers.

'Rothach is just as beautiful as anything in Gothenburg,' he said seriously. 'The village is charming, with its coloured cottages and slate roofs, and the rocky beach with the gentle sea.'

'Not always gentle, but it's sheltered in the sound. I could show you the cottage Valentina's bought, right on the Quays, if you fancy a walk in the dark and the snow. It's a mess now, but I think it will be spectacular after she's spent a small fortune on it.'

'Is she moving here?' His thumbs caressed the backs of her hands.

She grinned. 'Valentina and Gary are lawyers. She works in corporations and he's in local government. They've moved closer now, and live in Inverness rather than Edinburgh, but it's still a city. That's their thing. She wants a weekend cottage here as a get-away-from-it-all place.'

'I'd love that,' he said.

She snorted. 'I've seen your "weekend cottage". Rothach Hall is not *quite* the same as Overlook Cottage.'

He made a show of looking hurt. 'Rothach Hall belongs to my parents. Not me. I don't even own an old fisherman's cottage.'

'Yeah, I'd forgotten how poor you are,' she said ironically. 'I'll clear things ready for dessert. It's already made and in the fridge.'

'You made dinner, so I'll wash up,' he said. 'How about we have dessert after that, with coffee?'

She agreed, scraping plates and handing things to him to wash, cheerfully elbow-deep in white suds while he asked her about Maxie and Vince.

'Lovely parents.' She was swept by the rush of mixed pleasure and pain that came whenever she thought of them. 'I have a playlist of things they worked on. I'll put it on.' She located it on her phone and played it through the speaker on the window recess. 'That's Dad playing guitar. It's the theme music for a film and the soundtrack got into the album chart.' She giggled, her hands slowing as she gathered up the tablecloth. 'As a child, I remember him singing what I thought were silly songs. Have you ever heard "Walking My Baby Back Home"? I had no idea it was about adults, especially the line about getting powder all over a vest. I thought it must be a children's bath-time song about talcum powder. Mum and Dad nearly cried laughing. That's how I remember them. Hanging on to each other and howling with laughter.'

Her birth parents must have those kinds of memories with Julia and Iona, she thought, a hollow opening below her ribs. The next song began and she shoved that thought away. 'Mum's a backing singer on this track. Amazing that

217

I once had that voice singing lullabies to me.' Needing to rinse her wiping cloth, she eased in beside him at the sink and plunged her hands into the water.

He shifted so that he had one arm either side of her and she was sandwiched between moist, sudsy warmth one side and hard, male heat on the other. A strangled giggle escaped her. 'Mats!'

'Mm?' Nuzzling the nape of her neck, he nudged her hair aside to find the soft skin with his lips. 'This is a great way to wash up.'

The bubbles that ran off her wrists sparkled with rainbows and Ezz felt as if she sparkled with rainbows too. 'Mm,' she found herself returning. And maybe there was a 'muh' and an 'ooh' in there, too, as her eyes closed, and all those sparkling rainbows of pleasure burst into a melting sensation that slithered down her back.

Instinctively, she turned in his arms and searched for his mouth. Mats' lips were warm and soft but excited and hungry, and his hips pressed into the cradle of hers. Time slowed. He didn't complain that her fingers were damp as they threaded through his silky hair, and she ignored her hip pressing uncomfortably against a drawer handle and it felt suspiciously as if water was filtering under her waistband. She pressed against him, loving the shock of her breasts against his lean body and the answering jolt that shook through him.

Nothing seemed as important as their kisses, making her heart thud in a way that echoed to the soles of her feet. His hands stroked her back and followed the shape of her waist. His hardness pulsed against her, as if it would dissolve their clothes to find its way inside her.

And, oh, boy, *that* was what she wanted. This man. In bed. All night long. He was leaving Rothach – she knew that – but not yet, not *yet*. 'Oh, yeah,' she breathed. More words wanted to pour out of her, to tell him how he was setting her on fire, how she hadn't felt like this for so long, if ever, but they stuck in her brain, which apparently couldn't process every message her body was sending.

Mats, breathing like a train, rained kisses on her face, squeezing her against his body. 'Whatever the question is, it's a yeah from me too,' he gasped, nibbling along the exposed, incredibly sensitive skin at her neckline, nearly sending her off like a rocket.

'Upstairs?' she gasped.

'Oh, *yeah*.' He eased their embrace, so they could crab their way across the now-damp flagstones towards the hall without disentangling.

'There's a step,' she panted, just as he tripped.

'Found it,' he reported wryly. Up the hall, slithering along the walls, then she felt for the light switch, and they stumbled up the stairs. When she murmured, 'My dress is soaked,' he turned, a foot on one step and a knee a couple of steps higher. Taking the opportunity for a long, slow kiss, he felt for her zip and whizzed it down, so her back felt the cool air. Slowly, exquisitely, he eased the fabric over her shoulders, her arms and down her legs, following with brushes of his lips that began the rainbow sensation all over again.

She shivered, and he wrapped her in his arms.

'Now you're cold.' He ushered her up the last few steps. 'Which room?'

'That one.' She pointed.

He paused at the bathroom to grab a towel, then swung her into her bedroom, where the glow of streetlights filtered through the glass. The fluffiness of the towel descended on her back, and began to draw soft, caressing circles.

Every vestige of chill left her skin. 'Curtains,' she murmured, not sure pub-goers could see in, but not sure they couldn't. He released her long enough to close the night out, while she lit a lamp.

Then they were facing each other beside the bed. He stroked her face, the side of her neck, her shoulder. 'Still yes?'

She loved a man who made sure. 'Yes, from me,' she whispered.

A tremor shook through him. 'A very big yes from me. Huge, urgent yes. Yes, yes, yes.'

They sank onto the bed together, his fingers pulling down her straps, unfastening her bra so her breasts, freed, swung into his face. 'Gorgeous,' he muttered. Then his mouth was hot and his hands sure.

'Shirt, shirt,' she insisted. 'I don't like being naked on my own.'

'One shirt coming off.' A deft motion and it was off over his head without unbuttoning, ruffling his hair. 'Trousers to follow.' A zip and a wriggle and he was out of them too, his erection hard against her through his boxers.

Ezz almost lost her mind at the feel of the scalding heaviness of him against her sensitive flesh. 'That's better. That's the best. That's awesome,' she murmured, thoughts scrambling, limbs trembling at the sublime sensation of hot skin on hot skin, teasing mouth on breasts as, between them, they freed themselves of the final items of underwear.

Ezz would probably have checked her condoms were in date and then gone for a burning, insistent, fast-and-fucky coupling, but Mats took several audible breaths and whispered, 'Let me stroke you.' He sounded as if he were saying it through gritted teeth.

She paused, thinking he might need a moment to establish control. Then every hair stood on end because his fingertips were skating over her body, as if mapping it to commit to memory. That felt good. That felt like heaven was a real place. His palms circled over her back, over the globes of her buttocks, her thighs – between her legs so gently, just tracing the shape of her. She was going to explode. His knuckles grazed her before he moved back to her breasts, stroking, kissing.

Although his breath came heavy, he managed whole words and even short phrases like: 'You OK?' And: 'That good?' and she gasped only, 'Uh-huh,' followed by her mind exploding.

Her hands refused to glide around in the measured way his did. Instead, she clutched his buttocks, then his waist, pressing her open mouth against his chest, then his neck, tasting his skin. Finally, urgency encouraged her brain and mouth to work together on a whole sentence. 'I have condoms in the bathroom.'

He paused in nibbling his way up her ribcage, which felt *incredible*, still breathing hard. 'Mine are in my jeans.' He leant out of bed to flail an arm in the direction of his abandoned jeans and hook them to him, one hand on her as if he was scared she'd run away. 'Why in the hell don't you keep your condoms in your bedroom?'

'I don't bring men here. Let me do it. I like doing it.' She slipped the square packet from his hand.

Rolling onto his back, he breathed, 'I love that.'

And ten seconds later she was sliding over him, sliding him into her, closing her eyes and gripping him while he rumbled, 'Urrr,' as if there wasn't enough air.

She lost track of herself. Moving on instinct, swapping places, changing pace, holding him hard, stroking him gently, as the slow lovemaking built and built until her orgasm ripped through her like an eruption.

Finally, she lay against him, her breathing no longer rasping in her throat, her muscles mush, her body heavy and happy. Voice low, he said, 'You don't bring men here?'

'Never.' She touched a kiss to his collarbone, then licked it.

He didn't press her further, but she felt as if he were smiling to himself that he was different. She smiled in the darkness too, but wistfully, counting the ways in which he was different. A man whose parents she worked for. A man who by no means had his own life sorted out. A man with kids. She'd even cooked for him. Holy shit.

A man who was leaving.

Later, when she awoke, he was nibbling her ear. 'Mm,' she mumbled, thinking he was waking her to make love again, but when she reached for him, her questing fingers found jeans and a shirt. 'Dressed?'

He kissed her. 'I need to be home before the kids wake up.'

'Oh.' She kissed him back. 'In that case, I hope the snow stopped. I don't want to drag myself from this lovely warm bed and help dig out your car.'

He chuckled. 'It was only half an inch of snow. I think I'll cope.'

''Kay. Then you're on your own.' She closed her eyes again.

'Are you busy with your family the whole weekend?' His fingers traced the line of her shoulder, as if his hands couldn't help touching her.

She shivered contentedly. 'I'm meeting Valentina and co at Overlook Cottage in the morning. And dinner later, I think.'

'OK.' He eased the duvet down to kiss a breast. 'Would it be bad if I took Alvin and Astrid to the beach tomorrow and, if I happened to see you, came over to say hi?'

222

'It would be good,' she assured him. 'Barnaby's about the same age as Astrid and he loves the beach too.'

After one last kiss, she listened to him treading down the stairs, imagining him pulling on his coat in the hall. The front door opened and closed. A faint crunching meant snow beneath his feet. She pulled the duvet around her and shuffled upright, then to the window, easing back the curtain to watch him sweeping snow from the Volvo in shimmering arcs. He was right that it was a light covering, but enough to make the street glow like moonbeams. Fence posts wore sparkling white hats and his footprints were the only things not painted white.

Finally, he stamped snow from his shoes, slid into his car and drove steadily away. She realised she should have told him not to carry on to Bridge Road before turning back along Friday Furlong to reach the road above, because Friday Furlong was steep and narrow. But then his headlights described a smooth circle where Chapel Road met Bridge Road and Creag an Lolaire, and he drove back past her cottage.

Finally, when he was out of sight, she shuffled back to bed and flopped onto the mattress, smiling as she waited for sleep to return. Tomorrow – or was it today? – felt full of promise.

Chapter Sixteen

Morning came too swiftly. Barnaby rang on Valentina's phone, shouting excitedly, 'Hello, Auntie Ezzie, it was snowing but now it's raining, and we've got a new house and are you coming soon?'

'Sure am,' she answered sleepily. 'It's raining?' She swung her legs off the bed and twitched the curtain aside to see that a freezing rain was washing away the last of the short-lived snow. Then she remembered the half-cleared kitchen she and Mats had abandoned last night in favour of the glorious hours in her bed. 'Got a couple of jobs to do and then I'll be with you. Shall I come to Thistledome? Or meet you at Overlook Cottage?'

Valentina's voice joined Barnaby's. 'Shall we meet at the cottage? Barnaby can't wait.'

'Fine.' Ezz smothered a yawn. 'Be there soon.' She showered and dressed, choosing her hiking trousers because they were showerproof, and she could wear leggings underneath. Outdoor wear was a practical choice in Skye, regardless of whether you actually hiked in your hiking trousers or walked in your walking boots. She ran downstairs. On the threshold of the kitchen, she almost fell down the step in surprise. The washing up was done, dried and left for her to put away, the table and surfaces gleaming. Mats must have already cleared in here by the time he came to take his leave of her in the early hours.

'Damn, you're good,' she said into the empty room. 'I could get used to you.' Except there was no point in that.

Leaving the fairy lights twinkling in case her family members joined her here later, she set out after breakfast. White clouds were smeared with grey, like cotton wool that had been used to clean off last night's mascara. The rain stung her face and only the occasional stubborn white line of snow still edged a cottage roof. Ezzie strode down Creag an Lolaire, the pewter sea looming closer. The tide seemed to be running hard and a handful of white boats had appeared in the sheltered mooring, as if their owners knew wind was coming. Skye's weather was capricious.

A strong smell of woodsmoke came from a chimney, and she imagined those inside reading beside the fire or watching TV. She was happy outside though, despite the raindrops flying on the wind making her screw up her eyes. It was a good-to-be-alive day, the memories of last night plastering a beaming smile on her face and her body heavy and pleasantly aching in important areas.

Hands jammed in pockets, she turned right onto Harbour View and hurried along its curve. Nobody else was in sight and she wondered if Mats would bring the children to the beach as planned now the rain was coming in horizontally off the sea, ice spicules amongst the drops.

Gary's enormous, blue, gas-guzzling SUV was pulled up outside Fishermen's Cottages, and the rain suddenly came on as if it wanted to beat her into the ground. The sea's surface whipped up like steam, the gulls rode the wind with shrieks of glee and Ezzie broke into a run.

Panting, she reached the decrepit front door of Overlook Cottage and twisted the doorknob, relieved when it opened and she half-fell into the narrow hall. Barnaby jumped through the doorway from the front room, his wellies making a clatter on the bare boards. 'Auntie Ezzie!'

'Barnaby!' Ezzie was about to hug him, then realised her coat was soaked, and contented herself with tousling his hair. 'This is awesome. I didn't think I was going to see you till Christmas.'

Barnaby beamed, his mousy hair sticking up at the front. 'Christmas is only three weeks away. But this weekend we're going to have dinner and spend time together, aren't we?'

Ezz grinned at this obvious parroting of his parents' promises. Or his mum's, anyway. 'We definitely are.'

'Hello.' Valentina's voice floated down the stairs. 'Be down in a minute.'

Gary loomed from the living room, his hair a darker version of his son's, without the cow's lick because he was receding. 'Great to see you, Ezzie.' He'd grown a moustache, which made him look older than his fifty-four years.

Ezzie turned her cold cheek for Gary to kiss, the moustache bristling against her like a punk caterpillar. 'Great to see you too,' she said brightly, though she and Thea were only ever happy to see Gary because it usually meant Valentina too. The way he called them 'girls' was patronising, as was the way he occasionally looked down his nose at . . . well, anyone who wasn't Gary. He wasn't good at shouldering his share of household tasks and though he and Barnaby obviously loved each other, he also dodged the more onerous parenting duties. Ezz said, 'Let me dump my coat . . . somewhere.'

'There are a few old nails sticking out of the wall for coat hooks,' Gary said drily. 'Valentina's drawing a plan of the bathroom for the builder. Elastic walls would be a good thing.' He laughed at his own joke. 'And I thought we were slumming it in Thistledome until we came down here. Whatever possessed Valentina—'

Ezz was stung by the 'slumming it'. 'Thea's given up her lovely cottage to you this weekend, when she's not even here to enjoy the visit. Newly pregnant and facing a long drive, she made time to change the bed so you could have it.' Probably Dev had done it, but that wasn't the point.

Gary undoubtedly thought his grin was boyish and charming. 'I know. But I'm much more Broadford Hotel than cramped cottage.'

Ezzie reminded herself that he was Valentina's husband and managed to smile. 'You must love the view from Overlook Cottage.' She brushed past him into the front room where the window looked over Causeway to the rocky beach and troubled sea. 'You'll be able to see every change in the weather. Even since I came in, a blue patch has miraculously appeared over the bay.' The rain had eased to no more than the occasional spot, as if feeling its work done after chasing her here.

'Great, if you like weather,' Gary answered off-handedly, turning from the window. 'I've no idea what we'll do in this freezing, grotty shell of a place all day.'

Tempted to ask why he'd come on the trip at all, Ezzie turned to Barnaby, who was suddenly looking around with a disappointed expression. Probably he hadn't noticed the cottage's shortcomings until Gary had pointed them out.

To a six-year-old, a car ride through the snowy darkness to the village where his aunts lived by the sea would be exciting. That he was bundled up in a fleece and boots against the chill inside the cottage wouldn't bother him. Hoping to reignite his excitement, Ezz said, 'Which is your room going to be, Barnaby? Will you show me? I wonder what it'll look like when it's painted and carpeted.'

'Yeah!' Smile restored, Barnaby spun around and Ezz followed in his wake, leaving Gary to hate the 'freezing, grotty shell' alone.

The staircase had been repaired, and now felt solid underfoot, the smell of fresh wood combatting some of the mustiness. Valentina emerged through a frame that was obviously destined to be a doorway now that one room had been partitioned into two, her hair in a bun, her top half swaddled in an enormous jumper that could once have been Gary's. Ezzie launched herself at her elder sister for a hug, realising only once she was in those familiar arms how good it felt; how right. To prevent her mind from darting up the parallel track of thinking about Julia and Iona, who she would presumably have loved as much as she loved Valentina and Thea now, had she been brought up by Kay and Rick, she explained, 'I asked Barnaby to bring me upstairs to show me which room will be his.'

'This one,' Barnaby shouted, capering on the spot as he waited for Ezz to follow him through the original doorway. The new stud partition wall was the only clean thing about the room. A patch of floorboards had been lifted to allow for the passage of wires or pipes. The walls had been scraped of wallpaper and revealed a patchwork of drab paint that attested to decoration through the years.

'It's great to see how much progress Mummy's made

228

already. What colour will your walls be?' she asked Barnaby brightly.

'Blue,' he shouted.

Valentina slipped her arm along his shoulder. 'Very shouty today, Barnaby. Just lower your volume a little bit.' But she smiled.

Barnaby gazed up at her. 'Blue,' he repeated softly. 'With Minecraft on the duvet. Or maybe footballs.'

Valentina gave him a squeeze. 'I bet we could have one of each.'

Ezzie suddenly felt envious of Valentina having a child of her own. The time had never been right for Ezz. When she'd left Ramsay, it had been a blessing, allowing her to leave him behind with no real ties to cut. Then had come a decade of singledom that was only now beginning to wear on her.

She shook herself. Nobody could turn back the clock. 'Fantastic news about Thea and Dev being pregnant, isn't it? I can't wait to be an auntie again. What do you think about having a little cousin, Barnaby?'

Barnaby pulled an elaborate grimace. 'So long as it's not a girl it'll be OK.'

'But she'd be your cousin, almost as good as a sister, and sisters are awesome,' Ezzie declared. Then she was washed by a wave of discomfort. Valentina was right here with her, and Thea would be back after a lovely weekend with Dev's family. But there were two more sisters she was deliberately keeping out of her life.

As if reading her thoughts, Valentina said softly, 'Any . . . family news?'

'Nothing new.' Ezzie's throat felt thick. It must be the dust, she decided, because she couldn't be sad about sisters she didn't know and parents who were virtual strangers.

She wondered suddenly about her original birth certificate and if Kay and Rick had a copy. If Kay's mother had been the nightmare she sounded, she might have insisted on 'father unknown' to insult Rick and make Kay's situation seem as awful as possible.

She swallowed. As Barnaby was at the window, peering through the salt-spray to the windswept beach and black clouds flying towards the island, she whispered, 'I just feel angry.'

Valentina slipped an arm around her, eyes dark with concern. She checked on Barnaby, who'd begun to draw a face on the dust on the inside of the glass. 'I get that you are, but I'm not exactly sure why.'

'Neither am I.' Ezz slipped her arm around Valentina too, enjoying the comfort of the big sister she could never remember being without. 'At first it was simple. They'd dumped me and kept the other two.'

Valentina protested. 'Not sure it could have been exactly like that . . .'

'I know. I'm harsh.' She summoned reason and logic. 'It was a teen pregnancy. A difficult situation. Nobody would have foreseen that eventually they'd end up together in a stable marriage. I understand in principle.' But it was hard to inject understanding into her voice. She laid her head briefly on Valentina's shoulder. 'I'm beginning to think I'm angriest with Kay's mother, who seems to have scared Kay into giving me up. Then, when I remember her alcohol problem I wonder if I'm being unfair. Then I try not to think about the birth family, because it feels disloyal to Mum and Dad.' And Mats had certainly distracted her.

'Are you going to get back in touch with Kay and Rick?' Valentina's voice swam with sympathy, her embrace tight:

230

a rock in a storm. She'd followed Ezzie's lead in referring to her birth parents by name. An adoptee would never use clumsy language like 'real parents'. They both knew their real parents had been Maxie and Vince Wynter.

'I haven't felt the urge yet.' Ezz sighed.

Barnaby bounded over. 'Can I go to the beach? I'll stay really near the house so you can see me, Mum.'

Valentina shook her head. 'Not alone, darling. We walked along the sand before we came into the cottage. Maybe we can go again, after I've talked to the builder.'

Ezz could imagine Barnaby feeling tantalised by the beach being only a few yards beyond his window. Also, she thought of Mats' intention to bring Astrid and Alvin. Even if that plan was now scuppered by the weather, she suggested, 'I can go with Barnaby, while it's not raining. Would you like that, Barnaby? We'll need our coats.'

Barnaby jumped as if riding an invisible pogo stick, boots echoing in the empty room. 'Yes, please! Mum, can Auntie Ezzie take me?'

Valentina laughed, slipping her arm from around Ezz to pull the little boy into a fierce hug. 'Of course. The tide's ebbing, so you'll be able to look at rock pools.'

Gary called suddenly from the foot of the stairs. 'I'll go for a drive while you speak to your builder. See you later. Bye, Barnaby.'

Barnaby shouted, 'Bye, Dad.' Then ran to the head of the stairs. 'Auntie Ezzie and me are going to the beach.'

Under cover of the subsequent conversation about rock pools and waves, Ezz whispered to Valentina, 'Is Gary OK?' which was polite language for *Why's he going off on his own?*

Valentina hesitated, then grimaced. 'He didn't want me to buy the cottage because of its dilapidation. And if we were going to buy a second home he thinks it should be in Spain or maybe Cornwall.'

'Sunnier,' Ezzie observed. 'But a trek for weekends.'

'Exactly. And not near my lovely sisters.' Valentina glanced through the window as an engine started up. 'At least him clearing off will leave room for the builder's truck.'

Ezz wondered why Gary had needed to bring the car down to the Quays at all, as Thistledome was only a ten-minute walk away, even for Barnaby. Not for the first time she reflected that Valentina saw something in Gary that had passed Ezz by.

Leaving her sister happily consulting bathroom brochures and snapping her tape measure, Ezz located Barnaby's coat on a nail in what used to be the kitchen and checked he zipped it up against the raw day outside, then shrugged into her own coat and stepped out into the icy wind. At six years old – nearly seven, Ezz realised, as his birthday was in March – Barnaby needed only casual chaperonage on the deserted beach. She wandered behind him as he leapt from rock to rock and then balanced on an enormous pebble before executing a splashdown into a puddle, protected by his rain boots. Strands of lime-green seaweed clung to black rocks surrounded by gritty sand, grey clouds scudded above the bay and the wind dashed Ezz's hair into her eyes.

'A fish!' Barnaby shouted, stooping over a rock pool, his hands on his knees, probably to brace himself against the wind bowling him face-first into the freezing water.

Ezz joined him, holding back her hair and peering at the darting silver-pink form stranded by the tide. 'That's a tiddler: a baby fish,' she observed.

'Where's his mum?' Barnaby sounded outraged at what he obviously saw as fishy neglect.

Ezz patted his back. 'I expect she's waiting for him in the waves.'

He straightened, frowning at the impatient grey water hissing up the beach before sighing out again. 'We could pick him up and put him in the sea.'

Although she pretended to consider the idea, to show she was listening, finally she said, 'I'd be frightened of hurting him with our big hands. We don't have a bucket or a net, and fish are slippery.'

Barnaby allowed himself to be steered to the next rock pool, which proved to be empty of anything but shells to tuck into his coat pocket. They zigzagged between rocks and pools, until Ezz caught sight of the familiar grey bulk of the Rothach Hall Volvo easing onto Harbour View and parking at the far end. Her heart skipped a beat. While Barnaby chattered about asking for wallpaper with fish on it for his bedroom-in-the-making, she watched Mats hop from the driver's seat. First he helped Astrid out of the back door, then reached for Alvin, swinging him out before depositing him beside his sister. As if hearing a starter's pistol, the children ran off the side of the road and jumped onto the beach. At least, Astrid jumped. Alvin floundered.

Casually, Ezzie said, 'There are some more children. I think they're Astrid and Alvin, who live at Rothach Hall, with their dad.'

Barnaby gazed up the beach. When Mats waved, he waved back. Apparently, it was all the introduction he needed, as he set off towards the little family, leaving Ezz to follow, waving when Astrid spotted her and shouted, 'Ezz! Ezz!'

When they met, she smiled into Mats' eyes and saw the shared memories of last night glowing in their depth. Then she greeted the children. 'This is my nephew Barnaby. He's here for the weekend. Barnaby, this is Astrid and this is Alvin.'

'I've got a fish,' Barnaby told Astrid importantly, calmly taking ownership of the hapless, stranded tiddler. 'It's in a pool. Want to see it?'

Alvin capered with excitement. 'Yes, yes.'

Astrid exhibited more beach cred. 'If it's in a pool, why is it your fish?' But she fell into step beside him as they discussed whether Barnaby could claim ownership of the fish because he saw it first.

Mats smiled at Ezz. 'Kids. One minute they're strangers and the next they're friends. So simple. And because I know Barnaby's gorgeous auntie, I don't even have to check that his intentions towards my daughter are honourable.'

She lowered her voice. 'Thanks for clearing up the kitchen. Do you realise we never ate dessert?' She dug her hands into her pockets and hunched her shoulders as the wind tried to sneak a few drops of rain down her neck.

'It was worth the sacrifice.' He let his shoulder nudge hers.

They joked as they strolled, keeping sharp eyes on straying children, particularly three-year-old Alvin, discouraging him from the receding waves and the tallest and toothiest rocks. The sky grew darker and the air colder. Ezz pulled up her hood as the rain intensified. They were almost up to the Causeway and the Quays now. 'That's Overlook Cottage, the one on the end. It'll be amazing when it's finished but so far, it is, as my brother-in-law observes, grotty. Ouch.' She winced as something stung her cheek.

The children began to squeal. 'Someone's throwing things,' Barnaby wailed, shielding his head with his arms as large white hailstones bounced on the beach around him.

Ezz hurried over to pull up his hood. 'It's a hailstorm. Let's shelter in the cottage.' She turned to Mats, who was adjusting his kids' hats and pulling their hoods over the top. 'You guys as well. Your car's right down the beach.'

'If your sister won't mind,' Mats said politely, but he scooped up Alvin and grabbed Astrid's hand and sped up the slope of Causeway beside her and Barnaby. They fell into the cottage, gasping and laughing, shutting the rickety door on the hail that was by now hissing ferociously to earth and clattering against the cottage windows.

Valentina appeared at the head of the stairs. 'Good job you were at this end of the beach.' Smiling in a friendly way at the children and an interested way at Mats, she said, 'I'm Valentina, Ezzie's sister.' She trod down the stairs.

Mats shook her hand. 'Mats Larsson. I hope you don't mind us barging in, but the hail was stinging the children.'

Although Valentina answered equally politely, 'Of course I don't mind,' she'd stiffened as she heard his name. She removed her hand from Mats' and gave Ezzie an obviously *WTF?* stare.

For an instant, Ezz was wrong-footed. Then she realised that last time Valentina was here, Ezzie had declared Mats a knob and probably an entitled arse as well.

'Come and see which is going to be my room,' Barnaby yelled, and all three of the children charged upstairs. At least, Astrid and Barnaby charged. Alvin stumbled along at the rear.

Mats, obviously catching the chill coming off Valentina, looked unsure. 'Shall I bring them down again? Sorry. They should have waited for permission.'

'They're fine.' Valentina sent Ezz a pointed look, as if to say, *What's he doing here?*

Ezz felt irritated. She'd put up with Gary for years and years, hadn't she? Impulsively, she turned to Mats. 'I'm afraid I haven't updated Valentina since Thea and I resigned. It had just happened when I last saw her, and I was miffed with you.'

'Ah. When I was an entitled arse, you mean.' His gorgeous eyes began to twinkle as he turned back to Valentina. 'We got off on the wrong foot and it was my fault. I got carried away with the idea of having *Garden Gladiators* use Rothach Hall as a location and jumped in with both feet. My mother was miffed with me too. She pointed out that she and Dad own the hall, and I'm just a guest.'

Valentina uncrossed her arms and managed a smile. 'Ah, I see. Presumably Thea didn't want to get involved with the *Garden Gladiators* crew again? I suppose they've told you all about it.'

Mats nodded. He lowered his voice. 'I could see Thea's reasons, once Ezz confided the truth about the accident they were involved in – which was incredibly brave of her – but it'll go no further.' He turned to smile at Ezz.

The smile faded when Ezz gazed back at him with her mouth hanging open. 'Oh, *Mats*,' she breathed. Frantically, she tried to summon words to explain away what he'd blurted out.

But it was too late. Valentina demanded, '*What* truth about the accident? What does he mean, Ezz?'

Ezz could only gaze at her big sister's confused and apprehensive expression. The days of Valentina being kept in the dark about what happened that night in Suffolk were over.

Beside her, Mats caught his breath. 'Oh, shit. Didn't she know?' Then, doing more damage as he blundered along, he whispered, 'I thought that's what she meant about you telling me all about it.'

'I *meant* about Thea's time as a TV star.' Valentina stared at Ezz with enormous, wounded eyes. 'But clearly there's something else. Some big secret.'

The following silence was loud. Ezzie whispered, 'Mats, perhaps you should take the children and go. I can't hear the hail now.'

He didn't immediately move. 'If it would help if I stayed . . .'

Ezzie shook her head, her gaze fixed on Valentina. 'No. But thanks.'

'Right.' He looked up the narrow stairs, where patches of new wood amongst the old made the house look as if it had vitiligo.

Silently, Valentina stepped aside to allow him past in the narrow space, then moved into the front room. Ezz waited in the hall, blood hammering in her ears, watching Mats tread up the bare wooden stairs, listening to him utilise his Dad voice. 'Astrid and Alvin, we have to go now. Farmor and Farfar are at home and might want to join us for lunch. Aren't you hungry?' Judging by Astrid's evasive answers, she'd rather run around Barnaby's empty room than eat.

Finally, they trooped down, Mats asking Astrid to hold the handrail and carrying Alvin. His anxious gaze settled on Ezz's face. 'OK?' he murmured uncertainly.

She nodded, forcing the corners of her mouth to lift. 'Sure. Bye, Astrid. Bye, Alvin. See you soon.' They shuffled awkwardly around each other in the tiny hall, apology and dismay still large in Mats' eyes. Another moment, then the front door shut behind him and his children.

Slowly, she trailed into the front room to face Valentina, but Valentina was speaking into her phone in a tight, unnatural voice. 'Please can you come back and take Barnaby to Broadford or somewhere for lunch? Yes, now. Yes, it's important. I need to talk to Ezz.' A silence, then her voice dropped. 'Exactly.' She stabbed the screen, then looked out of the window as a shadow fell across it. 'Damn. The builder.' She spun and headed for the doorway where Ezzie hovered.

Her expression had become so fierce that Ezzie jumped out of the way. 'Valentina—'

'If you could entertain Barnaby until Gary arrives to pick him up, that would be useful.' Valentina jerked open the front door and greeted the builder, 'Hello, Keith.'

Keith was a big man with a weather-beaten complexion under a black woolly hat. His work jacket was ripped at the shoulder, and his boots were speckled with plaster. 'Hello there,' he greeted her pleasantly.

Barnaby ran to the top of the stairs, obviously eager to see who'd arrived. With a feeling of unreality that Valentina apparently couldn't even look at her, Ezz forced a smile. 'Where's your coat gone, Barns?'

He glanced back into the room he'd just vacated. 'On the floor.'

Nice and dirty, then. 'Pop it back on, please. Dad's coming to take you for lunch while Mum talks to the builder, so you and me can wait on the beach.' She made sure to make it sound like an enormous treat, rather than that Ezz was being lined up for such a major bollocking that Barnaby had to be shielded from it. Barnaby ran downstairs and then Valentina escorted Keith up.

Ezz convinced Barnaby that he really did need his coat,

then cried, 'Let's see if the fish is still there,' as if it were the most exciting event of her year.

'Yeah!' Barnaby took off through the front door, jumping off the side of the causeway onto the gritty sand, then racing around trying to find the right pool. 'Where is it?' he demanded, scowling at Ezz as if it were her fault. 'My fish has gone.'

'A huge wave must have come and washed him back into the sea,' Ezz improvised, pointing dramatically at the frothing shallows withdrawing sullenly down the beach. The poor little fish must have become a seagull's lunch, unprotected in such shallow water. 'How about we look for shells?'

'Got some.' Barnaby patted his pockets and sighed, as if at the idiocy of adults. Perhaps he'd picked up on the tension between Ezz and Valentina and it leaked out of him in moody kicks at the sand and stringy seaweed. Ezz felt like doing the same. Why on earth had Mats opened his mouth? He should have made quite sure he'd understood Valentina before he spoke. It was like the *Garden Gladiators* thing all over again, saying exactly what came into his head without thought.

It seemed a long half hour before the blue SUV appeared in Harbour View, and Ezz didn't think she'd ever been so glad to see Gary. 'Here's Dad,' she said. But Barnaby was already running, and Ezz hared after him, grabbing his shoulders to keep him safe. 'Just let the car stop.'

Gary, of course, had seen the human missile that was his son and halted the car in good time. He jumped out and opened the back door. 'Jump in, Barns. We'll go to a lovely café.'

'Awesome.' Barnaby scrambled into his seat without even glancing back at Ezz.

Gary checked he was buckled in, and then closed the door. He narrowed his eyes at Ezz. 'What's up with her this time?' He must have left his coat in the car, and he shivered in his cardigan.

'This time?' Ezz queried, surprised.

Rather than answering, he sighed. 'I'd better get off.' In a minute he'd turned the car and driven away. At least Barnaby gave Ezz a wave as he sailed by.

Alone now, she looked back at the cottage. Keith's pick-up was still outside. Her face felt frozen, and the rain was beginning again, a fine drizzle that stung her eyes. Should she go home? Hanging around out here felt as if she were a bad dog waiting to be forgiven. Letting herself back into icy Overlook Cottage with nowhere to sit didn't seem much better. But, as she debated, the cottage door opened and Keith ambled out, listening to Valentina and clutching something that looked like one of her bathroom brochures. Heavily, Ezz began stumping back along the road towards the cottage, frozen despite her outdoor wear.

Soon, Keith's pick-up truck was reversing up the Quays until it could swing round in the mouth of Portnalong Way. He gave Ezz a friendly nod as he drove past. Ezz responded, then trudged on, angry at being treated like a naughty child at her age. Mentally, she reviewed arguments she thought she was going to need when Valentina let her feelings be known. *Panic of the moment . . . knew I'd go to prison . . . I've always regretted the trouble I caused Thea.* The process stoked her resentment so that she shoved open the cottage door not feeling anywhere near as apologetic as when Mats had first spilled the beans.

But when she stepped inside, she found her sister sitting on the stairs, sobs shaking her shoulders, tears pouring between the fingers that covered her eyes. 'Valentina,' she gasped, dropping down beside her to pull her into her arms.

Valentina shoved her away and scrabbled in her pocket for a tissue. She mopped her eyes, blew her nose and gave a great sniff. 'Why was I excluded?'

Slowly, Ezz rose. She'd expected demands for explanations of Ezz's sin, not recriminations for protecting Valentina. Her hands clenched. 'Because it would have put you in a tricky position. You're a lawyer.'

Valentina rose, found her coat in the front room, and withdrew a travel pack of tissues from the pocket. It was very Valentina compared to the couple of sheets of kitchen roll Ezz usually carried around. She blew her nose again then turned to face Ezz, perfectly composed apart from red eyes. 'What does that matter? Are you going to let me into the secret now? Or not?'

Ezz almost snapped, 'Not,' because she felt prickly and cornered, in the wrong but not confident of a sympathetic hearing from a clearly furious and upset elder sister. It reminded her of childhood spats over what Valentina saw as the natural role of the eldest while Ezz termed it bossiness. But she tried to put herself in Valentina's place and realised that she was anguished by Ezz and Thea keeping a secret.

At her hesitation, Valentina began to put on her coat. 'Your silence is my answer, even though Mats – a stranger you don't even like – assumed you'd told me whatever it is.'

Ezz sighed. 'He's no longer a stranger and I do like him, but that's not the point. The point is that Thea and I did something criminal, OK?'

Valentina stilled, eyes wide but mouth still a furious line, while Ezz confessed. 'It was me who was driving. I'd been

241

partying the night before, so I thought I'd probably be over the drink-drive limit. Thea offered to pretend she'd been behind the wheel, because she was adamant that I'd go to prison. I let her. I brought trouble to Thea that I've regretted ever since.'

'I think you would have gone to prison,' Valentina said in a shocked voice. 'You'd lost your driving licence for drink-driving before. Someone was hurt.'

'Yep.' Ezz snipped her off. 'I know it. You don't have to lecture me.'

'What the hell did you think I'd do? Turn you in?' Valentina barked.

'No,' Ezz barked back. 'I thought you'd be embarrassed, mortified and ashamed. We tried to protect you. Lawyers don't generally want their relatives in prison, do they?'

'You didn't go to prison.' Valentina was only getting angrier.

'Because I compounded my possible offence by covering it up. Just out of interest, what would you have said if I had come to you?' Ezz met her sister's blazing eyes. 'That I'd been stupid? That I shouldn't have accepted Thea's help? That I should expect a prison sentence? Fuck it, Valentina, I *know*. What good would it have done to put the whole sorry mess on your conscience, too?'

Fresh rain spat against the window, making marks in the salty dirt. Gulls bickered. The atmosphere inside Overlook Cottage became colder. 'We'll never know, will we?' Valentina said at last. 'My view of what happened is clouded by a decade of being left out.'

'It's not a party we didn't invite you to,' Ezz wailed, exasperated. 'We were trying not to involve you in something bad we'd done. And please don't be angry with Thea. She did what she did for me.' She felt suddenly exhausted by

242

the emotion of the day, by the sex of the previous night, even by being well overdue her lunch. 'I'm sorry you're upset. I'm so, so sorry. If I could go back, I would refuse Thea's help and take my chance with the breathalyser. I still wouldn't drag you into my shitty mess, though.'

Valentina finished putting on her coat and pulled a hat from her pocket. 'We won't go out tonight because I won't be able to treat you normally. I'll tell the others you have stomach ache.' She pulled on the hat and tucked in stray hairs.

Although aware that she was being dismissed, Ezz held her ground. 'Don't you see why I didn't tell you?'

'Because you thought I wouldn't be able to keep the secret?' Valentina asked in a hard voice.

'No. The same reason I should imagine you're not going to tell Gary. You're ashamed. Plus, it would put him in a difficult situation because he's a lawyer too.'

Valentina strode to the front door and yanked it open. 'He is *not* your sister.'

'And also,' Ezz said pointedly, as she stalked through the open door, 'Gary would have a strong opinion and judge us. He might even try and make decisions without discussion.' Even as she made the dig, she knew she was making the situation worse, but she couldn't seem to stop her anger pouring from her mouth.

Valentina sent her a particularly fierce glare. 'I suppose you mean because I just made a decision about dinner tonight.'

'Exactly. You thought you knew best so you acted. You're probably right that we shouldn't go out to dinner, but don't pretend you might have had useful advice when I made a huge mistake and panicked. *Because there was no way out of the mess.*'

243

Then she pulled up her hood, put down her head and trailed home in tears.

It was much later in the afternoon, when she'd soaked in a hot bath and then comforted herself by eating both desserts from last night, that she checked her phone and found a string of texts and voicemails from Mats, all of the *so incredibly sorry* and *feel like a shit* variety.

She texted back. *Not really your fault.*

Can I see you? Or call? he returned.

Not feeling great, she replied, truthfully but ambiguously.

Because you're so close to your sisters I stupidly assumed I knew what Valentina meant. Of course, there's a big difference between sharing the secret with the sister involved and with the one not involved. I'm a moron. Screaming emoji. *Is Valentina very upset?*

For several minutes, Ezz contemplated returning, *Yes, stupid assumption. Yes, you're a moron. YES, she's upset!* Eventually she just returned, *Can't change history. I'll be at work on Monday.* She didn't want to see him tonight or the second advent Sunday gathering tomorrow at Rothach Hall. Her first priority was to sit down with Valentina and talk properly. She could hear the echo of her father Vince when she and Valentina had butted heads as children. *The trouble is with you two that you both think you're right, and that's rarely possible.* And he would slip his arms around them and gently referee two strong characters sharing equally strong opinions.

But Vince was gone. An image of Rick Colville floated into her mind, the sad lines on his face on the three occasions she'd seen him. She couldn't imagine him being as good a dad as Vince, because she couldn't imagine having a dad *other* than Vince. Even if Rick was living proof that she did have.

She lay on her turquoise sofa, trying to decide what to do about Valentina. Ezz could have just turned up at Thistledome, but when your big sis was so pissed off that she refused to dine with you, it was obvious that she needed time to cool down.

Finally, late in the evening, she sent Valentina a text. *I hate this. Can we meet up Sunday a.m. and talk, please? You could come here so we won't be disturbed. Xx*

But no text pinged back across the village.

Slowly, Ezz turned out the fairy lights in the lounge and the kitchen, and went to bed.

A text alert woke her at eight on Sunday morning. Blinking the sleep from her eyes, Ezz scrabbled to read Valentina's reply. *Sorry, we left early. We're at Dornie already.* Typical of Valentina, there were no fibs such as *didn't see your message till now* or *we have to get back because Barnaby has a play date*. No. She'd left early and was more than half an hour away already.

It was, in anybody's eyes, a snub.

Unfortunately, the bad news wasn't over, because Thea phoned, uncharacteristically subdued and anxious. 'I'm going to need time off.'

Ezz, who'd made it out of bed but not out of her pyjamas, smothered a sigh and reached down a coffee mug from the kitchen cabinet. It felt as if it was going to be a constant-coffee type of day. She'd intended to wait until Thea was safely home this evening to break the news that Valentina knew Ezz had been driving Thea's car that fateful day, and was furious, but mainly with Ezz. Now it sounded as if there was something else to deal with first. 'What's up?'

Thea's voice caught. 'I had some bleeding. I've been in Dumfries hospital. I've had a scan and the baby's heartbeat's still there, but they've advised me to stay off work and rest, and not to travel home yet.'

Instantly, everything else vanished from Ezz's mind and her heart went out to Thea, imagining the crushing threat of loss and disappointment on the horizon. Her eyes pricked with tears. 'Oh, no. But the heartbeat's everything. Cling on to that, sweetie. Can you stay with Dev's family?'

'There's not much room, so we've taken an Airbnb, so I can rest quietly. Dev's nieces are lovely, but noisy.' Thea's voice dwindled to a thread.

Ezz gripped her phone, feeling it cut into her palm. 'I'm so sorry this has happened, Thea. Don't worry about work. I'll sort it out.' And no way would Ezz let on about Valentina's huff now. The last thing Thea needed was stress. 'What else can I do?' she asked, feeling as if her life had turned to a bad dream in the past couple of days. 'Shall I tell Valentina for you?' If Thea said no, Ezz determined that she'd try and call Valentina before Thea could, to tell her not to give Thea shit, imagining Valentina seeing Thea's name on her screen and jumping straight in with her hurt feelings even before saying hello.

But Thea said a dreary, 'Yes, please.' Ezz breathed a sigh of relief. 'Dev's with you all the time, is he?' she asked, feeling as if she had some headspace now for anxious enquiries. 'Are you in any pain?'

'Yes, he's here, and there's no pain,' Thea said. 'I'm just going to flop on the sofa and watch TV.'

'Let me know if there's anything I can do,' Ezz urged. 'Sending you all my love.'

When she'd ended the call, she brushed away her tears, sustained herself with several gulps of coffee, then called Valentina, who at least picked up straight away with a neutral, 'Hello.'

Ezz gazed out of the kitchen window at her weather-flattened grass and bare trees. 'I'm not on speaker, am I?'

'No.' Valentina sounded quiet and strained.

Plunging on, Ezz said, 'This is about Thea, not me. She's just been on the phone and she's not sure she's going to be able to hang on to her pregnancy.' She provided the details she knew.

Valentina sounded as if she was trying not to cry. 'That's horrible. Thanks for letting me know. Obviously she didn't feel I warranted my own phone call.'

Any patience Ezz had snapped. 'Stop laying it on. I was protecting *her* from calling you and finding out that you're upset and angry, and *you* from letting her know you're upset before she had a chance to tell you that she has worse things to worry about. We've got to think about her and the baby at the moment.'

Valentina's silence lasted several seconds. Then, sounding as if she might have thawed a couple of degrees, she said, 'OK. I understand.'

It was obvious that Valentina was a long way off seeing things from Ezz's point of view yet, but Ezz was sure her lovely big sister would forgive her sooner or later.

It just might be later.

Chapter Seventeen

Mats greeted Monday with scant enthusiasm. As Ezzie hadn't shown up for *fika* on Sunday nor answered his most recent texts, he lay in wait for her to arrive for work. When she spotted him lurking in reception under the guise of chatting to Orla, she said, 'Good morning,' then strode into her office, pulling off her long overcoat. Though her face was wan, the rest of her was as immaculate as ever.

He followed her in. 'Are you OK?'

Her blue eyes bleak, she answered indirectly. 'Thea's having difficulty with her pregnancy and has stayed in Dumfries. I need to concentrate on that and work stuff.' She didn't actually add, *So please don't talk to me about the crappy mess you dropped me into*, but her tone suggested that she didn't want to rehash his motormouth moment in front of Valentina on Saturday.

'I'm sorry to hear it.' He was shaken, imagining how he'd have felt if either of Inger's pregnancies had come under threat. 'Now I feel worse than ever.'

She settled herself at the desk without acknowledging his feelings. 'I'll send Grete a formal email. Then I must speak to Sheena about working around Thea's absence.'

'I understand,' he said hollowly, getting the hint that she was manager and she wasn't in favour of him informing his parents. After a pause to see if she'd add anything, he returned to the family quarters, hanging around until Grete received the email on her phone and read it aloud to him and Erik, her voice full of concern.

Erik knit his thick eyebrows anxiously. 'We must hope for the best for Thea.'

'Indeed.' Grete phoned Ezz to ask her to come to the home office to discuss the staff situation once she'd spoken to Sheena. When Grete and Erik settled themselves there to plan for the rest of the family arriving on Sunday, Mats joined them.

'Two hire cars will be waiting at Inverness Airport.' Grete, perhaps not wanting to dwell on poor Thea's situation before they knew the outcome, beamed at the prospect of seeing all her children and grandchildren together.

Mats listened to his parents discuss food and drink, and days out around the island. Affectionately, he said, 'You'd think there were ninety extra people coming, not nine.' But he was glad to see his parents putting their heads together. They'd been so natural and relaxed with each other since their heart-to-heart after Erik's arrival that he was nurturing hopes they were sorting out their differences.

Grete treated him to a look of mock-reproof. 'But they are nine very special people.'

They were laughing as Ezz knocked at the half-open door, her pallor exaggerated by her sombre black suit.

Mats rose to give her his chair, while he took another at the side of the room. For some reason, it gave him satisfaction to think that she'd be able to feel the residual warmth of his body.

'Any news from Thea?' He wanted to show her that he was focused on her main concern.

She shook her head. 'I've talked to Dev this morning, but Thea was sleeping. He said that it's just a question of waiting to see.' Her gaze switched to Grete and Erik. 'I've spoken to Sheena.'

Erik smiled. 'The gardens can be left in winter?'

Her blonde hair danced as she nodded. 'To an extent. Tree surgeons are coming this week, so Sheena will oversee them. Other jobs on the gardeners' planner up until New Year are pruning of shrubs and the grapevine, clearing leaves and things like that.'

'Nothing world-ending,' Grete observed kindly.

'No. Though Thea loves that grapevine.' Ezz managed a tiny smile. 'The one thing that can't be neglected is the feeding and general care of Clive and the ponies.'

Mats heard himself say, 'I can do that. Then Sheena can concentrate on the gardens.'

All the eyes in the room swivelled his way. 'Good, Mats,' approved Grete.

'Very helpful,' added Erik.

An actual smile shone in Ezz's eyes. 'That would solve a small but important issue. Sheena will show you what supplementary feed they need in winter and how to check their water's filling. It's piped automatically but can freeze.' She turned back to Grete. 'You thought perhaps some of the older children might like to ride. Haggis and Scotch have tack in one of the outbuildings. I don't think they'd mind coming out of retirement.'

Grete pursed her lips. 'But we have done nothing about helmets. I think we do not tell the children that Scotch and Haggis have saddles until summer.'

Mats stored away the information that his mum expected at least some of the family to be at Rothach this summer and wondered if he'd be among them. At present, it was easy to arrange his holidays as and when they suited him, but if he left Larsson Fiskeri because of the long hours he'd been working then that might change. He studied Ezz as she listened to the conversation, the tiniest tuck between her pale brows, and wondered how much it would hurt to leave her behind when he went home to Sweden in the New Year. How had he fallen so hard and fast for the beautiful British blonde, the first woman he'd felt anything for since his divorce? Would he return in the summer and discover that Ezz had found a new man? A green spear of jealousy pierced him at the idea of her sharing with someone else that fierce, sensation-seeking passion that had gripped them both on Saturday night.

Grete spoke again. 'I have texted to Thea our good wishes. She must not worry about work.'

Ezz blinked rapidly. 'Thank you. I'm sure she appreciates your kindness.'

The sombre exchange made Mats think that both women feared the worst for Thea's pregnancy. He wanted to take Ezz's hand but knew how little she'd welcome it. *Already dropped her in it with her sister by blabbing the biggest secret of her life? Why not let her employers know that she's been sleeping with their son into the bargain? Awesome job, Mats.*

Ezz's tepid texts might not have blamed Mats for his stupid indiscretion, but the way her gaze skated away from his suggested the opposite. He half-listened to a conversation about Orla from reception leaving on Friday. His dad was in rumbling mode, questioning whether they needed more help, holding up his big hands to count off on his fingers. 'No assistant manager until February. No receptionist. No head gardener. Perhaps the Larssons are horrible?' He gave one of his giant, beaming grins, but sobered quickly. 'You are OK, Ezz? We distress if you are not OK with much work.'

Her smile for Erik was obviously genuine, and it was obvious that they got along well, despite Erik's ungrammatical English. It dawned on Mats that if Erik had arrived at the hall at the same time as Mats, Grete and co, she might never have been so stiff and anxious to please. Ezz answered, 'I haven't met any horrible Larssons yet.' She hesitated, frowning. 'I'll have to take back some of the routine tasks I gave Orla. Updating spreadsheets and collating statements for the accountants ready for the end of year and the fourth-quarter VAT return, for instance.'

Mats found himself volunteering again. 'If you show me the spreadsheets, I can do those.' When she looked taken aback and her mouth opened as if to refuse, he added, 'I'm a finance officer. I can take a few hours of work off your desk.'

'Good boy,' said Erik, as if Mats was five years old.

Grete awarded him her twinkliest smile.

In the face of their approbation, Ezz capitulated. 'That would be a great help. Thank you.'

Ten minutes later, he was in her office while she whizzed through the relevant spreadsheets, showing him where to pick up the data, and what to cross-reference. There was not even the slightest acknowledgement that he was anything more to her than her bosses' son. He made notes on her pad. 'What else can I do?'

She hesitated, then seemed to give a mental shrug, as if she might as well make use of him. 'The employment records need checking. We do it once to December 31st for the year end and again in April for the tax year. The staff records are in a password-protected area.' She took the pad from him and wrote the access details he'd need. 'If you take the assistant manager's office, the computer there has the accounting software.' She added the computer password to his notes.

He let his body angle towards hers, enjoying the citrus scent of her skin, wondering whether it was soap or body lotion. Despite her so obviously being in work mode, he dropped his voice, so she had to lean in to hear him. 'Did I cause real trouble between you and Valentina?' His arms itched to close around her and hold her as he had on Saturday, feeling her beautiful body melt into him like butter on hot toast.

She put up a hand, as if she anticipated the embrace he was itching to bestow . . . and didn't want it. 'I'm afraid Valentina's hurt and upset. We're very close, you see . . .' The words caught in her throat.

His heart gave a great, wretched heave. 'I'm so sorry.' When she didn't answer he rose, deflated. 'I'll make a start while Josefin has the children out at the playground.' He returned his chair to its spot on the other side of the desk, and then sought out the tiny assistant manager's office, furious with himself that impetuosity had once again got him in trouble and no matter how profuse his apologies, Ezz was the one suffering for him speaking before he thought.

His first night with Ezz might have been his last.

* * *

Mats' family gathered in the kitchen for lunch, everyone grabbing things from cupboards or the fridge and adding them to the table to share, like a chaotic *smörgåsbord*. Astrid and Alvin had been racing around outside, and Alvin was almost asleep in his bread and cheese, a sausage clutched in one small hand. Although he considered himself too old for daytime naps, he did occasionally grab one.

Astrid licked her fingers, having just consumed a tomato from her hand as if it were an apple. 'Daddy, can we talk to Mummy?'

He nodded. 'Let me text her to set up a time.' Video calls with Inger were fine with him, but he first intended to make it clear that, in the children's hearing, it would not be appropriate to repeat her request that he whisk them to North Tunisia for Christmas. They'd start running around whooping about visiting Mummy on a yacht with zero understanding of what that would entail and no care for existing plans for a Skye Christmas. He slipped Alvin onto his lap to snooze. The little boy smelled of sausage and the outdoors. Mats dropped a kiss on the baby-soft hair as he texted Inger: *The kids would like to FaceTime you. When is convenient?* He added his request for circumspection regarding impossible Christmas plans.

Erik switched to his native Swedish. 'It's good Alvin gets some sleep before his cousins arrive. Especially Walter. I've never known a seven-year-old who can keep going from dawn till dusk like he can.'

Grete laughed, giving Erik a little push with her fingertips. 'He's as mischievous as his grandfather.' It was good to see them interacting with some of their old closeness.

Josefin took Astrid up to the playroom so she wouldn't disturb Alvin's nap, and Grete went to talk to Gwen, probably armed with yet another shopping list as she thought of treats that might be desired by members of the family arriving on Sunday.

Mats crossed an ankle over the other knee to support the arm cradling Alvin. Erik made coffee and then returned to the table. 'We should talk about work.' He smiled at Alvin, pink-cheeked in sleep.

Mats stifled a sigh. He'd been enjoying not even thinking about work – apart from the small tasks he'd taken on to please Ezz. 'I need to be more available to my children,' he said bluntly. 'If I have to keep working such long hours, then you'd better replace me.' It felt less aggressive than saying: *I'll leave.*

But Erik only nodded. 'You must get your priorities right.'

Mats felt as if the whole of Rothach Hall held its breath in shock. He stared at his father, who was still gazing down at Alvin. He'd expected an explosion, or at least a warning rumble. Agreement threw him. Cautiously, he tried to be clearer, in case Erik hadn't properly understood. 'I want to be home to put my children to bed regularly, and even early enough to build a snowman or watch a swimming lesson.'

'Your little ones are important.' Erik sipped his coffee, and the rich aroma wafted to Mats. Then, with an air of self-consciousness, Erik added, 'I am to cut my hours too.'

Mats' heart flipped right over at this welcome news. 'Seriously? To be with Mum?'

'Well, I don't like being without her.' Erik sipped more coffee and then smacked his lips. 'She said I made work everything. If that were true, I wouldn't have missed her so much. And I missed her *so* much.'

Mats reached out and clasped Erik's shoulder, still firm

and strong even at Erik's age of seventy-one. His father was one of the most vital men Mats knew, yet apparently a lesser person without his soulmate beside him. 'That's great, Dad. Mum's been low without you.'

Erik looked gratified. 'That's something.'

Then Mats' phone beeped, and Alvin woke up, twisted in Mats' arms and blinked at his father and grandfather. 'Text,' he announced accurately, slipping instantly from sleep to waking, despite rumpled hair and heavy eyes.

'Clever boy.' Mats read the text. 'Mummy's ready to FaceTime. Shall we find Astrid?'

'Yeah!' Alvin wriggled from Mats' lap. They left Erik to join Grete in the lounge before the cosy fire and the shimmering Christmas tree, while they climbed the stairs together. Soon, they'd collected Astrid from the playroom and were snuggled together on Astrid's bed, Mats' iPad propped up by a cushion on his legs.

When Inger appeared on the screen, the sky was blue behind her head and her bare shoulders looked tanned above a yellow top. She cooed, 'Oh, darlings, how lovely to see you.' The children instantly fell back into Swedish, and Mats listened to them outdo each other with stories of the woods, ponies, sausages and all the joys that floated to the tops of their young minds.

'The beach,' Alvin shouted, scrambling to his knees, obviously bursting with the need to be first on the topic. 'We went to the beach, and it rained stones.'

Astrid laughed. 'They were hailstones,' she clarified. 'And they hurt. Ezz was there with Barnaby – we looked at his fish, but it wasn't really *his* fish, because it came from the sea – so we all ran into her house. No,' she corrected herself, 'her sister's house. It's very dirty and doesn't have anything in it.'

Inger laughed, white teeth flashing. 'That's a strange house.'

'Barnaby's mother, Valentina, has bought a cottage to do up,' Mats put in. 'It's not at its best.' And he wished like hell that he hadn't visited it, because then he couldn't have blabbed Ezz's secret to her sister and ballsed things up.

Inger didn't show much interest in the property. Probably 'cottage' didn't sound grand enough. 'So, how old is Barnaby? Is he a new friend?'

The children agreed that he was, and Mats interpolated, 'He's about Astrid's age.'

'And if Valentina's Barnaby's mummy, who is Ezz?' Inger shifted in her seat, and the backdrop became the quay of a marina briefly, then settled back to being a cloudless blue sky.

Astrid looked at Mats for guidance. Ezz was just Ezz, he guessed, so far as Astrid was concerned. He supplied, 'She's the manager at the hall. You probably met her when she was assistant manager. Barnaby's her nephew. They were playing on the beach at the same time we were, and then the hailstorm began, so we all sheltered for a few minutes.' To turn the subject as he wasn't particularly mad on discussing with his ex-wife the woman he'd just slept with, he asked, 'Still in Tunisia?'

'We turned north, so we're in Sardinia now.' Inger waved an airy hand at scenery they couldn't see. 'Then it's Corsica and Monaco. Andreas has friends in Monte Carlo, and they've invited us to their villa. They own a lovely restaurant where the Formula One drivers go. Monaco's filled with rich people because it's a tax haven.' Inger sounded very used to Andreas' privileged way of life now.

Alvin jumped back into the conversation. 'We saw the ponies today. One's a donkey.'

Mats didn't bother pointing out the difference between ponies and donkeys, but let the children chatter about the sea, ponies, donkeys, gulls, fish, the hall, the village, the snow-topped mountains and the wintry weather.

He listened idly, an arm around each child, thinking that luxurious as Inger's surroundings appeared, he was happier squashed up on a couple of pillows with the two most amazing little people on the planet.

He was even happier when they reached the conclusion of the call without Inger once again mentioning him bringing the kids for Christmas.

Chapter Eighteen

Friday the thirteenth might traditionally be an unlucky day, but for Ezz it meant the first ray of light in the entire week when Thea rang.

She sounded breathless, but her voice was lighter. 'I haven't bled for several days. We've had another scan, and we still have a heartbeat, so the hospital says I can come home. We've got the Airbnb until Tuesday seventeenth, so that's when we'll drive up.'

Ezz had to blink back tears. 'That's the best news,' she said thickly. 'You sound happier.'

'Cautiously optimistic,' Thea confirmed, with the breath of a laugh. 'Dev's treating me as if I'm made of antique crystal, his mum and grandpa have bought me flowers and his nieces made me get-well cards. I've been told to see my GP for a sick note until after Christmas,' she finished apologetically.

'Very sensible,' Ezz replied firmly, to quash any guilt. 'Grete and Erik will only care that the baby's OK.'

'That's great.' Thea sounded relieved. 'Valentina's just called, so she already knows things are looking better. We were chatting about her having been around my age when she was pregnant with Barnaby. Luckily, they didn't have any issues.'

Ezz listened for any hint of alarm in Thea's voice, but detecting none, felt comfortable that Valentina hadn't told Thea she knew the truth about the accident or that she and Ezz had quarrelled. At least one relationship seemed intact. She ended the call feeling glad about that, at least.

As it was Orla's last day, Ezz had bought her chocolates and presented them to her with a hug. 'Thanks for all your work during your time at Rothach Hall.'

'Oh, my goodness.' Orla smiled, though her eyes were bright with tears. 'Mrs Larsson has already given me flowers and a card, and Gwen gave me Skye shortbread from the Nature Garden Café to remind me of home.' She had to pause and blow her nose. 'I feel so bad at leaving when you haven't got an assistant manager either. But my husband's job—'

'You're doing the right thing for you,' Ezz said, with a huge smile she didn't feel. 'I'll be fine.'

She waited until evening, when she was home in her cosy cottage, to call Valentina, timing her call for when Barnaby would be in bed. Attempting to thaw the frost between them, she began, 'Great news about Thea, isn't it?'

Valentina sounded tired. 'Better, anyway.' Before Ezz could try and improve on this stiff start, she went on crisply. 'But her situation cements my decision not to come to Rothach for Christmas. Thea needs to be quiet and there are Christmas activities that Barnaby will miss out on if we're away.' She didn't even mention Hogmanay celebrations, which had once been planned to be at Valentina's, but had seemed forgotten lately.

Ezzie's heart plummeted so hard it made her queasy. 'Not come?' she repeated. 'Not even for a couple of days? You're serious?'

'I think it's better.' Valentina might have been talking to Gary about whether to switch their brand of coffee, for all the emotion in her words.

Ezz's own voice quavered. 'You're punishing me? Or you don't want to stay with me and now you can't stay with Thea?'

'It's not because of you.' But Valentina's words lacked conviction. 'I've given my reasons.'

'Have you told Thea?' Every word stung Ezz's throat. 'Did she believe you?'

Valentina answered with a vague: 'Of course. But I asked her to leave it to me to tell you.'

'Well. OK.' Ezz knew she sounded as glum as Eeyore. After a silence, which Valentina made no effort to fill, Ezz said goodbye. She sat on her sofa for several minutes, gazing at the wall.

Valentina wasn't coming for Christmas.

It seemed tough on Thea, who was at risk of being collateral damage from the sudden cracks in Ezz and Valentina's relationship. Happily, her focus would be on her pregnancy and with luck, this would be the last Christmas morning that she and Dev would wake up alone.

It had been a beautiful wintry Skye day, clear and frosty and, as happened so often, Ezz had found little opportunity to be outside and enjoy it. Now, unable to bear the

261

constraints of the familiar walls, she dressed warmly and strode out into the dark evening, where frost gave every twig a white glittering coat and iced-over puddles waited like traps for the unwary. The Jolly Abbot looked very jolly indeed, festooned with coloured lights, every window in the pub ablaze, but Ezz turned away, fearing the comfort she might let herself indulge in there – a large glass of wine. Or three.

First, she crossed the village to Loch View. Thistledome was dark and deserted but she had a key, so she went in to check that everywhere was clean and tidy for Thea's return. On the kitchen table lay a note in Valentina's handwriting. *Stripped the bed and put on clean sheets. Emptied the bin. Thanks for letting us use your lovely home. See you soon. Loads of love, V Xxx*

It sounded like the real Valentina: brisk but warm and loving. Nothing like the stiff, angry Valentina who was showing herself to Ezz. A sudden, fierce longing for their normal relationship grabbed her by the heart and she paused to ride the wave of pain. She checked around the house, but Valentina seemed to have left nothing for her to do, so she let herself out.

Loch View was so high up in the village that she paused to admire the moonlight on Rothach Bay, silvering the black sea in a wandering path that fanned out towards the shore. She lifted her gaze higher, to the black velvet sky spangled with an impossible number of stars, twinkling and blinking back at her like diamond dust. She remembered her whimsical idea that there was a constellation called Birth Family of which she was part. Two other stars in her constellation were now known to her – Rick and Kay, whose teenage passion had accidentally created her life – and she had names for two more, Julia and Iona. A constellation was small compared to the galaxy, the universe, and anything bigger than that, but each individual star was beautiful, shimmering down on the Isle of Skye and one lone woman feeling sorry for herself.

Finally, she roused from her reverie and crunched away down the frosty lanes to her warm but empty home.

Ezz remained on duty all weekend. The rest of the Larssons arrived late on Sunday afternoon and she was on hand to greet dark-haired Maja and blond Nils with their children Walter, Liam and Ronja. While Astrid and Alvin raced around in a fever of excitement and Mats and his parents exchanged beaming hugs with the new arrivals, Ezz unobtrusively unloaded luggage from the hire car. Mats came to help, and she thought she felt his hand brush her back. She didn't look his way, but just drove the now empty car to the parking place behind the hall. A few minutes later, Jonas and Ebba, Emil and Filip bowled up the drive, tooting the car horn and waving through the windscreen. Ezz did the 'greet then fade into the background' thing again.

Astrid was loud in her excitement, and everyone chattered in Swedish, which only added to Ezz's sense of exclusion.

The family made a laughing group, carting what luggage Ezzie hadn't already hauled up the steps. This time, before she could move the car, Mats approached. 'Please join us for *fika*,' he said, giving coffee and cake the Swedish name. 'Mum asked Gwen to provide us with something yummy.'

Despite herself, her heart gave a tiny skip. 'I don't think—'

'Please.' His smile was warm and hopeful. 'I hate us

being so distant, Ezzie. I know I made a horrible mistake, but I would never hurt you intentionally.'

Involuntarily, she flinched. She'd made a much bigger mistake ten years ago. In his grey eyes she saw what she knew only too well herself: regret. And something she felt seriously short of: affection. Her smile muscles wavered into life. 'Thank you. That would be lovely.'

'Leave the car,' he said. 'Jonas or Ebba can move it.'

Half an hour in the big lounge with the oversized tree and the crackling fire turned out to be incredibly cheering, where the children gathered noisily around the table full of cakes and drink while the adults kept casual watch over them. Mats' sister Maja buttonholed Ezz. She favoured Erik in her colouring and had gorgeous smiling eyes. 'We'd love to see something of the island in winter. I'm sure you know lovely places to recommend.' She spoke the same perfect English as Mats.

Ezz had met Maja only occasionally when she'd been assistant manager, but now she warmed to the other woman. 'There are glorious places to visit like Fairy Glen or the Fairy Pools. The island's just one enormous scenery fest with the snowy mountaintops. If you're feeling less energetic, there are lots of nice cafés in Broadford and the capital, Portree, all sparkling with Christmas lights.'

Jonas, Maja and Mats' brother, joined them. He too was dark, a more compact man than either his brother or his dad, with a short, easy-care haircut and a face that looked ready to crease into laughter. 'I've read that there are dinosaur footprints on Skye, but have never seen them.'

'There are,' Ezz assured him. 'Though I can't explain the geological process that preserved them. They're not far from Portree. Behind the reception desk we have a box of leaflets that other visitor attractions send us. I could get you some.'

'If I know my dear sister Maja, she'd enjoy digging through the box herself.' When Jonas grinned, he looked more like Mats than she'd thought. Maybe they both got the lovely smile from Grete.

Maja looked unabashed. 'True. I'll do that. I expect you've met my husband Nils before?' She smiled as Nils arrived, with thin blond hair and an adoring expression whenever his gaze fell on his wife or children. 'He's a teacher for the younger children in Grundskolan, which is the school for six to fifteen years old.'

Then Jonas' wife Ebba drifted up, brown hair gleaming like horse chestnuts. Maja explained that they'd been questioning Ezz about what they might do on Skye, prompting Ebba to declare solemnly, 'We need to tire the children out each day, so we can have peaceful evenings.' Her English was good, but, like Josefin's, more accented than that of Mats and his siblings.

As Ezz chatted, she saw Josefin appear and pause to speak to one of the children – Ezz thought it was Walter – who was eating shortbread as if frightened it would be snatched away. She waited to catch Josefin's eye and exchange smiles, but Josefin seemed to avoid her gaze. Ezz wondered whether she'd warm up if she realised that Mats had dropped her in the disaster zone with Valentina and that sat between them like a giant, immovable boulder.

Then she realised Mats was watching her from across the room. She turned hot – nothing to do with the warm gingerbread Gwen had just passed round, but because of the unguarded desire in his eyes. Their night together rushed back at her in a wave of blood-boiling lust.

Of course, *then* Josefin chose to look up and catch the exchange. She looked away, her expression shuttered.

On Monday, Ezz was in her office when Gwen brought in a young woman with a ponytail and rainbow-framed glasses. 'This is my sister's granddaughter Caitriona, who's starting today. She has her ID for your records.'

Ezz smiled at Caitriona, who was a similar height to Gwen, slighter, but with a similar can-do air. 'Welcome to the team. It's only nine days until Christmas Day. You're prepared to work where requested throughout Christmas, are you? Mr and Mrs Larsson and their family don't require twenty-four-hour-a-day hotel service, but as well as providing occasional meals, there will be constant clearing of the kitchen, making cakes, snacks and sandwiches to stock the fridge, cleaning as required, and frequent shopping.'

Caitriona nodded enthusiastically, her ponytail dancing. 'Aye, my great aunt explained. I don't mind working through Christmas and Hogmanay. It's to help me pay my way next term at uni. I'd love work during the Easter and summer holidays too, if it comes up. I'm at Abertay in Dundee, and I get casual work there but I've my studying to do.'

Ezz understood that though the Scottish enjoyed the unparalleled luxury of free university tuition, living costs had still to be found. 'Then let's get you on the seasonal workers list,' she suggested, waving Caitriona to a chair. 'I'm not sure about Easter yet, but we'll certainly need help in summer.'

Not long after the formalities had been completed and Caitriona had departed in Gwen's wake to be introduced to Grete and Erik and then shown the kitchen, Astrid,

Alvin and what looked like all the Larsson children but baby Ronja burst through the white door and tumbled across reception and into Ezz's office.

'This is our Ezzie,' Astrid said possessively, as if Ezz hadn't been present at *fika* yesterday. Probably the children had all been so excited to see each other that another adult more or less hadn't been noted.

Pleased by the 'our', Ezzie smiled round at the children, who bobbed before her desk in a sea of mini humanity. 'Hello again, everyone. Should I start by seeing if I can remember all your names?' As they all nodded expectantly, she began with the tallest. 'You're Emil, the eldest? And this is your brother, Filip.'

Filip, as dark as his father Jonas, nodded. 'I'm eight and Emil's ten.'

Ezz worked her way through the others. Liam was three like Alvin, and Walter was seven, a bit older than Astrid. 'And we've got a baby,' Walter said, dismissing his little sister Ronja. 'But can you take us to see the ponies? Mormor says there are two new ones.'

'He means Haggis and Scotch,' Astrid said, showing off that she was in the know. 'And he calls Farmor "Mormor" because she's his mother's mother.'

'Thanks for the reminder.' But Ezz assumed an expression of regret, as if there had been any realistic chance of her taking off with almost every child in the place without arrangement. 'I'm afraid I have to stay here to work. Maybe Josefin will take you?'

Astrid gave an elaborate shrug, small pink palms upturned. 'Josefin's gone home. Farfar's driving her to the airport.'

Shocked, Ezz stared. 'I thought she was spending Christmas with you all.' Then, remembering Josefin's unsmiling countenance yesterday, she wondered whether she'd received bad news.

The white door opened again, then Mats strode over the lobby to gaze at the children severely, while they all grinned cheerfully back. 'You're not supposed to bother Ezz.' Then with a smile, he supplied her with details that Astrid had omitted. 'Josefin's son's travelling home to Sweden for Christmas after a bust-up with his partner, so she's gone to share the festivities with him. We have plenty of adults around to look after kids after all. Dad drove her to Inverness early this morning. I expect he'll be back soon.'

Ezz was surprised and a touch hurt that Josefin hadn't so much as texted a goodbye. Though Ezzie felt for her if she had a crush on Mats, Josefin had lived with his family for some time without him showing interest, so it seemed hard if Ezz had copped the blame. Evidently, Josefin and Valentina could form a club called 'Ezzie's on my shitlist'.

Mats broke into her dismal thoughts. 'Children, I'm going to take the feed down to the ponies, so let's check it's OK with your parents for you guys to come.'

'Yeah!' Five of the children spun around and raced for the white door.

But Astrid lingered, her blue eyes on Ezz. 'Will you come too?'

'Unfortunately,' Ezz began, ready to reiterate her need to work.

'Do come,' Mats butted in. 'It's a nice day. We'd love your company, wouldn't we, Astrid?'

'Yes!' Astrid performed a pirouette, as if that underlined how much.

Glancing out of her window at the high blue winter

sky, Ezz was tempted to join in the stroll across the park, feeling sorely in need of daylight. She'd count it as an early lunch hour. And, she realised, being wanted was balm on a heart bruised by Valentina so pointedly rejecting her. What Mats had done was tactless but inadvertent. Valentina backing out of their Christmas plans had seemed uncharacteristically calculated to hurt. Ezz couldn't remember another occasion when Valentina had been vindictive. 'OK, thanks.'

It was twenty minutes before Mats and the children bundled back into reception in outdoor clothes. Ezz had changed into boots and needed only to grab her coat and scarf.

Outside, Alvin paused at the top of the stairs and squinted at the innocently blue sky, demanding suspiciously, 'Will it rain stones again?' Evidently, Ezz's presence had reminded him of the hailstones on the beach.

She laughed, putting out a steadying hand in case he showed signs of toppling from the top step. 'Not today. But snow's forecast again soon.'

Mats must have been out earlier as the garden cart waited at the foot of the steps, laden with a bale of hay and a bucket of feed. He popped the two smallest children, Alvin and Liam, into the cart too. 'Hold tight.' He pushed the cart, keeping an eye on his human cargo, and gave the kids a beginner's guide to pony care, probably the result of Sheena's coaching. 'The hay's called forage and I'm to break it into piles, at least one more than there are animals, so they won't fight. Same with piles of bucket feed. If snow does come, I need to at least double the forage because they won't have grass. I'm to check their water twice a day in case it freezes, and I mustn't groom the animals because they need their winter coats thick and oily.'

Paying scant heed, the children on foot paired up, Emil jogging along with his brother Filip and Astrid and Walter galloping like horses. The headland dropped away, revealing boats on the Sound of Sleat, the water glittering in the sharp winter light. 'Boats, boats,' Alvin shouted, waving as if the people on board two fishing vessels might see him and wave back. Little Liam, beside him in the cart, did the same. Ezz wasn't sure if he spoke English as much as the others as she hadn't heard him say much of anything. He seemed content just to gambol along with his brother and cousins.

It was a beautiful walk down the drive and over the bridge and then the grass to the paddock. Mats said, 'I rode as a child, but Maja was best. Jonas and I liked ice hockey in winter or brännboll in summer. That's a bit like rounders.'

She liked hearing about his youth. 'Were you fast? You look like a runner.'

The look he sent her made her think he appreciated her noticing. 'Yes, I played left wing in ice hockey. Anyone playing for the offence has to be quick.'

Rather than list her own childhood pursuits, Ezz said, 'I was surprised to hear that Josefin's gone.'

'It was a bit sudden.' He shrugged. 'But I can understand her getting homesick for Sweden once she knew her son would be there.'

Walter galloped back to them, Astrid panting beside him as if galloping was a bit much but she wanted to keep up with her cousin. 'Is Haggis the biggest pony? Or Scotch?'

Ezz couldn't really tell, so she hazarded, 'Mary might be bigger than either if she didn't sag in the middle.'

Astrid giggled.

'Filip, Emil, slow down, please,' Mats called to the two

eldest boys forging ahead. 'Don't frighten the animals.' Mary and Clive, as was their custom, hung over the gate to watch them arrive. Or, more likely, watch the arrival of a cartful of food.

Mats' attention was on the safety of the children. 'Please stay outside the gate while I put out the hay and the buckets. You could easily get knocked over by a pony eager for lunch. You four older children can sit on the gate, and Alvin and Liam stand up in the cart, so you can all see.'

The children arranged themselves exactly as asked except Walter. It took Ezz all her time to dissuade him from jumping down and following Mats around the field. 'Don't you ever sit still?' she asked, holding on to the back of his coat.

He gave it some thought before answering with a solemn, 'No.'

Emil grinned at Ezz. He was as dark as his parents Jonas and Ebba. 'His dad, Uncle Nils, says Walter has no fear. He dislocated his shoulder trying to fly downstairs, and he broke his ankle when he jumped into the paddling pool from a tree.'

'I think your Uncle Nils is right,' she commented, wondering how the quiet, serious Nils had ended up with such a madcap son.

Once the animals had their heads down eating, Mats told the children they could come in, but not run around or get near any hind legs. 'Particularly Clive Donkey, because he has his ears back, which is threatening.' That was the signal for Walter to run directly at Clive, but Mats was ready for him and swooped him up and posted him back over the gate. 'Stay there until you calm down,' he said easily.

271

Walter gazed angelically up at him. 'I'm calm now.' Ezz had to smother a snort of laughter. Walter was obviously an imp, but so funny and loveable. She caught herself wondering whether Thea's baby would be a boy or a girl, but then it felt like a jinx, so she just wished for it to be healthy.

After a few minutes she checked her watch. Mats was holding Alvin and Liam a cautious distance from Scotch, who was waffling his nose in their direction as if wondering if they had more food. She called to him, 'I need to get back now.'

He looked disappointed, but she just called her goodbyes, remembering all the children's names. Walter shouted after her, 'You could ride one of these horses home.'

'Maybe another time.' As if she'd mess up her suit and overcoat on the back of a disreputably shaggy pony.

She hurried back to the hall with the wind trying to unwind her scarf and steal it. When she gained the calm of the reception area, she found a pile of envelopes and a small parcel on the desk. The post van must have visited while she was out. Carrying the stack into her office, she hung up her coat and changed back into shoes before sorting through it. The junk mail went straight in the shredder. The small parcel proved to be a lightbulb that Gwen had ordered for the large kitchen oven. An invoice came from a company that evidently hadn't embraced the age of email, and the last was a long cream handwritten envelope addressed to Ms Esmerelda Wynter c/o Rothach Hall, Rothach, Isle of Skye – private and personal.

Frowning, she opened the envelope and smoothed the two sheets of writing paper inside.

Dear Esmerelda,

Mum and Dad say you're known as Ezz or Ezzie. We don't feel we can use your short names when we don't know you but we're your birth sisters and we want to say hello. We don't have your email and didn't want to use the contact form on the website of Rothach Hall, hence this letter.

The bones seemed to vanish from Ezz's legs and she sank into her seat.

We are Julia Colville and Iona Berio née Colville. Our parents have very recently told us about the baby they made before we were born.

So, they really hadn't known till now!

It's so odd to think of them having a teenaged pregnancy (but not so odd hearing that Nan was NOT sympathetic) and we all cried when they told us. We would say 'even Dad', but actually Dad cries at anything. He wells up at people winning races or dogs needing forever homes. You might expect Mum to be the soft one, as she's so small and quiet, but she's also a coper.

We don't know what to think about having a new sister. What do you think about having two?? We understand that it didn't go well when you met Mum and Dad – or met Mum again, and Dad for the first time. That's a shame because they're lovely people, and obviously, there's stuff you don't know.

Ezz wondered what that 'stuff' might be, and glanced at the back of the letter as if someone might have written a clue there, before reading on.

It's understandable that you were upset but we don't want you to think that no one wants to hear from you, because that's not true. Regardless of what happens with Mum and Dad, we – Julia and Iona – would like to get to know you in some way, so we can decide whether we like each other based on reality rather than on assumptions.

Ezz paused to read this twice, realising it was a conclusion she might have reached herself . . . if she hadn't gone off like an emotional firecracker.

So, I'm Julia. I'm 39. I'm a therapist, but the kind who gives facials rather than the kind that counsels people who need help. I'm not tall and willowy, as Mum and Dad say you are. My doctor told me snarkily that I'm 'below average height but above average weight', but my partner, Hamal, says I'm curvy, which is a nicer way of putting it. My daughter Edina is four, and we're looking at schools for September. Do you have children? Mum and Dad said they didn't think so, but they don't think they actually asked. They were pretty scared when they met you.

Ezz stopped again. She hadn't thought of Kay and Rick being scared. They'd just seemed tense.

The handwriting changed, becoming less loopy but more sprawling.

Hi, this is Iona here. I'm 37 and I teach art at a senior school. Everyone says I'm like Julia to look at, so I won't repeat her description, but they also say I'm different in temperament. I don't know about that. We

274

like a lot of the same things, like art shows, Green Day and chocolate, but I suppose she's quieter. Honestly, if you want to get anywhere with a class of thirty fifteen-year-olds, being quiet's not really the way. I'm married to Vido. His grandparents were Italian, which is how he got the cool name.

We'll put our contact details at the end. We don't want to pressure you into doing anything you don't want to, but it would be great to be in contact. Great for us, anyway – we're not trying to make up your mind. It just seems wrong not to know you at all. If you feel like sending a message or a letter or anything, please, please do.

Warmest wishes,
Julia
Iona

Email addresses, street addresses and phone numbers followed each of the names.

Ezz read the letter again. And then again, trying to make it feel real.

Her birth sisters had written to her.

They wanted her to reply.

With no idea for how long she sat staring at the cream paper and blue ink, she jumped when the front door clunked open, and Walter pelted into reception. '*Hallå*,' he called breathlessly to Ezz, then seized the knob of the white door in both hands and twisted it open, vanishing inside. Filip, Emil and Astrid followed hard on his heels. After a few seconds, Mats appeared with Alvin and Liam. Mats glanced into her office, and when he saw her, he frowned. He vanished through the door, and she heard him calling to someone. In less than half a minute he was back in her office, minus coat and hat.

'What's up?' he murmured, rounding the desk. 'You look as if you've seen a ghost.'

Wordlessly, she showed him the letter that trembled in her hand.

He scanned it quickly, crouching beside her chair. 'Wow.' He looked at her. 'Another surprise. How do you feel?'

Before Ezz could attempt to describe the tangle of wonder, astonishment, fear and trepidation inside her, the white door opened and Erik's voice boomed, 'Mats?' and then something in Swedish.

Flustered, Ezz scooted her chair away from Mats.

Mats accepted the rejection, though his muttered, 'We've done nothing to be ashamed of,' was sharp. Then he raised his voice. '*Ja*, Pappa.' And he gave the letter back to her and strolled out of her office, then back into the family area, contriving to carry Erik along with him as they chatted in Swedish.

Ezz was grateful to be left alone and not obliged to explain her state of shock to big, buff Erik. For the remainder of the afternoon, her mind returned not just to the letter from Julia and Iona, but to Mats' comment that they'd done nothing to be ashamed of.

Did that mean he wouldn't have *minded* his dad discovering him so close to Ezz? Her mind buzzed as she tried to get to grips with professional boundaries versus personal, but all she concluded was that everything in her life was changing and nothing was certain.

That evening, Mats turned up at Ezz's cottage in Chapel Road, allowing her no opportunity to tell him not to come by messaging or phoning first. When she opened the door and saw him, shoulders hunched against the near-arctic wind searing off the sea, her expression lightened, but she hesitated. He jigged on the spot. 'It's cold,' he pointed out politely.

A smile ghosted across her fine lips. 'Then you'd better come inside.'

He was happy to be shown into her small lounge, where the woodstove roared, orange flames licking at the glass door. Somehow it seemed a good omen when he noticed that the stove was a Swedish make. Less so when he noticed her Christmas lights were unlit. He discarded his coat and, after waiting for her to choose her sofa to sit on, he joined her on it.

'How are you?' He angled himself towards her. She was dressed in plum-coloured cord leggings and a thick, cream, oversized sweater. He thought he liked her better in the soft lounge wear than even in her sexy black work suits.

'Fine.' Her smile was perfunctory.

But he hadn't come out into the cold to be fobbed off like an acquaintance, when nine nights ago she'd shared her body with him in one of the rooms above their heads. 'Are you still angry with me?'

She touched her temple, as if it ached, and closed her eyes. 'Don't start apologising again.' It wasn't forgiveness, but it felt like a step in that direction.

He softened his voice. 'Not if you don't want me to. But is Valentina still angry?'

Her eyes remained closed, allowing him to admire the smoothness of her pale skin, and the twin fans of eyelashes resting on her satin cheeks. Her bottom lip quivered. 'She's not coming for Christmas. She says it's because Thea needs a quiet time and because Barnaby has a hectic social calendar, and that she's not punishing me. But . . .' She lifted her palm in a plain gesture of disbelief.

Morosely, he said, 'I'm a moron not to have even allowed for the possibility that she didn't know.'

'Yeah,' she agreed, but without heat.

Slowly, giving her ample time to fend him off, he slid along the cushions until he could slip an arm around her. For a moment she stiffened . . . then she relaxed against him. 'I'm not going to answer the letter I showed you right away. It makes sense to me to let it settle for a day or two, but I think I will write back.'

This small confidence sent a flush of pleasure through him. Valentina and Thea were her usual confidantes, and though he knew that one was royally pissed off with her and the other absorbed in protecting the nascent life she carried, he still felt privileged that she'd volunteer something so meaningful, so delicately personal. Feeling his way, he said, 'I thought the letter heart-warming. A straightforward reaching out.'

She looked at him from the corner of her eye. 'It was,' she agreed. 'But I still feel all at sea.'

He shared both parents with his siblings, but he tried to jump into her shoes and examine how he'd feel if more brothers and sisters turned up. 'Would interacting with Julia and Iona make you feel disloyal to Valentina and Thea?'

'Maybe.' Her troubled gaze settled on the woodstove, as if her future could be read in the dancing flames. 'When Thea found her birth family it was just her mother, Ynez, who has only a partner, Jean-Jacques. No siblings.' Her hand rose to her head. 'And though I told Thea I wouldn't mind if she had half-brothers or sisters, actually I was glad that Ynez hadn't had more children, as if Thea wouldn't have enough love for me if she had siblings who shared her blood.'

He frowned as he mulled this over. 'But Thea has Ynez, and her partner Dev, and now she's having a baby. Does any of that mean she won't have enough love for you?'

Her shoulders relaxed a shade, and she managed a faint smile. 'No,' she admitted. And then, as if to turn the tables by bringing up something equally personal about him, she asked, 'This might seem an odd time to raise this, but I'm bothered about Josefin. Do you realise she has a crush on you?'

It was an unpleasant jolt. 'Not a crush,' he objected immediately, reviewing Josefin through this new prism and not liking the picture. Then he remembered the day at the Nature Garden Café and honesty made him add, 'Once or twice, outsiders have taken us as a couple because we were with the children and I did think she liked that. But the liking was all on her side.'

'That must make her sad.' She settled herself more comfortably against him. 'She talked about you *a lot* when she was out with me. And recently, I felt . . .' She dipped her head and fiddled with the hem of her top. 'I'm pretty sure she detected something between us and was sulking. Then she went home without even saying bye to me.'

'Oh.' He was dismayed. 'She could feel that way, I suppose, and I only have her word for it that she wanted to leave because her son was unexpectedly in Sweden. When she asked if she could take some of her leave, I said of course. All my family had arrived, and it was natural that she'd want to be with her son.' Then, spotting an opportunity, he mused, 'Of course, Josefin's employed by *me*, not my parents. Whereas you are employed by *my parents* and not me, so there was no need for you to shove me away like a muddy dog when Dad came looking for me today.'

A pink blush crept up her cheeks. 'I didn't shove you, I just moved. I was at work. It would have been the same with any man.'

He shrugged, as if unconvinced. 'OK. I won't take it personally. And my parents, my brother and my sister have all asked me whether we're seeing each other, and I sort of said yes, hoping that we were. Word's obviously been getting around. They all wanted to talk to you when you came for *fika*.'

She rose vertically and landed facing him, her face a mask of horrified astonishment. 'You "sort of said yes"? Is this your impetuosity again? I *work* for your parents, Mats. That's . . . that's . . .'

'Honest?' he supplied helpfully.

'Outrageous,' she corrected him. But then, as if unable to resist: 'How did everyone react?'

He grinned. 'Just, "Oh, OK." And, "Seems nice". Dad said, "She is very pretty", in an "I'm not surprised" kind of voice.' He sobered, running his fingertips over her cheek. 'Mum pointed out that we live in different countries, but she was reminding me, rather than being against you.'

Slowly, she subsided, taking up her place within the circle of his arm again. 'She's right.'

'Yeah.' He sighed.

After a moment, she asked, 'Was that why you said we shouldn't be ashamed? That there's something between us and it's OK that we spent the night together?'

'Exactly.' He felt a lift in his sensitive areas at this

reference to the most amazing lovemaking of his life. 'And . . .' He paused, not sure whether to voice his thoughts.

'And . . . ?' she prompted, treating him to her blue-eyed stare.

He decided to go for it. 'And you shouldn't feel new shame about the accident because of Valentina's reaction, Ezz. What you did was against the law, but you acted in the heat of the moment. Did you ask Thea to stand in for you?' He was stroking her hair rhythmically now, enjoying the silk beneath his fingers.

'No,' she admitted. 'But I shouldn't have let her.'

'No,' he conceded, though the potential for this beautiful, vibrant woman to be locked in a cell made him queasy. 'But no one has ever laid blame on the car driver, and there's no proof that you had too much alcohol in your blood from the night before.' He transferred the attention of his stroking hand to her collarbone. He could just extend his caress far enough to touch the skin of her neck. 'Is Valentina always so judgy? You and Thea are so warm and friendly.'

'No, not normally,' She sighed. 'I'm shocked at how hard and horrible she's being. She must be really hurt.'

Haunted by the grief in her voice, he snuggled her closer.

Though he stayed till well past midnight, they didn't make love, but cuddled on her squashy sofa watching a movie and drinking coffee. Mats loved it. Just holding her, warm and soft, was a delight. It felt as if he'd been forgiven, and he thought perhaps she found some peace in his arms.

Later, when he was preparing to leave, he said, 'Will you come with us to Portree again tomorrow? Astrid wants to show everyone the Christmas lights, eat millionaire shortbread and drink hot chocolate.'

'I don't know—' she started.

He kissed the tip of her nose. 'Everyone's hoping you will, and nobody will think you should be at your desk. Consider yourself our local guide.'

A smile grew in her eyes. 'Then, yes. Thank you.'

He drove home feeling as if he'd just won a particularly finely balanced lottery.

Chapter Nineteen

The promised snow arrived on Tuesday and Ezz woke to a view of the peaks on the mainland completely white as if sculpted from icing, beyond the grey, fidgety sea. Across the road, the Jolly Abbot looked as if someone had dressed it in a white beret and the lights of the Christmas tree outside gleamed through a gorgeous snow jacket.

She dressed in leggings under green and purple hiking trousers, snow boots and ski jacket, with a pearly grey knitted hat.

Before she left for Rothach Hall, she called Thea. 'We've got a couple of inches of snow in Skye. Are you still driving up here? I'd love to see you home, but not if it means taking risks.'

'Already in the car,' Thea reported cheerfully. 'Dev's driving. We have a dusting but we're on the motorway and hope to at least get past Glasgow. Once we're on smaller roads, if the snow's a problem we might stop over.'

Ezz felt relieved. 'Good plan. How are you?'

Thea sounded happy. 'Currently no further cause for concern, so we have our fingers crossed. See you soon.'

Reassured, Ezz went out to clear her car, enjoying the rasp of the scraper and the creak of snow beneath her boots, even the chill air biting her cheeks. The sky was grey in the early light, pearly and luminescent. Breaking her usual habit, she approached Rothach Hall via the front drive and over the stone bridge to drink in the best view of the gorgeous grounds in a blanket of gleaming, twinkling white, where every tree and bush had been kissed all over by snowflakes. The hall wore snow on its sills, like ermine trim on its usual grey-stone robe, and the turret's roof looked like an incongruous white beanie hat. Was Mats in his room in the turret now? Or in the shower? It was an interesting thought.

She changed gear for the slope up to the hall. Rothach Hall had big luxurious shower enclosures with jets that fired at you from all angles . . . A jolt to the steering wheel made her realise that her car had popped a wheel off the drive and into a flowerbed. Oops. Hurriedly, she straightened up. Good job Thea wasn't in the car. Removing her mind from showers with Mats, Ezz drove more carefully up the carpet of snow and around the back of the house.

She did turn her computer on that morning but had barely worked through her email when Mats popped his head in the door with a grin and a bright, 'Ten minutes, OK?' before vanishing again.

The Scandinavians made light work of even Skye's narrow roads in the snow. Mats drove the Volvo with Ezz, Astrid, Alvin, Erik and Grete on board, and his siblings piled their families into their respective hire cars. It took longer than usual to reach Portree in that weather, but they had to pause to drink in views of the mountains, white but for pale blue shadows on their shady sides. Once they'd crossed the moor to Broadford, pausing to take selfies with a dazzling white Beinn na Caillich rearing up behind them, they drove the winding, undulating coastal road. The pewter-grey sea scurried beside them, hustling around Scalpay and the Isle of Raasay, sending a fishing boat pitching and rolling on its journey.

Portree looked like something from the front of a chocolate box in its mantle of snow. The buildings rose like cakes on tiered stands. With snowy roofs, as well, those with white walls truly looked made of icing. The coloured buildings of the harbour were Christmas-card pretty, and the church they passed wore snow on one side of its bell tower, and even on the bell, like a white balaclava. Across the water, the Isle of Raasay glinted like a giant iceberg.

In the town, the tall Christmas tree twinkled with fairy lights and snow glittered along its boughs. Groups of people, presumably fellow tourists, queued to take photos with it. Ezz soon discovered that the greater the number of fairy lights festooning a shop or café, the more the children clamoured to visit it. Mats told Emil and Filip, 'I'm going to buy you kilts for Christmas, so you'd better choose your tartan.' They were shocked into silence, eyes enormous.

Finally, Emil protested, 'It'd be like wearing shorts in winter – freezing.'

A smiling shop assistant with 'Fiona' on her name badge exhibited the sporrans and knee socks that traditionally went with kilts, but Emil looked unconvinced by Scottish traditional dress. Even livewire-Walter uttered a polite, but firm, 'No, thank *you*.'

As they meandered from shop to shop, the pavements fast turned to slush with the passage of many feet, even in the freezing air rising from the harbour. Ezz gradually realised she was being treated as if she were 'with' Mats, his family leaving her a place beside him when they stopped at a cute café for hot drinks and scones. Even Grete and Erik left an Ezz-sized space beside Mats to walk with him when they left the café again.

Just after two o'clock, she received a text from Thea. *We've stopped overnight at Loch Lomond. It's a more expensive hotel than we usually manage, but Dev thinks the baby needs the luxury! X*

Ezz returned, *I agree. X* She put away her phone, happy that baby jokes indicated optimism from Thea.

They left just as Skye's early sunset was casting a rosy tint over the snow and bouncing blindingly from the sea. Ezz and Mats were the only ones in the Volvo to stay awake. The pink-cheeked children flaked out in their car seats, and Grete and Erik sagged gently towards each other in the back row as they dozed. Ezz began to glance through her email on her phone while Mats drove but he rested one hand on her thigh. 'Enjoy the last of the day,' he suggested, indicating the lavender dusk creeping over the island and the headlights illuminating the glistening snow beside the road.

She thought of invoices, orders, voicemails, staff records, the year-end and the thousand other things that presently came under her remit without an assistant or a receptionist, and grimaced. But she knew that she'd be able to lengthen her hours when the Larssons had gone. Then she'd only have work to worry about . . .

apart from her birth family, her new niece or nephew, hopefully, and her row with Valentina. She put away her phone and enjoyed watching the sun set above the snow.

On Wednesday, Thea and Dev stayed put in their cosy Loch Lomond hotel to let the snow pass, then on Thursday, rain poured in from the west, swamping the Outer Hebrides before moving on to deluge Skye from angry purple clouds. When Mats appeared through the white door, Ezz held on to her desk as if he might try to detach her bodily from it. 'You Scandinavians might consider it just the weather for another sightseeing trip, but I'm staying in my nice warm office.'

Mats gazed mournfully at the rain sluicing over her windowpanes. 'I have to go and feed the ponies alone?'

'Yep.' She grinned. 'And keep the cart on the drive as far as possible because the ground's going to be icy mush with thawed snow and now this torrent.'

'Thanks for the tip,' he said drily. 'If I don't get washed away, I'll carry on with the spreadsheets later if the kids are occupied with their cousins and other adults will keep an eye on them.'

'That would be great.' She blew him a kiss and he trudged off to get his rain gear.

After working steadily all morning, undisturbed by the landline, stray Larsson children or even Mats, she was thrilled to receive a call from Thea, upbeat and bouncy. 'Hi. We're finally home. We stopped at the supermarket in Broadford and got drenched with freezing Skye rain, and now I'm going to nap.'

Ezz's heart melted with relief. 'You're OK? Baby behaving?'

Thea heaved a sigh. 'Seems to be. We've got everything

287

crossed that we've survived a nasty scare. I'm to see my midwife on Friday, when I'll be fifteen weeks.'

Ezz opted for cautious optimism. 'Aw, Thea. I'm so thrilled for you. Would you and Dev like to come to dinner this evening at mine? Save you cooking?' She decided to invite Mats too, but, in a spirit of mischief, thought she'd keep that as a surprise.

'That would be great.' Thea yawned noisily. 'I'll probably have had two more naps by then. I'd never realised that pregnancy was so tiring.'

Settling down to work after texting Mats about dinner, Ezz made steady inroads into negotiating with a printing company for next year's pamphlets designed to attract visitors to enjoy Rothach Hall and its grounds and then paid invoices from the tree surgeon and the company that supplied cleaning materials.

Immediately after Ezz had eaten a sandwich at her desk, Gwen arrived, her long raincoat open over her striped housekeeper's uniform. 'The wee 'uns can eat more than a plague of locusts,' she announced with a broad smile. 'Caitriona and I are going shopping. Young Walter consumes so much Irn-Bru and shortbread, I think he must be trying to turn Scottish. Is there anything you'll be needing?'

'Fresh basil, if they have some please,' Ezz answered, thinking about this evening's dinner, and passed over the money.

Mats arrived about three, wandered into her office, kissed her just below her ear and said, 'Spreadsheet time. Yes, please, to dinner. Mum says to remind you about *fika* on Sunday, the last advent before Christmas.' Then he strolled out again in the direction of the assistant manager's cubicle, leaving her smiling.

For the rest of the afternoon, she was aware of the tapping of his keyboard reaching her faintly whenever hers was quiet. At five-thirty, she shut down her machine. She had a meal to prepare, and her routine had been disrupted so much lately that she was behind with laundry and other household chores.

Rain was still lashing the window when Ezz heard the opening of the hall's front door and it closing with a bang.

Then Mats' voice exclaimed, 'What the hell are you doing here?'

Ezz paused, frowning. Who? And why did Mats sound so curt?

A calm female voice answered. 'I've come to see my children.'

A horrible sensation seized Ezz's chest, as if her heart had turned to rock and was rolling slowly towards her toes. The voice was familiar and Ezz had a nasty feeling that it was Inger, Mats' ex, Astrid and Alvin's mother.

'How did you get here?' Mats sounded bewildered.

The female voice neared Ezz's office door. 'We sailed to Monte Carlo after Corsica, as planned, but Andreas and I had a major disagreement.'

Shit. It *was* Inger. Ezz froze at her desk, thoughts flying.

Inger continued impatiently. 'His friends kindly lent me a car and I drove up through France, stopping overnight in Calais. Then I got the ferry across the Channel, drove through England, encountered snow in Scotland, so stopped again. Today I drove to Mallaig and took the car-ferry to Armadale. And here I am. Where are Astrid and Alvin?'

'In the apartment,' Mats began. 'But—'

Then suddenly, Inger was standing in the door to Ezz's office in a white overcoat with its hood thrown back, dark hair and full-face make-up immaculate. She didn't smile. 'My luggage is in the boot. When you've seen it's brought in, perhaps you could park my car around the back for me. Thanks.' And she tossed over a set of keys.

Ezz had to catch them or let them hit her in the face. Stupefied, she watched Inger turn, stalk across the lobby and open the white door. Apparently, if she'd changed in the year and a half since Ezz had last met her, it was only to become yet more entitled.

'Inger!' Mats barked. 'Just hold on.' He appeared in Ezzie's line of sight, casting her a quick, grim: 'I'll be back in a minute,' then chased Inger through the door and out of sight.

Ezzie gazed at the door that snapped shut behind him. Her fingers still stung from fielding the rudely thrown car keys. Inger was here. If she'd spent her long journey planning how to remind Ezz that she was an employee, she couldn't have done a better job.

When Mats didn't reappear, she rose and slipped into her outdoor things. She strode from her office, across reception and through the front door, flinching as the rain flew into her face. At the foot of the steps stood a small but sporty white car – an Alpine, its badge said, a brand she'd never heard of, but it looked expensive. Five suitcases were jammed into the boot and on the seats. Five! One by one, rain seeping coldly down her neck, she hauled them up the steps and left them in a neat row outside the white door, remembering that she'd performed exactly the same task when Mats, Grete, Astrid and Alvin had first arrived.

Back at the car, with measured movements, she climbed into the driver's seat – which was on the left – and drove around the building and parked. Then she took the back way into the hall and positioned the car keys neatly atop the largest case. Numbly, she retrieved her bag from her desk, and left for the evening.

Driving home along Manor Road, which had become single-track by virtue of the huge puddles at its edges, she supposed drearily that there would only be three for dinner. Mats would be busy.

Chapter Twenty

By the time Mats had yanked open the door, Inger was striding along the downstairs hall calling loudly, 'Astrid? Alvin? Mamma's here. Isn't this a lovely surprise? I've driven for *three days*, just to see you.'

There was the barest moment's silence before two small bodies shot into the hall from the kitchen, squealing, 'Mamma!'

Mats halted, watching Astrid fly up the hall, her eyes full of love and joy. Alvin was only a second behind, expression urgent as he raced towards Inger, who dropped to her knees to receive her babies. Two pairs of arms curled fiercely around her neck while their high-pitched voices filled the air, with happy Swedish.

'We've got new ponies!'

'Walter and Liam, Filip and Emil are here. And Ronja.'

We're having *fika* on Sunday for advent.'

'Are you here for Christmas?'

Inger, to Mats' silent fury, answered the last question

first. 'Of course, I'm here for Christmas. Someone's bringing in my cases, then you can help me unpack.'

Astrid yelled, 'Yay!' and capered on the spot, blonde hair jiggling.

Mats would have liked to shake Inger. By promising the children her presence over the festivities, she'd left him powerless. Other members of his family began emerging from the kitchen and lounge. Grete and Erik's wide-eyed gazes darted between Mats and Inger. Jonas gaped at Mats with a distinct *What the hell?* in his eyes. Maja said, 'This is a surprise,' but without noticeable pleasure. Nils, Maja's quiet husband, stared at Inger with raised eyebrows. Ebba, Jonas's pretty wife, gazed at Inger unsmilingly.

Walter stuck his head into the hall, called back to whoever remained in the kitchen, 'It's only Auntie Inger,' and vanished again.

Inger rose and stared around defiantly, apparently not deeming it necessary to offer, *Sorry to drop myself on you,* or *I hope this is OK,* despite her clear lack of welcome from anyone but her children. Astrid began to look worried at the silence, and Alvin bewildered.

Gathering his wits, Mats said calmly, 'Well, at least Mamma can have dinner with us before she and I have a talk. Why don't you take her to set another place at the table, Astrid?'

Inger didn't endear herself when, though she let Astrid tug her along, as she reached the doorway she exclaimed, 'Ugh. Are we eating in the *kitchen*?'

Mats had to lean against the wall while his blood stopped roaring in his ears. He didn't think he'd ever been so furious, not even when Inger had first told him that she was having an affair with Andreas and wanted out of their marriage.

'This is a shock,' said Grete grimly.

Erik's opinion was blunter. 'It's bullshit.' He jutted his jaw.

Maja took Mats' hand. 'You look winded. She's just turned up without warning?'

Mats swallowed, nodding. 'She borrowed a car and drove all the way from Monte Carlo.' Even to his own ears his voice sounded shaky, as if he'd just been given terrible news. Well, yes. Inger being here was definitely not good news for him.

Jonas muttered, 'Bitch.'

Although Mats knew he should follow Inger to witness what else she might be telling the children, he was desperate to find Ezz. Her shock and resentment at Inger speaking to her like a dogsbody hung before his eyes. He hoped she didn't think he'd known that Inger was about to descend on them.

'I need a minute.' He turned on his heel and hurried to the door to the lobby. When he yanked it open, however, he was confronted by Inger's car keys along with her suitcases, and saw the light was out in Ezz's office. Might he catch her in the car park? He debated, but then realised it was unlikely. As a stopgap measure, he texted her. *I had no idea Inger was on her way. Apologies for her appalling behaviour.* He didn't say 'for treating you like staff' as that would only resurrect the discussion about Ezz being staff and him being family. 'Us and them' discussions rarely resulted in a smoothing of tensions.

He snapped the door shut on the suitcases and strode to the kitchen, where his family was congregating for an early dinner. His adrenaline level was so high that he had to jam his hands into his pockets to hide their shaking. He found Grete and Erik carrying dishes to the table. Gwen and Caitriona had vanished, so presumably his parents had requested privacy. Baby Ronja banged her spoon on her highchair and Maja spoke to her softly while Nils settled Liam, while calling, 'Don't stand on your chair, please, Walter.'

The only adult smiling was Inger, stroking first Astrid's head and then Alvin's while she chatted gaily with Emil and Filip about what they'd done for Lucia Day at school last Friday, pausing to listen as Astrid chimed in. 'We didn't have Lucia this year, because they don't have it in Scotland.' If there was an Oscar for playing the doting mother, Inger would be presented with the golden statuette without delay.

As the showdown Mats planned would have to wait, he sat at the table. He took little food, as unless Gwen had a crystal ball, she wouldn't have catered for him or Inger. The roast chicken and potatoes tasted like ashes in his mouth anyway. He'd meant to eat with Ezz, Thea and Dev this evening. Ezz hadn't replied to his message. He wasn't surprised.

Dinner seemed endless. Afterwards, Inger promised Alvin and Astrid, 'You can stay up tonight, as we haven't seen each other for so long.' The children didn't even look at Mats for agreement but towed their mother upstairs to see their room and the playroom, with Filip, Emil, Walter and Liam pouring after them while baby Ronja crawled after a brightly coloured ball on the floor at Nils' feet.

The kitchen rang with silence until Erik rumbled, 'This is difficult.'

Mats was still too angry to speak calmly. 'She's cornered me! How can I tell the kids that she can't stay for Christmas, now?'

'You can't.' Grete shook her head, while Maja, Nils, Jonas and Ebba murmured in agreement.

Jonas frowned anxiously. 'Mats, what about Ezz?'

His gut felt as if someone was tightening his belt. 'That's difficult too. Inger ordered her around like a lackey.'

The silence grew. Finally, Grete changed seats, so she was sitting beside him, sliding an arm around his shoulders. 'It was going to finish sooner or later,' she said kindly. 'Because Ezz lives here. You have Swedish children with a Swedish mother. You love your children too much to relocate to a Scottish island that takes so long to reach from Sweden.'

'I know.' But his throat was tight with something that felt like despair.

'What a bitch Inger is,' Maja said sadly. Nobody disagreed, not even Nils, who could usually find something nice to say about anyone.

It was after nine when Astrid and Alvin were finally in bed and Mats could usher Inger from their room and into the corridor. Pulling away, she danced along to the turret room, took two steps inside and gazed around in exaggerated dismay. 'Oh. No one's brought my cases up.' She smiled expectantly.

He ignored her little pantomime. 'What the fuck are you doing here?' he demanded in a hiss designed not to be overheard. 'What happened to your superyacht Christmas? Where's Andreas? How dare you just turn up and *tell the children that you've come for Christmas*?'

Inger lifted her chin. 'I told you. I had a major disagreement with Andreas.'

'So major that you had to leave the yacht?' He glared into her rebellious hazel eyes.

'Precisely,' she drawled, as if glad he'd finally caught on. 'So major that I gave him back his ring.' She waggled her naked finger, where once had nestled a rock of a diamond.

'Also, when I said you could have the children this year, I underestimated how much I'd miss them.' She blinked sorrowfully.

'I don't doubt your love for Astrid and Alvin,' he ground out. 'But it comes at convenient times, depending on whether they interfere with your pleasure – like when you wanted to go on a cruise.'

Tremulously, she murmured, 'That was a mistake.'

He stormed on in an angry whisper. 'Now you've argued with Andreas, you barge into Rothach as if you were still part of the family.'

Her jaw dropped. 'But . . . I'm the mother of your children. How can I not be part of the family?'

He glared into her face. 'By divorcing me.'

Her bottom lip began to tremble. 'That may have been a mistake too.'

'Balls,' he spat, and flung away from her. 'You don't want me back, and I don't want you back.'

Inger's lips rounded into an O of surprise.

He drew in a long, shaky breath. 'You'd better stay in Josefin's room. She's gone home, so it's been cleaned and made up.'

He manoeuvred around her to open the door before she could suggest that he give up the turret room, with the expensive, flamboyant fabrics and wallpaper she'd chosen.

'I know Josefin's gone home,' she said, not making the least effort to leave the room they used to share. 'She told me she was going. Just as she told me about your girlfriend.'

Fresh fury burned through him, but he managed to wipe it from his face before he turned back to her. 'Good,' he said, with false affability. 'Then there can be no misunderstanding. And as you plainly know who she is, if you talk to her again the way you talked to her tonight, I shall look for every opportunity to humiliate you in return.'

Her gaze slid away. 'I have every right to monitor women you involve my children with—'

'Bullshit,' he cut in ruthlessly. 'At least, yes, you do, but only what's reasonable. Ezz has only ever been pleasant and friendly, and given the kids attention.'

Her nostrils flared. 'Josefin made it sound as if they can't get enough of her.'

He paused, hearing a note of jealousy in Inger's voice. 'Ah. That's it. It's not me you don't want her to be fond of. It's Astrid and Alvin. Well, I can see why that made you realise that you left them for too long.' Then he bustled Inger along the corridor, before opening the door to Josefin's room. 'At this moment, I don't like you much. And I'm not pleased with Josefin either, so next time the two of you have a cosy little chat, be sure to tell her so.'

Dimly, he was aware of Inger staring at him in shocked dismay. Feeling he'd said more than enough, he muttered, 'I'll get your suitcases.'

He brought them up but left them outside her closed door. He didn't think he'd ever been so angry and disappointed in his life. It seethed inside him like black bile.

Everything Grete had said earlier about him having to part from Ezz soon had been true, but it was only now that their short time together was in danger of fizzling out that he realised how much he wished things could be different.

* * *

At dinner, Ezz was aware of Thea and Dev exchanging looks and knew herself to be abnormally subdued and abstracted. She picked at her food. Her tiny table wasn't meant for three, especially when one was Deveron's size, so she'd brought her patio set indoors and set it up in the lounge and set the fairy lights twinkling. Now she could see the sofa and kept remembering Monday evening curled up there with Mats, his body warm against hers as he stroked her hair.

When Thea dropped her cutlery and blurted, 'Ezz, is it Christmas?' it startled her from her despondency. Daisy, who'd been dozing before the fire, jumped up and glared around the room.

Ezz blinked. 'It's six more days to Christmas,' she answered uncertainly.

But Thea's brown eyes were anxious. 'I meant, are you upset because Valentina won't come for Christmas as I need a quiet time?'

Dev looked apologetic too, though he slipped an arm about Thea. 'We're sorry if it means a boring Christmas for you. We're probably being overcautious, but if Thea doesn't rest, and then something happens . . .'

Guilt flooded Ezzie, as *she* was the one who'd made Valentina change her plans and then use Thea needing rest as a convenient excuse. 'I'm not upset. I've been to the post office in Armadale to send the gifts for Valentina and family.' Not letting it show on her face how it had hurt to wrap games for Barnaby and clothes for Valentina and Gary in shiny paper, knowing she wouldn't see them opened, she patted Thea's arm, and then because Dev's hand was on Thea's shoulder, patted that too. 'The baby's much more important than Christmas. And you know I have loads to do with the Larsson family in situ.'

Thea regarded her beadily. 'So, why are you so quiet? It's as if something terrible has happened.'

A vision rose of Inger the Entitled wafting around giving Ezz orders, and she suppressed a shudder. Balling up her napkin, she let out a groan. 'Mats' ex-wife turned up today and I'm pretty sure that ends things between Mats and me. And I feel so bloody uncomfortable under her supercilious nose. I was just wondering whether to put up with her bossing me about or to have pretend-flu until she's gone.' She pictured herself taking to her bed for a couple of weeks with a stack of Christmas reads. Quite appealing, actually . . .

Thea sat up straight, eyes wide. 'There are "things" between Mats and you?' She wagged her eyebrows. '*Thing*-type things?'

Belatedly, Ezz remembered that Thea had been away. She settled her chin glumly on her fist. 'Yes, those things. A winter romance until he goes back to Sweden.'

'Ooh.' Thea contemplated her sister with twinkling eyes. 'Wow. You have been busy.' A frown replaced her smile. 'But if he's divorced, his ex-wife being around should count for nothing.'

Ezz shrugged. 'Of course he's divorced, but he'll do what's best for the children. He's made that clear. Do you remember being a small child? How would you have coped with both your parents in the same house, and a girlfriend around, too? He won't want it and neither do I.'

Seeing Thea was about to argue, she changed direction. 'Anyway, I've something more important to discuss. I didn't want to say anything till you were safely home, and I could see with my own eyes that you were OK.'

Thea's hand went to cover Dev's. 'What?' she asked apprehensively.

'It's nothing awful,' Ezz hastened to assure her, thinking that at some time Thea would have to learn that Valentina was now in possession of the truth about the accident, and was scarcely talking to Ezz. But not while Thea's pregnancy was vulnerable. Ezz didn't want Thea to get even a hint of *that* upset. 'I had a letter from my birth sisters. I thought . . . can I show it to you?'

Thea breathed, 'Oh, blimey, yes,' managing to look relieved, apprehensive and agog, all at once. 'Do they seem OK? Do they want to meet you?' Then, expectantly, 'What does Valentina think?'

Ezz hurried into the hall where she'd left her bag so Thea couldn't see her face. 'I haven't talked to Valentina. I only received it a few days ago.' She returned with the cream-coloured envelope and handed it over.

Thea took out the sheets of paper and she and Dev pored over them, their heads close together and arms touching. The written word didn't come easily to Thea, and she frowned as she read. Finally, she lifted apprehensive eyes. 'This reminds me of when I first saw a photo of Ynez. You have the evidence of your birth family right there, but it feels unreal. You know your adoptive family is your real family, but still doubts and questions float into your mind.' Thea slipped her arms around Ezz. 'It's OK to have a birth family, Ezz. I know my birth mother, Ynez, is a bit of a character, but I've enjoyed connecting with her. It's kind of poignant that Julia and Iona say your birth parents were scared. It humanises them, doesn't it?'

Ezz nodded, fighting a lump in her throat at the sympathy in Thea's voice. Shrugging as best she could in the middle of her sister's bear hug, she admitted, 'Maybe.'

Thea sat back. 'Let's FaceTime Valentina. I'll bet she says the same.' She beamed at the prospect, because that's what the three sisters were used to doing – talking things out, even when they were geographically distant.

Ezz cast about for an excuse. Facing Valentina even on screen filled her with dismay, which made her feel sad, but also awoke her anger that Valentina hadn't made the least attempt to understand why Ezz and Thea had kept their secret from her. 'You're tired,' she prevaricated. 'And to be honest, tonight I just need to process what's going on with Mats and feel sorry for myself.'

Thea looked sympathetic, but then smothered a yawn. 'OK. I suppose you're right. My appointment with the midwife is at nine a.m. so I can't lie in. Just—' she hugged Ezz again '—I'm sure Valentina will agree you shouldn't hold back because of us.'

Dev helped Ezz carry the patio table back outside, their breath hanging in clouds in the wintry air, then he and Thea got their coats and clipped Daisy's lead to her tartan collar. Ezz hugged them goodbye, so glad for them that they still had a happy event to look forward to.

After they'd gone, it didn't take her long to clear the dishes. Then she settled on the sofa. She'd been ignoring Mats' messages, but now she read them all. *I had no idea . . . Inger's appalling behaviour . . . I need to talk to you . . .* And, just a few minutes ago: *I know it's getting late, but can I call you?*

Closing her eyes, she tried to get a sense of what she should do. Surely it would be better to accept the end had come early for her and Mats and be philosophical about it . . . ? But somehow, her eyes opened, and she found herself typing, *OK.*

Immediately, her phone rang. Contrarily, she felt like declining the call, in case he confirmed her own thoughts that it was better to call a halt. Licking her lips, she answered. 'Hi.' It came out as a croak, and she hoped he didn't think she'd been crying.

'Ezzie.' His voice was a caress. 'I'm so sorry Inger turned up. She says she's quarrelled with Andreas and misses her children more than she anticipated. I had to stay home tonight to manage the situation. I'm sorry I let you down.' He paused, and she pictured him raking his fingers through his hair. 'I'm afraid . . . look, I might as well be up front.'

'OK.' She braced herself.

But his words weren't about accepting a premature end to their winter romance at all. Instead, he said, 'Josefin's been feeding Inger information, so Inger knew I was seeing you, and that the children like you. I think that last bit's alarmed her.'

'Oh.' Ezz took a moment to process this unexpected information. 'I understand how Inger might feel uncomfortable.' Especially in view of Ezz being a member of staff, with no blue blood or gold-plating or whatever Inger valued.

Mats snorted. 'She's outrageous. I've had to put up with Andreas, and she has to put up with me seeing someone. But I'm sorry if it hurts your feelings that Josefin's been so underhand when you were friendly. I've emailed her a warning about discretion. I think she knew what she'd set off by running to Inger with tales, so returned to Sweden to be out of the way.'

Ezz sighed. 'I'd already realised that Josefin's not feeling friendly towards me. It's sad, but she changed as soon as she realised we were seeing each other.' Before he could speak again, Ezz went on gently. 'Inger's a different prospect, though. I can't disregard the beady eyes of your ex-wife – especially if she's going to continue to put me

303

in my place. I don't want bad feeling.' She swallowed and realised that she was going to have to be the one to say it. 'You're going home in the New Year, anyway.'

For several seconds, Mats was silent. Then, despondently, unconvincingly, he said, 'I'm divorced. I've left Inger in no doubt that her behaviour was inappropriate.'

Though sad for the frustration in his voice, she headed him off. 'You can't let Christmas be ruined by quarrels and an atmosphere. It's not fair on your family. They've travelled all this way to relax and have fun. Their Scottish Christmas, remember?'

'It doesn't have to affect them,' he retorted mulishly, if without conviction.

Wearily, she swivelled around to lie along the sofa, her head on the arm. 'Well . . . what are you doing tomorrow?'

'I don't know. Does it matter?' He sounded exasperated.

'Yes. Because if it's a day out, you'll be in a tricky situation,' she explained softly. 'You can't invite both Inger and me because the atmosphere would be terrible. You can't leave her at Rothach alone, because that's mean. And neither can you stay at the hall with me, leaving your family with her.' Just in time, she avoided saying 'stuck with her'. She made her voice softer still. 'And if everybody stays at the hall . . . a repetition of the way she treated me today would be unacceptable.'

He didn't argue, just said morosely, 'To quote Dad, this situation's bullshit.'

She couldn't argue. They talked on for a few minutes, but there was no way forward in their situation, so she said goodnight, and took herself to bed.

After an hour tossing and turning, she got up again. What she needed was to give her mind something else to work on, something just as significant and emotional as getting used to the idea of no longer being involved with Mats.

Wrapped in her dressing gown and enormous fluffy slippers, she fetched her laptop and the letter from Julia and Iona and returned to bed. She typed both their email addresses in the 'to' line, then began.

Dear Julia and Iona,

Your letter took me by surprise but thank you for reaching out. She paused, rereading those few words while she wondered what she wanted from her stranger-sisters. She must at least be open to a thread of contact, or she would have tossed their letter in the bin.

She began with easy stuff, uncertain how much Rick and Kay would have passed on. *I'm forty-four and I was brought up near Bury St Edmunds in Suffolk by my parents Maxie and Vince Wynter, who were musicians.* Their faces floated before her eyes, Maxie's long hair and Vince's rioting curls, and she was deluged both by a fruitless yearning to feel their arms around her, and anxiety that by emailing Iona and Julia she would be betraying those parents who'd loved her so much. She shook herself. Maxie and Vince weren't here to ask, but she didn't think they'd have stood in her way. *My parents died when I was twenty. I'm the middle child, with my sister Valentina older and Thea younger. Thea and I work at Rothach Hall, while Valentina's career took her to Edinburgh and now Inverness.*

She took a breath before going on. *You asked me how I feel to have two new sisters . . . well, I don't know. Part of me wants to know about your upbringing; another part doesn't. I'm still reeling from Rick and Kay turning up. I was prickly, hurt that you'd been kept, while I'd been given away. Yet if I'd*

305

been brought up with you, I would have missed out on Maxie and Vince, Thea and Valentina, who I love very much. So I don't know what I feel or what I want – except that I am Ezzie Wynter, not Lindy Loveless. Lindy ceased to exist at a few weeks old.

I assume the woman who you call 'Nan' is Kay's mother. Rick explained that she had alcoholic rages. He obviously wanted me to feel sympathy for Kay, but instead I felt guilty, because I once had problems with alcohol too. She stared at the last sentence, her finger hovering over the delete button. Then she shrugged. Why shouldn't they know the worst of her? She went on. Kay was raged at, overwhelmed by shame and censure, and so she let me go. Rick was shut out of the pregnancy and birth but subjected to the gossip. With that history, it's nice for Rick and Kay that they married once she was eighteen, but I suppose I expected a story of a one-night stand or worse, not a happy-ever-after for everyone but me. This may not be rational.

The moments outside the hall with Rick floated back to her, him staring up at the hall. She added, Rick's the first person I've met who looks like me – blue eyes and quite tall. And he showed me a photo from when he had hair like mine before it receded. He seemed interested in Rothach Hall, a place I love, and said he wished he could have been an architect. And as I'm responding to your letter, though much of this email sounds wounded and bitter, it's clearly not ALL I feel. I feel curiosity about my birth family.

I also feel fear about the future. If we ever meet, will we connect? Or will I be looking in from outside, like a trial run for your family, the Colvilles, that was discarded? There I go with the wounded and bitter again. Evidently, I feel vulnerable.

Best wishes,
Ezzie

A wave of fatigue engulfed her. Yawning, she sent the email, then closed her laptop and turned out the light. Tomorrow, she'd have to deal with the Mats situation but for now, she thought she could at last fall asleep.

In the morning, she woke to two emails. The first read:

I'm so sorry about you losing your parents so young. Thank you so much for responding to us. Totally understand that you must feel a mixture of emotions that are difficult for others to understand. I'd like to email you again when I've had time to mull over what you said.
Very, very best wishes,
Julia

The second was shorter:

What Julia said. We're so lucky that we have our parents whenever we want them.
Iona

It wasn't until Ezz was showered and dressed that it occurred to her that Iona's comment had a double meaning. Ezz's parents were Maxie and Vince, much missed. But Iona had said 'our parents', which Ezz had blithely taken to mean Iona and Julia's parents. But Rick and Kay had created Ezz, just as much as they'd given life to Julia and Iona.

Iona was saying that Ezz had living parents who wanted to know her.

If only she knew whether she wanted to know them.

Chapter Twenty-One

There seemed no hope of Inger hopping back into her borrowed car and once again vanishing. For Astrid and Alvin's sake, Mats knew he should be glad, as they were thrilled to have their mum around – although they were also focused on Christmas or screaming around the hall in breathless games with their cousins.

On Saturday, all the family but Grete, Erik, Jonas and Ebba were breakfasting together in the large, homely kitchen when Astrid turned to Inger. 'Can you take us to see the ponies?'

'And the donkey,' Alvin added, always reluctant for Clive's non-pony status to be overlooked.

Emil, the eldest of the cousins and so often the leader, tried to take charge. 'I'd rather go to the copse where we made the mud slide.' Emil, Filip, Astrid and Walter had been allowed a little way into the copse on their own yesterday and returned looking like piglets who'd found a muddy wallow. Mats had threatened to hose them down in the courtyard.

Inger answered cautiously, apparently attracted by neither a paddock nor a mud slide. 'I'd rather do something indoors.' Her hair was coiled behind her head and her smooth, glossy fingernails were painted the scarlet of her cashmere sweater. Mats contemplated her. She'd succeeded in avoiding being alone with him since the evening she arrived, when his anger had prevented him from paying close attention to her explanations.

'Bah,' baby Ronja contributed from her highchair between opening her mouth for spoons of porridge. Nils was feeding her while Maja supervised Liam and Walter munching crumpets, which all the older children had chosen this morning, and slathered with Nutella.

Astrid redirected her pony quest to Mats. 'Can you and Ezz take us?' Then, discontentedly: 'Ezz hasn't come out with us for ages.'

'She's busy,' Mats said casually, knowing Ezz had been coming to work, albeit with a professional smile and a remote expression. He didn't miss Inger's lips tightening. 'But I'll be feeding the ponies and Clive, so any of you children who want to come, can. Just finish breakfast and get your outdoor things.' In less than a minute, all the children but Ronja had run off, Walter still holding a crumpet in each hand. Ronja looked after them in surprise. 'Gone,' she observed.

Mats glanced at Inger. 'What was it you and Andreas argued about?' he asked abruptly.

Inger patted her mouth with a napkin, her eyes cutting to Maja and Nils, who were trying to free Ronja's starfish-hands of excess porridge. 'Not a subject for public discussion.'

309

Maja and Nils exchanged looks, lifted Ronja from the highchair and hurriedly exited the kitchen.

'Bye,' Ronja called, waving over Nils' shoulder.

'Bye.' Mats returned the wave. 'You've avoided being alone with me,' he reminded Inger, keeping his tone mild when he felt anything but.

She tilted her nose. 'Because you were so angry.'

'Still am,' he returned frankly. 'And I think that considering the amount of disruption you've caused me, I deserve a fuller understanding of your actions.'

Suddenly, an expression of desolation showed through her make-up. 'OK,' she sighed. 'We argued about me missing the children. I said Andreas didn't understand because he isn't a parent, which he didn't like. He accused me of being more interested in you than the children. He knew Josefin had told me about what you were up to with your precious Ezz—'

Words leapt from him in a low, furious growl. 'If Andreas is genuinely stupid enough to think there's anything left between you and me, I'd be happy to tell him that we're *completely* over. As you and Andreas cheated on me, "what you were up to with your precious Ezz" is insulting. And I'll "get up to" anything I want.' If only Ezz wasn't holding him at a distance. He'd called her last night to invite her to the final advent Sunday tomorrow, when the children would get satsumas and nuts on ribbons to hang on the tree. She'd refused, regretful but firm, saying it felt wrong. There had been no shifting her.

Inger paled at his brutal honesty. 'Well, he was angry,' she continued stiffly. 'As was I. I said maybe he wasn't ready to be a stepdad and then I walked out and left him ranting. The wife of his friend said I could borrow her car, and I left.'

Mats pictured the scene. Even allowing for Inger pausing long enough to pack a heap of suitcases, it didn't sound like a structured leave-taking. 'Have you told him where you are so he's not picturing you dead in a ditch?'

Sulkily, Inger snapped, 'I've messaged him. He knows I'm here and OK.'

Mats wanted to say, *Were you always such a brat? I can't believe I ever loved you.* But he resisted. 'Then all we can do is put on a front for the kids until you can leave.' He meant to ask her to make her exit between Christmas and New Year to give him a few days with Ezz before returning to Sweden in early January, but the slap of shoes on the hall tiles advertised the return of a herd of children. 'Ready! Can we see the ponies now?' Astrid panted.

Mats rose. 'OK, kids. I'll get my coat on our way out. Who's going to push the cart?'

'Me, me, me!' Every child claimed to want the pleasure. They flowed up the hall like a river and out through the door to reception. By the time Mats gained the lobby, only half into his coat, they were bobbing about in Ezz's office. 'Want to come and see the ponies?' Astrid demanded, in her *what a treat* voice.

'And the donkey,' Alvin added.

Ezz's hair swung and glistened as she swivelled her chair so she could smile regretfully at the hopeful faces lined up before her. 'I can't today. Have a lovely time, though, and give my best pats to Haggis, Scotch, Mary and Clive.' Over their heads, she gave Mats a polite and perfunctory smile.

He tried to tell her with his eyes that he wished they were back to where they'd been before Inger had turned up to spoil everything but her attention was on Astrid skipping around the desk to give Ezz a hug. 'I don't like it when you stay in your office. Will you be with us on Christmas Eve?'

Mats jumped in to support Astrid's invitation. 'Mum and I were outvoted about having a Scottish Christmas, so the gifts are to be given out on Christmas Eve, as we do in Sweden, and the food will be a mixture of Scandinavian and Scottish. Gwen and Caitriona are kindly preparing most of it and then going home for their own Christmas, and we'll look after ourselves until after Boxing Day. But you'd be very—' he paused for emphasis '—*very* welcome to join us. Or to meet any of us in the village,' he tacked on hopefully.

'Thank you very much, but I can't make it.' Ezz hugged Astrid again and buried her face in the blonde curls for an instant. Her voice emerged muffled. 'Sorry, my lovely.'

Mats couldn't force her, so he said, 'I understand,' in a voice that turned to a growl in his throat. 'We'd better get the hay and feed, kids.'

When he cast a last look back as the children raced for the front door, he caught her dashing a tear from her cheek, and his heart ached. When they returned an hour later, her office was empty.

He hadn't been back in the apartment for more than ten minutes when he discovered why. Grete took him aside, her eyes shining with compassion. 'Ezz asked if she could take time off. I thought it best to agree.'

Mats felt winded. 'From now? Till when?'

She made a rocking motion with her hand. 'Maybe the twenty-eighth. She tells me almost all the work that can be done before the year-end is complete, and she'll catch up . . . later.'

'Shit,' Mats muttered. He knew most of the preparation for year-end was done, because he'd helped her do it.

'Shit,' Walter shouted happily. 'Uncle Mats said shit.'

His mother demonstrated her sympathy for his unhappiness by refraining from telling him off for swearing in front of the children, but giving him a hug instead.

Chapter Twenty-Two

Ezz spent much of the run-up to Christmas alone, not even telling Thea that instead of working over the festive season, she'd abandoned the Larsson family to their own devices.

For a couple of days, she stayed in bed and read, losing herself in the lives of the characters that peopled the pages of books filled with glorious, happy Christmases, as if some might rub off on her. Mats sent a few messages: *Thinking of you. Are you OK? Can I call?* Eventually, she sent a terse, *I'm fine.*

Valentina remained stubbornly silent but for a Christmas card signed '*Love from Valentina, Gary and Barnaby*' and a present Ezz placed on the mantelpiece, as she didn't feel like putting up a tree. Ezz hadn't tried to contact Julia or Iona any further, and neither had they been back in touch.

On Christmas Eve, she decided she was being pathetic and should get up and shower. Unsure what to do after accomplishing that feat, she took herself for a drive down the Sleat Peninsula, right through Armadale Bay to park at a spot that seemed half beach and half mud near Ardvasar – just the place for a wintry hike. When she left the car, the iron-cold air stung her exposed skin and sleet landed like icy grains of rice on her coat. The sea was the colour of ice, too, and the mountains on the mainland dodged snowy heads in and out of pillowy clouds while ducks swam on the sea amongst the seagulls.

She didn't feel Christmassy, but Skye was still beautiful in its wintry clothes as her hiking boots carried her away from the sea, and into the hilly scenery. Heather, bracken and the longer grasses had turned amazing ambers and ochres. A swathe of spruce and pine looked like a big green grin with an occasional dead tree like a bad tooth; and white birch trunks were spotted with lichen, like off-colour Dalmatians. Sheep munched unconcernedly on the hillsides, barely glancing up as she panted up the steep incline of their field.

When she turned to retrace her steps, she paused to admire the way the clouds parted to allow the winter sun to illuminate one particularly snowy mountaintop across the silvery waters of the Sound of Sleat. It was easier walking back down, of course, and peaceful with the rushing of the wind combining pleasantly with the occasional 'Baa-a' from a sheep.

The sharp air at least gave her an appetite. She stamped mud from her boots before driving back up the peninsula and over the moor to Broadford, watching the Cuillin Mountains drawing closer, Beinn na Caillich in the vanguard of her white-headed mountain friends. Ezz joined the thronged aisles at the supermarket to buy supplies for the next few days. She deliberately hadn't made Christmassy suggestions to Thea and Dev, and they hadn't either, so she presumed they wanted a quiet time together. Then she crossed the main road to a café and found full Scottish breakfast was being served, complete with haggis and black pudding to go with eggs, bacon, sausage and mushroom.

After eating a healthy portion, she felt more herself.

When she finally reached home, she shouldered her way indoors with her bags in either hand and discovered an A4 envelope on the doormat, her name on the front. Dumping her bags, she found that it was packed with Christmas cards bearing *God Jul* and *Merry Christmas*. She read each one, unsure whether to be glad or sorry that she'd been out when the envelope had been delivered. Astrid had made a card depicting a wobbly Santa from her and Alvin – who had scribbled an A and a V and added something in brown crayon that Ezz suspected was meant to be Clive the donkey. Walter had crayoned a picture of a Christmas tree from him, Liam and Ronja, and Filip and Emil had managed a card each, with Christmas stockings on the front. Grete and Erik had written in a shop-bought card thanking her for all her hard work all year and enclosing a generous gift voucher.

Mats' card she left till last. He'd found one handmade by one of the island's crafters, a small watercolour sketch of Rothach Bay, with rows of cottage roofs peeping between the trees and tiny boats out on the water. Inside he'd written, *I think of you every day.* And added a long row of kisses. She propped all the cards carefully on her mantelpiece.

Tears wobbled down her cheeks because, too busy feeling the loss of Mats before he'd even left, it hadn't occurred to her to write cards to anyone at Rothach Hall. She wondered who'd put the big envelope through

316

her door; whether the children had been there and been disappointed not to find her at home. And Mats. How he'd felt. She hoped he realised her absence from Rothach Hall was for the best now Inger had joined the family for Christmas. Just the thought made her heart feel as if it had lost a layer of skin.

Later in the afternoon, Thea rang. 'Have you finished work for the day?'

'Oh, um.' Ezzie decided on the truth. 'I've taken a few days off after all.'

Thea sighed. 'Because of Mats? Oh, Ezz, I'm sorry it ended badly. But will you come up and FaceTime Valentina? I'm feeling much better now. Everything looks fine with the baby and the midwife says I should enjoy a gentle Christmas. Spend the rest of Christmas Eve with us. Dev and I have been baking. We bought this eating-for-pregnancy cookbook and it's amazing. I feel full of beans. Well, I suppose I am full of beans, and broccoli, and fruit, nuts, and lean organic meat.' She giggled.

Ezz forced her mind to think of Christmas foodie treats. And family. 'Of course,' she said brightly. 'How lovely. Does Valentina know we're FaceTiming?' Wrapped up in her regrets, it hadn't occurred to her that Thea would expect the sisters to spend virtual time together, but Thea had specified 'a quiet Christmas', not 'ignoring Christmas altogether'.

'Absolutely,' Thea said. 'She and Barnaby will be ready at seven, so wrap up warm and get your bum up here. I'll mix you a festive mocktail and Dev's put chocolate bananas in the oven. Don't dress up because I can't wear anything that doesn't have an elasticated waist, or I have to leave the buttons open for my belly.' Thea sounded delighted and awestruck at this indication of progressing pregnancy.

317

Ezzie felt an infinitesimal lifting of her heart. 'Very happy to hear both about the chocolate bananas and the belly.'

So, she wrapped up warm as instructed and strode through the village, where a Christmas tree seemed to sparkle from every window. Ribbons of mist floated along the street as she pulled her collar higher against the burning cold. A man hurrying the other way smiled and called, 'Merry Christmas, Ezz,' and she realised it was Gus, one of the Regular Drinkers from the pub.

She called back, 'Merry Christmas,' as if it was merry. Then she offered the same greeting to two couples also heading towards the Jolly Abbot, and a woman clutching a handful of envelopes, presumably engaged in last-minute Christmas card deliveries.

Ten minutes later, Ezz was ensconced before the fire in Thistledome, with Thea presenting her with a cranberry mocktail, and Dev passing her a plate containing a long foil parcel. 'I made you your favourite.' He grinned, his teeth white through his dark stubble.

'Yum, chocolate baked banana.' Ezz lost no time unwrapping her treat, warm and soft, with melted chocolate oozing from a slit down the middle of the fruit. 'Oh, my,' she breathed, taking a forkful. 'It's delicious.' Daisy the fluffy dog sat at Ezz's feet, gazing fixedly at the plate as if hoping the contents would roll off and into her mouth.

'And very healthy if it's made with good-quality chocolate,' Thea assured her, picking up her own fork. 'Or, at least, not too *un*healthy.'

Ezz halted, her own fork poised, while she studied her sister critically. 'Thea,' she breathed in awe. 'You're *showing*.'

Blushing, Thea cupped her stomach. 'I'm fifteen-and-a-half weeks, so I'm allowed to show, aren't I?' Then the two sisters were hugging, trying to keep their plates level so as not to drop their bananas and let Daisy get the chocolate, which was very bad for dogs.

'I'm so thrilled for you. You're going to be such an awesome mum,' Ezz choked, feeling a belated stirring of Christmas spirit. All her problems, however hurtful or insurmountable, could not outweigh her joy that Thea had been able to keep her baby. She emerged from the hug with tears on her cheeks. 'Look at me getting all emosh.'

They finished their bananas, but then Thea received a text. She frowned. 'Valentina's not available this evening after all. She says: "This evening's crazy. Will explain tomorrow." Bummer,' she added disappointedly.

Although, in one way, Ezz felt as if she'd received a reprieve from having to talk to Valentina in front of Thea and pretend that everything was normal, she also wondered whether Valentina had simply felt unequal to faking a smile for Ezz. 'Oh, dear,' she commiserated. Then she feigned needing a bathroom break so she could text Valentina without Thea knowing.

If you've put off FaceTiming because of me, why don't you FT Thea first thing in the morning, on her own? We can pretend you did the same for me, if you want. And she added two kisses, because she wanted Valentina to know she still loved her, despite Ezz having been sent to live in the doghouse.

The reply arrived as she was washing her hands. *It's not that. X*

Ezz sent back an *OK*. If the problem wasn't her and she still merited a kiss, that was something she supposed.

She found Thea lying in wait for her on the landing,

her dark eyes filled with concern. 'Are you OK?' she demanded. 'You're so quiet and sad. You must be more upset than I realised about Mats Larsson.'

Glad that Thea hadn't tuned in to the discord between Ezz and Valentina, she went for a simple – and truthful – response. 'Yeah, but I'll get over it. Sorry if I'm bringing the party down.'

Thea tiptoed to give Ezz a big hug. 'Let me show you the nursery to cheer you up. Though it looks like an empty room rather than a nursery just now.' She led Ezzie two steps up the landing to her tiny spare room, which currently boasted bare floorboards and an uncurtained window. 'The old furniture's gone to a charity so we can paint the walls before choosing a new carpet,' Thea explained, beaming. 'We're going to get one of those things that start as a cot and then become a bed later, because it's such a titchy room. There's a wardrobe to match. I'll show you on my phone.'

While Thea located the appropriate website, Ezz slipped an arm around her lovely little sister. 'Next Christmas will be a lot different, won't it?' she said, concentrating on the good things. 'I'll be able to spoil your baby with an entire sackful of gifts.'

And a whole year would have passed – ample time for Ezz to have got over Mats, when he'd returned to being a very occasional visitor to Rothach again.

Christmas Day began slowly. Ezzie awoke wondering what Mats was doing and whether the children at the hall had loved their presents. She pictured Mats lying on the playroom floor, helping Astrid with her Lego princess palace and then, more painfully, imagined Inger joining the family for the festive meals.

Luckily, Thea, Dev and Daisy arrived to take Ezz for a wintry walk. 'We didn't suggest it yesterday because I never know if I'm going to wake up with morning sickness,' Thea explained candidly, her hood pushed back from pink cheeks. 'But as I'm OK, we thought a walk, then you come to us for a Christmas brunch of home-made pancakes, fruit and yoghurt, and we can give you your presents. After that I'll probably get tired, so can we bring our food down to you and we all have Christmas dinner together? Maybe we'll be able to get Valentina then. I tried again this morning, but she didn't answer. Have you tried?'

Ezz was able to answer with perfect truth, 'No, but I haven't been up long. Those Christmas Day plans sound great. I can cook dinner while you chill.'

'We'll do it together,' Dev said.

Daisy whined, probably wanting to get on with her ramble around the village.

After the walk in a perfect frosty day that made the bracken and heather amber and bronze, transformed the burn into a snake of ice and hung the rocks with icicles, the idea of brunch at Thistledome was even more appealing.

'I'm in charge of pancakes,' Dev announced, and spooned out batter to make beautifully even circles that turned golden first on one side and then the other as he flipped them.

'I made fruit coulis yesterday,' Thea explained. 'It's got sugar in, obviously, but not too much. Would you like to put out these strawberries, the fresh pineapple and yoghurt?'

Ezz inspected the feast. 'I think it needs chocolate.'

Dev's face lit up. 'Let's grate some.'

After brunch, they gathered around Thea's Christmas

tree – a 'wee one', as Dev called it, because Thistledome was 'wee' too. Ezz gave her gifts first, wrapped in gold paper with red ribbon. Thea's was a red, snuggly fleece dressing gown. 'It's wraparound, so there'll be plenty of room for baby,' Ezz said.

To Dev she gave crystal whisky tumblers with pewter bases. He beamed. 'I'll have a wee dram later.'

And she gave them both the knitted rabbit-ears hat and bob-tailed bootees that she'd bought in Portree for the baby. 'I know it'll be a summer baby, but you can get chilly summer days here on Skye.'

Thea's eyes glistened. 'Aw, Ezz.'

Dev grinned and walked the bootees over Thea's stomach to make them all laugh.

When Ezz unwrapped her presents from them – the wrapping paper bore pictures of Highland cows in Santa hats – she found the most gorgeous smoky blue angora hat, with thick faux-fur trim, and navy-blue sweatshirt bearing the legend 'Auntie' on the front.

After such a large brunch, it was early afternoon before they loaded up Dev's car to transport the turkey, veg and Christmas pudding to Ezz's place. 'You've done more Christmas food shopping than me,' Ezz said guiltily. 'I wasn't feeling very Christmassy when I shopped.'

Thea just beamed. 'You can do it all next year when I'm busy with the baby.' That made Ezz's eyes fill with happy tears.

Ezz and Dev carried in the supplies while Thea put Daisy's bed in the kitchen. Then Thea was despatched to the sofa to doze before the TV while Ezz put the turkey in the oven. She'd just said, 'Dev, do you think you could wash the patio set ready to bring into the lounge later?' when her front door banged open.

Daisy gave a shocked, 'Arf, arf, arf!' and rose vertically from her bed.

Then Barnaby jumped into the hall wearing a pirate costume, complete with plastic cutlass, bellowing, 'Merry Christmas! I'm Captain Jack Sparrow.'

Ezz jumped so hard she hit her hip painfully on the front of the oven. 'Barnaby?' she asked faintly, wondering if she was seeing things.

Thea appeared in the lounge doorway. 'Barnaby? What are you doing here?'

'It's Christmas,' said Barnaby, plainly puzzled by the question. Then, as if it might make a difference to his welcome, he doffed his pirate hat and bowed.

'Merry Christmas,' Ezz, Thea and Dev all said at once, rushing to hug Barnaby's warm little body. He smelled of chocolate.

Through the open front door, Ezz spied Valentina, festooned with bags, plodding up the path. Deveron hurried out to help, while Thea threw herself into Valentina's arms. 'Have you come for Christmas after all? This is awesome.' Then, slowly, drawing back: 'Is everything OK?'

'Let me get in first.' Valentina smiled but her voice was flat. When she and the bags were indoors and the front door shut against the wintry chill, her eyes sought Ezzie's. 'I'm sorry,' she said. And, after a hesitation: 'To land on you like this. It's been a difficult few days.'

'It's OK,' said Ezz, with no idea what was going on but alarmed at the anguish in her sister's eyes.

Barnaby clapped his hat back on. 'Grandpa's ill so Dad's gone to be with him and Grandma.'

Valentina patted his shoulder. 'That's right. So, we wanted to come here, didn't we, Barns?'

'Yep. We've brought most of my presents, so I've got

lots to play with.' Barnaby pointed at a Santa sack with his cutlass. His body language was totally different to Valentina's. He was bouncing and beaming, clearly confident that wherever he went, Christmas would come too. She looked as if she'd been hit by an emotional truck, face pale and eyes haunted. Every line of her body drooped with exhaustion, yet was strung tight with strain.

'What a wonderful surprise,' cried Ezz. With Barnaby present, Valentina wasn't about to confide further details about their sudden appearance. 'What would you like to drink, Barnaby? Fizzy orange? Or hot chocolate? Sit down, Valentina, and I'll get you a drink too.'

'Where's your Christmas tree?' Barnaby demanded indignantly, peeping into the lounge.

'I didn't know you were coming, so I didn't put it up,' Ezz answered. It had seemed a pointless exercise, when she'd only wanted to get Christmas over with as soon as possible. Feeling she'd been a grinch, she sidled into the lounge and switched on the golden fairy lights over the mantelpiece. 'But if you ask Uncle Dev nicely, he might get it and the decorations out for us, and you could put it up while I cook dinner.'

'Yeah,' breathed Barnaby. 'Please, Uncle Dev?'

The look Valentina sent Ezz brimmed with gratitude, yet at the same time she appeared to be fighting back tears. She whispered, 'Can I grab an hour alone?'

'Of course,' Ezz whispered back, feeling strange to be talking to her as if their quarrel hadn't happened. So, Valentina vanished upstairs under the guise of putting up the camp bed for Barnaby, while Ezz peeled and parboiled potatoes and made sauce for cauliflower cheese, listening with one ear to laughter from Barnaby, Dev and Thea putting up the tree in the lounge, and with the other to Valentina moving around above her head.

Later, Dev brought the patio set into the lounge, and the five of them squeezed around it, with Daisy at their feet in the hopes of scraps of turkey or sausage stuffing raining down. 'But where are the crackers?' Barnaby demanded.

'We'll just tell each other jokes instead,' said Ezz. Crackers were on the long list of things she hadn't bought.

'I've got a joke book.' Barnaby scrambled down and yanked it from his bag, proceeding to eat his dinner with one hand while he held the book in the other and read out such gems as, 'Why did the teddy bear have no pudding? Because he was already stuffed,' while the others ate crunchy roast potatoes and dark green Brussels sprouts and laughed in the right places. The fact that Valentina said not one word about Barnaby's unorthodox mealtime behaviour told Ezz just how wrong something must have gone. She exchanged anxious looks with Thea.

After dinner, Dev and Ezz cleared away the dishes. 'I'm too full for pudding,' said Barnaby, summing up the feelings of all, with the possible exception of Valentina, who'd pushed her food around her plate more than eating it. 'Mum, can you help me work out how this car transforms into a dinosaur?'

'I'll help too,' Thea volunteered, patting Valentina's arm.

After he'd helped Ezz with the clearing up, Dev tried to get Barnaby to come out with him to walk Daisy in the dark. 'We can count Christmas trees in windows and leave your mum and her sisters to chat.'

But Barnaby might not have been as oblivious to whatever was going on as he'd seemed, because first he said, 'I want us all to go.' Then he burst into tears. 'I want Daddy.'

Valentina hugged him tightly. 'You'll see Daddy again soon.' And then they all went out together, the stars twinkling down from a clear sky and the frost twinkling up at them. The Christmas tree count was over thirty, which wasn't bad for a tiny village. It was nearly nine p.m. before Valentina finally got Barnaby to bed, his tears dried, his joke book and his dinosaur car on the camp bed with him.

While Daisy snored in the kitchen, Ezz, Thea and Dev waited in the lounge for Valentina to come down, passing around the Christmas chocolates. Finally, she trudged in, great shadows below her eyes, and flopped on a sofa. Thea gazed at her. 'What's happened?'

Valentina dropped her face in her hands, her voice emerging dreary and muffled. 'Gary had an affair. I've known for a couple of months. He says it's over and wants – expects – forgiveness but I can't force myself to feel it. He's gone to spend the rest of Christmas and New Year with his parents and brother. That's what he says, anyway. He's been lying a lot. We had a row after Barnaby was in bed last night because Gary left his phone on the sofa and a message came up on his lock screen with a number rather than a name. It was just "Merry Christmas, sweet man" but he blushed like fire, so it was obvious who it was. He blustered that he'd blocked her, and she must have changed her number to get round it, so I was making a fuss about nothing. I lost my temper and said I couldn't face the Christmas holiday with him. He agreed to go to his parents after he'd seen Barnaby unwrap his presents on Christmas morning, and so began the whole "Grandpa's ill" subterfuge. I hate to think what his parents, Pearl and

Frank, think about it – probably that somehow it was my fault.'

'Oh, Valentina, that's shitty,' Ezz breathed, horrified.

Thea slid her arms around Valentina in a big, wordless hug.

Dev muttered, 'What an arse. And she was obviously trying to be disruptive, so she's not a nice woman.'

Valentina propped her face on her hand. 'Ezz, I owe you an apology.' Her eyes were dull. 'When you came to Fishermen's Cottages with Mats, I'd been planning to get you alone to talk over the whole affair thing, because Gary said I ought to be trying harder to get past it for Barnaby's sake. When, instead of unloading onto you, I had to listen to you confess the truth about that accident, I turned into a shitmonster. I'm so sorry. I was just lashing out.'

'What?' Thea whispered and turned her gaze on Ezz. 'Valentina knows?'

'Oh,' said Dev, hollowly, his dark eyes apprehensive as his glance flicked between Thea and her sisters.

Ezz pulled an agonised face in case it would be Thea's turn to give Ezz the cold shoulder. 'Mats accidentally spilled the beans. Valentina was really hurt at being excluded, but I didn't want to tell you because of the baby. Sorry if I did the wrong thing, but if you'd got upset and something had happened . . .'

It was Valentina who came to Ezz's rescue. 'Don't be angry or upset, Thea. She's had enough of that from me. I somehow turned all my Gary-rage on Ezz, refusing to listen to her reasons for me being left out of the loop and just being bitchy to her instead.'

After a long moment, Thea breathed out loudly. 'OK. I can see why you didn't tell me, Ezz,' she admitted. 'If it was while I was in Dumfries, scared to death that we'd lose the baby, I wouldn't have thanked you for laying extra anxiety on me.'

Ezz had to swallow before she could speak. 'It's been horrible.' A lone tear trickled down her cheek, chased there by all anxieties and disappointments of the last couple of weeks. But now wasn't the time to rake it all up again. She regarded Valentina anxiously. 'What's going to happen, do you know? Is being apart temporary? Or . . . ?' She let her question hang in the air.

Fresh tears quivered on Valentina's lower lids. 'I suppose that's what I'm here to think out.'

They chewed over her situation in hushed voices, repeating, 'I'd never have thought it of Gary,' at intervals, then Thea reluctantly let Dev chivvy her to the car to drive home. She'd never got her planned afternoon rest and was in danger of yawning her head clean off. 'OK,' she said, as she let him help her into her coat. 'But you'll be here tomorrow, Valentina?' Yawn. 'Yes, I'm coming, Dev.' Yawn.

'I'll be here if Ezzie doesn't throw me out,' Valentina promised. 'I'll see you then.'

After Thea had let Dev usher her out, Valentina let her head roll back to rest on the sofa. 'I am sorry, Ezz.'

Ezz could now move onto the same sofa as Valentina. 'I know. So am I.' Her heart knew that it was everything they needed to say to each other on the subject for now. Perhaps forever. 'I'm just so sorry about Gary being a rat.'

A tear seeped from under Valentina's eyelid. 'I tried to forgive him. I failed . . . but maybe I can forget. He's Barnaby's dad, and they love each other. Perhaps we can live in the same home and be civilised.' She sounded incredibly tired.

Ezz, not having a child to put first, thought of Mats

in Rothach Hall up on the headland. He and Inger were back to sharing a home with their two children, even if it was an enormous home. Despite everything that had happened, did part of him look at his children and think they were happier with her around? If Andreas was out of the picture, might Mats make the same pragmatic self-sacrifice that Valentina was apparently viewing as a possibility and return to the family home? 'I can't blame you for doing what's best for your child,' she said. She couldn't blame Mats, either. She wondered about the woman Gary had had the affair with. Had she known he was married with a young child when she fell for him? Had she been able to help herself?

And did her heart hurt as much as Ezzie's did?

'After all,' she went on dully. 'I don't know what it's like to be a parent. At forty-four, my time's almost certainly past. I hadn't realised quite how much until Thea explained why she might not be able to stay pregnant.'

She sensed rather than saw Valentina turning to her. 'Regrets?'

Ezz sighed. 'Sometimes, when I see how parents feel about their children. I never made the decision not to have any, but the last decade went by so fast.'

'The decade since the accident?' Valentina asked carefully.

'Yes. That changed my life in more ways than rejecting alcohol. I knew that if I met someone to begin a family with, I'd have to confess what I'd done, and what I have on my conscience. That's a lot of trust to put in someone's feelings for me.'

A log in the wood burner shifted and fell. A car passed in the road outside. 'But you trusted Mats. What's happening with him?' Valentina asked. 'I've been so wrapped up in my own crappy situation that I haven't even asked you where he is.'

Ezz groaned, though she was relieved Valentina hadn't circled back to why Ezz had trusted Mats and not Valentina. 'At the hall. And so's his ex-wife.'

Valentina gave a shocked exclamation. 'That sucks. How did it happen?'

As Ezz prepared to tell her, she suspected that neither of them would be early to bed. But it was great to have her eldest sister as a confidante once more.

Chapter Twenty-Three

On Boxing Day, Ezz gave Barnaby breakfast while Valentina took a shower and dried her hair. Ezz heard her voice once and wondered if she was on the phone to Gary.

Barnaby, getting ready to attack his third slice of toast, asked, 'Can we go to the beach?'

'Probably.' Ezzie topped up his apple juice. 'I expect we need to confer with your mum, Thea and Dev.'

'Daddy says that word . . . *confer*. Is he coming back from Grandpa's today?' Barnaby's hair stuck up as if he'd been doing headstands in his sleep.

'I'm not sure. Maybe Mummy will tell us.' Ezz sipped her coffee. She couldn't blame her nephew for wanting to know what was happening in his life. She supposed she'd have to think about her own life soon – post-Mats.

'Will Astrid and Alvin be on the beach again?' Barnaby demanded.

For a second, Ezz let her skin prickle pleasurably at a vision of meeting Astrid, Alvin and their lovely dad amongst the rock pools and Mats taking her hand. She wiped her imagination clean. Whatever the Inger situation, Mats would still be returning to Sweden shortly. 'It would be a coincidence if they were. But I bet your mum will want to look at the cottage.'

Valentina entered in time to hear this. 'You read my mind. Keith's fitted the new front door and says he'll drop off the key in the next hour. I just caught him before he went off to relatives on the mainland.'

'So, we'll be near the beach?' Barnaby queried hopefully.

'We will.' Valentina gave him a big hug and tried to flatten his hair.

A quick telephone conference with Thea resulted in them all meeting an hour later on Harbour View, complete with new key. 'That looks amazing,' said Ezz, as they approached along the curve of the bay. The door was a tasteful navy blue – very Valentina.

'There are two new upstairs windows at the back, too.' Valentina turned the key and the new door opened smoothly in its frame, so they could crowd in behind her. They admired the new windows but, other than fresh plaster boarding and wiring, there wasn't much more to inspect. They walked along the beach, exhilarated by the rushing wind, though Barnaby was the only one who ran round in circles, screaming back at the gulls circling above, probably hoping for a human to discard food.

Thea held back her hair with a gloved hand. 'Have you shown Valentina the letter, Ezz?'

Ezz shook her head. 'She's had enough to . . . think about.' She'd been about to say 'worry about', before catching Barnaby's enquiring brown eyes gazing her way.

Thea obviously understood. 'Barnaby, shall we look in some rock pools? Coming, Dev?'

So, while the waves whispered on the beach, Ezz told Valentina about hearing from her birth sisters. 'I haven't really been able to update you,' she finished, regretting anew the recent estrangement.

Valentina slung an arm around her. 'Oh, Ezz. You decided not to find your birth family, but they found you. Even if your s-sisters' emails were brief, having come so far to search for you, your family won't just lose interest.'

Ezz burrowed her hands into her pockets, unhappily aware how Valentina had stumbled over the word 'sisters', and how odd it felt that her birth family, all her life a vague shadowy backdrop, had formed into real human beings. 'How do you feel about it?'

For several seconds, Valentina stared out to the mouth of the bay, where moored boats slithered about as if the surface of the sea was oily. The mainland had its head in the clouds. Then she turned back with a smile. 'As long as they don't hurt you, then great. If they do hurt you, I'll beat them up.'

Tears pricked in the backs of Ezz's eyes. 'That's against the law, and you're a lawyer.'

Valentina's hair was loose for once and flew around her head in the wind like the gorgons' snakes. 'Even the law isn't more important to me than family.'

They spent the rest of the day together, lunching on soup then playing a board game Barnaby had received for Christmas on the floor – though Thea got up onto the sofa after a while and napped.

Then Gary rang, and Barnaby chatted excitedly about the new front door, the beach, the dinosaur car and Thea falling asleep. Watching the love and light in his eyes as he poured out all the important stuff Gary had missed in Barnaby's life in just a couple of days, Ezz understood Valentina saying she might have to try again with her husband. Children grabbed you by the heart.

The next day was Friday. Once again, Thea had come down to Ezz's cottage in Chapel Row, leaving Thistledome to Dev, who was working from home. Barnaby watched TV in the lounge so his mother and aunts congregated in the kitchen, comparing schedules.

Thea said, 'I see my GP a week today, the 3rd of January. If everything's OK, I expect she'll say I can return to work on Monday the 6th. I'll be seventeen weeks.'

'As long as the doctor's reasonably confident the danger has passed.' Ezz consulted her electronic calendar. 'I told Grete I might go back on the 28th, but that's a Saturday, so I could leave it until Monday the 30th. But that's nearly New Year, and with the 1st and 2nd being public holidays in Scotland, I could stay off until the 3rd or even the 6th. I've enough annual leave, Grete says she never expected me to be constantly on duty while the family visited, and we're not open to the public over Christmas and New Year.'

Valentina eyed her shrewdly. 'And Mats would be gone by the 6th?'

'I think so,' Ezz agreed with a sigh. Then her phone began to ring in her hand, and when *Mats* flashed up on the screen, she nearly dropped it into her coffee. 'Hello,' she answered shakily.

'Hi.' Mats' voice was low and warm. 'You have visitors at the hall. It's Rick, Kay, Julia and Iona. They're asking whether I can put one of them on the phone. But it's entirely up to you,' he added.

'Um . . .' Over the sudden panicked beating of her

heart, she imagined her birth family listening, waiting. 'I suppose . . . well . . . um, Rick, please.'

After a pause, Rick's voice sounded in her ear, tentative and cautious. 'We . . . Hello, Ezzie. We were wondering if we could see you?'

Emotions flapping around like gulls on the beach, Ezz couldn't make herself answer.

She heard him sigh. 'We don't want to intrude. But we'd agreed to come on a fam . . . on a holiday.' He'd probably been about to say 'family holiday' but thought better of it. 'We were going to Cumbria. But then we found out we could change hotels, so we came to Skye, hoping to see you. We found Rothach Hall closed, but this gentleman came out when he saw us and we asked if he'd give you a call.'

'Right.' Ezz's voice squeaked in her throat. 'Well, I'm with my . . .' She found the same reluctance to say 'family', because Valentina and Thea *were* her family. But then the man on the phone was her father.

'You're busy,' he guessed sadly. 'Maybe later in the week? Julia and Iona said we should have told you we were coming, but . . . we didn't want you to say no.'

Ezz imagined him standing on the drive again, in his big black coat, Kay watching on anxiously with Julia and Iona. Imagined them changing their hotel booking and undertaking a much longer journey north than to Cumbria, even knowing she might refuse to see them.

She swallowed, screwed up her eyes and, before she could change her mind, said, 'I'll come up and see you.'

'That would be *fantastic*.' Joy rang suddenly in Rick's voice. 'We'll wait here for you.' And he rang off quickly, as if not allowing her time to change her mind.

Ezz was left gazing at Thea and Valentina, who gazed

335

back. From their big-eyed expressions, they'd heard both sides of the conversation. 'Wow,' Thea whispered. 'That's huge.'

Valentina smiled. 'Told you they'd be back.'

Finding herself shaking, Ezz whispered, 'Will you come with me?'

Both sisters shook their heads. 'Another time,' Valentina added kindly. 'You need to get to know them on your own first.' She gave Ezz's arm a squeeze. 'But we'll be here when you get back.'

'Right. OK.' Ezzie gazed at her now-silent phone. Then: 'OK,' again. 'I ought to change—'

Thea rolled her eyes. 'They're hanging about in the freezing cold. They won't care if you're not wearing your best jeans.'

'Right.' In a dream, Ezz put on her boots, coat and hat, and picked up her car keys. Valentina and Thea gave her long, bracing hugs, then she let herself out into another raw day, with tiny snowflakes flying in the wind, and drove out of the village, turning onto Manor Road and then onto the estate, parking at the back. She floated across the courtyard and in through the back door, expecting to cross the lobby and exit again to find her visitors waiting on the drive.

But Mats intercepted her, waiting beside the lobby Christmas tree. His blue sweatshirt hugged his shoulders, and his hair shone. His eyes ate her up, though his smile held a note of apology. 'Mum didn't want them to freeze outside, so she brought them into the lounge. Caitriona's made hot drinks. I'm to take you to join them.'

'Oh.' Ezz's steps faltered as it flashed through her mind that Inger could sashay in and give Ezz orders while Ezz was trying to find her footing in a slippery situation.

336

But it was as if he could read her mind. 'Mum's making sure everyone else stays upstairs. I didn't tell Astrid and Alvin you'd be here, or they'd come flying down to see you.'

Her eyes heated. She wished she could see the shining little faces and maybe have a hug, but she just nodded, and followed him through the white door she spent so much of her working day viewing from the outside, turned left down the corridor and then into the spacious lounge, where the fire crackled and the other Christmas tree shimmered with lights and tinsel.

Pausing on the threshold, she watched Rick rise slowly to his feet, followed by Kay, looking anxious, and two smiling women of Kay's stature and curly hair. From behind her, Mats whispered, 'I'll be in the kitchen if you want anything.'

Ezz croaked, 'Thanks.' Uncertainly, she took a couple of steps further into the room.

One of the smiling women said softly, 'I'm Julia.' She wore jeans with boots, and a pink, fluffy jumper.

'Iona,' said the other, who wore leggings and a dark green ribbed tunic. Then, when no one else spoke, she sighed. 'How come you got the gorgeous blonde hair and long legs?'

Ezz smiled at the sally, but then her lips did something wobbly and she slapped her hand over her mouth.

Rick cleared his throat. 'Shall we sit down?' he suggested gruffly. 'It's kind of your employers to invite us in like this, Ezzie.'

Silently, she nodded, floating over to an armchair and sinking into it, but then finding her voice to say, 'Well. Hello, everyone. I can't believe you're here.'

'Hamal and Vido are looking after Edina in Broadford,' Julia supplied. 'That's where we're staying.'

Finally, Ezz met Kay's eyes, knowing they'd be anxious and beseeching as they had been before. She knew what the counsellors on the TV show *My Ghost Kingdom* would have told Ezz. Kay was the one who'd given Ezz away, causing a chasm between mother and daughter that Ezz didn't feel able to cross.

Kay's forehead was furrowed. On a side table stood a pretty blue mug with a gold rim, and when she picked it up and sipped from it, her hand shook. 'It was me who wanted us all to come,' she said after she'd put it down again, her voice thready. 'We've talked and talked. Julia and Iona want to get to know you, but Rick and I feel there's something else we need to say.'

'Oh?' Ezz queried politely.

Julia gazed at Kay with suddenly tear-filled eyes. 'Do you want me to do it? It might be easier. Or Dad.'

Kay shook her head. 'It should be me.' She tried to smile, but the corners of her mouth wavered. She gripped her hands together till her knuckles shone white. 'Ezzie, when Rick and I saw you before, we told you how it came about that you were adopted. I know Rick's told you more about my mother since then. It's true—' her breath hitched '—that she was difficult, because of her drinking. And I was a wimp.'

Rick made a noise of protest, but Kay's brown-eyed gaze remained on Ezz. 'It's also true that we didn't try and find you until after Mum died, but we didn't come *because* Mum died. She's been dead for five years.'

Ezz thought back over that conversation, when anger and hurt had made her launch the accusation that they'd only come looking for Ezz once it was convenient. 'I see.'

Apprehensively, Kay went on. 'I'd made up my mind never to search for you. We left our names on registers in case you searched for us, but if you didn't, well that meant you didn't want to. I'd given up any right to expect it. Dad died. Mum died. Those things didn't change my mind. But something else has.'

Rick took out a tissue and blew his nose.

Ezz glanced at him, and then back to Kay. 'What?'

Kay drew in a long, slow breath. 'Ovarian cancer,' she said simply. 'That was the trigger. Once I realised there might not be much time left to wait for you to make the first move I was swamped by the need to see you again. To see for myself who you are and tell you I've always loved you . . . in case you wanted to know.'

Ezz went cold. She stared at the small woman in disbelief. 'Are you going to die?' The words seemed to scratch her throat.

Faintly, Kay managed a smile. 'We're all going to die. It's just a question of when. Last time we came—'

Ezz interrupted. 'But do you know when?' Then she heard the bluntness of the words and winced.

Kay said calmly. 'I'm doing OK at the moment. My hair's grown back. I'm being monitored.' Her shoulders rose and fell. 'The only thing I know is that I want to hold you in my arms again.'

Ezz looked at Rick, Julia and Iona, all grave and watchful, and felt as if she'd been asked to undress in a roomful of strangers. Faintly, she said, 'I'm not Lindy. I haven't been for forty-four years.'

Kay rose. 'And I'm not fifteen. Ditto.' She held out her arms in the wordless, 'are we hugging?' gesture. Her expression was hopeful, determined, apprehensive . . .

Ezz was shocked. Alarmed. Horrified. But 'there was' something about Kay standing there, risking rejection. Risking everything for a single hug. Slowly, shaking, Ezz

339

rose. Then somehow a small woman was in her arms, holding on to her fiercely. Someone sniffed loudly, and she thought it must be Rick. It was like hugging Thea, she thought dazedly, stooping to embrace someone smaller. But it wasn't Thea.

It was someone else who loved her.

Something she hadn't even known she carried around her heart chipped off and fell away.

She dipped her head and kissed her mother's hair. And they just stood there, connecting, feeling, and letting everything else in the room fade. Except Rick blowing his nose, loudly.

Driving back to the village later, Ezz hardly knew what she was doing. If there had been a breathalyser test for driving under the influence of emotion, she would have failed it. Luckily, the hedgerow didn't jump out in front of her and the only other cars she saw in the village were parked, so she made it home in one piece.

Valentina and Thea were lying on the floor, doing a jigsaw with Barnaby, who leapt up when he saw her. 'Can we go to the beach now? And get a burger? My jigsaw's got monkeys all over it and you have to match the colours.'

Charmed at the way he shared everything he could bring to mind, Ezz gave him an affectionate hug. 'There's no burger bar in Rothach, but I have burgers in the freezer, so we could cook those.'

Thea and Valentina had scrambled up and were gazing at her with matching questions in their eyes. 'Are you . . . *all right?*' Thea asked. 'Do you need emergency chocolate or anything?'

Barnaby instantly changed subject. 'Can I have emergency chocolate too? Please,' he added, with a glance at Valentina. 'Is that as well as burgers? Or instead?' He paused. 'What *is* emergency chocolate?'

Thea threw an arm about him. 'It's the kind you don't just want, but you *need* to get through the day.'

'Ooh!' Barnaby looked delighted. 'I never knew about it.'

Valentina laughed. 'I think it's a women-only thing.'

He glared at her in outrage. 'That's sexist.'

So, they all had emergency chocolate, though Valentina cautioned, 'Don't expect this all the time, Barnaby. Now, how about you go back and work on your puzzle while we get lunch? Or would you like to help in the kitchen?'

'Puzzle,' Barnaby said hastily, getting back down on the floor while his mum and aunts exited to the kitchen, where they could have a conference before they began grilling burgers and shredding lettuce.

Thea squeezed Ezzie's hand. 'How did it go?'

Valentina pushed the door almost closed. 'You looked like a ghost when you came in.'

Despite the emergency chocolate, Ezz felt trembly. 'It's knocked the stuffing out of me.'

'*Oh . . .*' breathed Thea and Valentina, in twin sighs of disappointment. Valentina slipped a comforting arm along Ezz's shoulders.

Ezz tried to laugh but her voice wavered. 'Kay and I . . . hugged. Then I hugged Rick, Julia and Iona too. I feel as if I've been on the wildest fairground ride ever invented. My heart feels strange. My breathing's gone all bumpy.'

Thea clutched her chest. 'That's so lovely, Ezz. You're *happy* about your birth family.'

Ezz gazed at her, seeing tears shining in Thea's dark eyes. 'I think I am,' she said wonderingly. 'Hugs don't resolve forty-four years of absence, forty-four years of wondering, but they did bring a certain amount of peace. Kay's been ill. That's why she suddenly searched for me.' She explained about Kay's cancer, and watched her sisters' faces melt into tears.

'I can see why that would change her perspective,' Valentina choked.

'When you're facing tragedy, you know exactly what it is you crave,' Thea added, sniffing. 'I can't blame her for wanting to hold her child.'

Finally, Ezz told them about what Mats and Grete had done to facilitate the meeting away from the freezing wind blowing off the sea and swooping up on the headland to batter Rothach Hall.

Thea slipped her hand into Ezz's. 'So . . . you saw Mats?' There was a hopeful note in her voice.

Ezz's happiness dimmed at remembering Mats emerging from the kitchen as she fumbled at the door to let Kay, Rick, Julia and Iona out of the Larsson's apartment. 'He's going home in the New Year. I asked him to say goodbye to the children for me.' She sighed as a new sadness weighed on her heart. 'I might need more emergency chocolate.'

Chapter Twenty-Four

Could we meet? You are on annual leave, I understand, and it is Sunday, so I impose, but I am happy to visit your house. Regards, Grete.

Ezz stared dubiously at the text message. They were at Thea's place, watching *How to Train Your Dragon*, and she was taking the weekend to recover from the unexpected visit from her birth family. Thea and Dev were cuddled up on the sofa and Ezz and Valentina each had a rocking chair. Barnaby lounged on a cushion on the floor, with Daisy sleeping over his legs, her pearly fur shedding all over his clothes. Ezz wanted to reply *Why?* But although she might no longer be the Stepford employee that Mats had decried, she didn't speak to her boss like that.

'Bum,' she muttered.

Barnaby looked round and laughed, before returning his gaze to the dragons on the TV screen.

In answer to her sisters' enquiring glances. Ezzie explained. 'Grete's asked to see me . . . today.' She uncurled her legs from beneath her. 'As my car's at my house, I'll walk from here. Shall I take Daisy with me?' It wouldn't hurt to look totally off duty.

In a flash, Daisy transformed from snoring gently to wide awake, apparently able to hear 'Daisy' and 'walk' together even in her sleep. Floppy ears perked, she placed her front feet together like a dancer and gazed up hopefully.

'Daisy says yes please.' Thea yawned.

Daisy gave a little dance. 'Arf!'

'OK. I'll just text Grete and tell her I'll meet her at the hall.' Soon, Ezz was wrapped up in her ski jacket and knitted hat, Daisy running happily on her stretchy lead that attached to her tartan collar. It took about twenty minutes for Ezz to stride down Glen Road and left up the steep footpath through the copse. It would be dark in an hour, but she had her torch on her phone if Grete kept her that long.

Grete must have been watching for her, because she opened the white door as soon as Ezz and Daisy made it into the lobby. 'Thea's little dog,' Grete said, stooping to fuss Daisy. Daisy laid back her ears and snuffled coquettishly.

'I hope you don't mind me bringing her,' Ezz said. 'It saved Thea having to walk her and I wasn't very near my house, or car.'

'Of course not. I have inconvenienced you.' Grete opened the door wider, and when Ezz and Daisy had stepped through, led them up the corridor to the home office. 'I apologise for breaking into your time, but soon must we make departure plans, and first I have something I wish to arrange.'

'Oh,' Ezz said hollowly, unable to refrain from glancing down the corridor towards the kitchen and the lounge.

Grete must have noticed. 'The rest of the family has gone out.'

'Lovely,' Ezz said mechanically, glad she wouldn't trip over Inger, and telling herself that it was for the best that she wouldn't see Mats, Astrid and Alvin. In the home office, she took a seat across the desk from Grete, Daisy at her feet.

'So.' Grete adjusted her glasses and twinkled through them. 'I am making a party, with Gwen's help. She tells me about Hogmanay and seeing in the bells with friends and family. I am a little confused about the "first footing" as she calls it, but she tells me Jonas can play this role, as he is dark. He is not tall, and neither a stranger, but we manage with what we have.' Her eyes creased almost to slits with the size of her smile. 'Wikipedia says the tradition may date back to the Viking invasion, when to have a blond stranger at your door was bad luck. But we are already Vikings, and we are already here, so I do not see a problem. At home, we would have fireworks, but I have not thought to buy any.'

Ezz found herself smiling. 'Still sounds great. It's only two days away, though, so do you need my help?' Bang went her time off, if so.

'Only to deliver some invitations.' Grete gave a satisfied nod. She opened the desk drawer and withdrew a stack of envelopes. 'This invitation is for you. And these – please will you give to Thea, and your sister Valentina? Mats tells me she is in Rothach.' She passed over three blue envelopes.

Surprised, Ezz read the fronts. *Ezzie. Thea and Deveron. Valentina and family.* They were all invited to the Larssons' Hogmanay?

Grete began to flip through more envelopes. 'I have also invitations for Georgia and Peony, Dilly from the café,

Sheena, Gwen and Caitriona, and Hadley who is every summer raising our plants in the greenhouse.'

'How generous.' Ezz was touched at Grete inviting employees to celebrate with her family. Then her heart began a downward spiral as she remembered that Inger would no doubt be there too. Ezz did *not* relish Inger finding ways to remind Ezzie that she was only staff.

Grete shrugged off Ezz's appreciation. 'Already, many will have their New Year arrangements. Possibly, Georgia and Peony have gone away. But we see who comes.'

'Well. Thanks again,' Ezz said.

Grete took up another envelope and tapped it on her fingers, regarding Ezz keenly. Then, slowly, she laid it on the desk so Ezz could read the addressees. *Kay, Rick and family.*

'Oh.' Ezz didn't know what to think or say. She'd agreed to meet her birth family again before they left on Friday January 3rd, but she'd havered over when and where. A pub might be too public, but her little cottage would be too crowded, especially if Thea and Valentina came, along with Julia's partner Hamal and daughter Edina, and Iona's partner Vido. She was still wondering what to do.

'It is your choice whether to give it.' Grete's eyes shone with compassion. 'We make them your guests, so you decide.'

'That's so kind,' Ezz murmured, tears pricking her eyes that Grete was once again providing an arena for Ezz to meet her birth family, neutral ground but not public property. She felt a warm affection for her employer, who she'd come to understand on a different level this winter. Ezz knew which hotel the Colvilles were staying at in Broadford. She could leave the invitation at reception, with an explanatory note. Though she was sure they would accept, it gave them the chance to discuss it amongst themselves.

Was that cowardly? Maybe. Or maybe she was, as always, just being pragmatic.

When the New Year's Eve party came around, Mats was tantalised by seeing Ezz always the centre of a group. Her hair shone almost enough to reflect the flame-coloured top that clung to her front and dipped at the back. He had to talk to himself sternly not to walk behind her and stroke the skin between her shoulder blades.

He hovered closer, watching her smile and laugh with Valentina, Thea and Dev. Gwen and Caitriona had prepared the food and drink for the party, laid it out buffet style, then removed their aprons and become guests. Sheena, Georgia and Peony had replied to their invitations by saying they already had plans. Ebba, Jonas's wife, was chatting to Caitriona, as she had a young relative who wanted to attend university outside of Sweden and was looking for information. Gwen was laughing with Dilly from the Nature Garden Café, Hadley and his wife. Barnaby was at the children's table. Grete had put out colouring things, but what the table was mainly being used for was children sliding along it on their bellies – even Ronja – and chattering in a mixture of Swedish and English.

Oh, well. Kids.

He double-checked that Astrid and Alvin were happy, then edged a couple of steps towards Ezz. Rick and Kay Colville hovered nearby as she chatted to Thea, as if just listening to her conversation was enough for them, glancing around the large room with the huge Christmas tree, looking awestruck and shy. It wasn't hard to believe that as youngsters they'd been swept along by parental wishes.

Then Valentina drew one of Ezz's birth sisters into the conversation, and Thea drew in the other. He watched the apprehension flit over Ezz's face as her eyes slid between her adoptive sisters and her birth sisters. One of her birth sisters included Rick and Kay in the group. Rick said something and Ezz laughed. Gradually her shoulders relaxed.

It was like watching a garden grow from seeds. It would take a while for it to ever truly bloom, but at least green shoots were showing.

As the group milled around Ezz, Mats edged closer, until he found himself next to Valentina. 'Lovely party,' she said politely.

'I want to apologise,' he said at the same time. 'My dad says I speak first and think later. It was unforgivable of me to assume you knew what had happened.'

She smiled, though it didn't completely erase the lines of anxiety on her face. 'Don't worry. I overreacted and didn't listen to Ezz or see things from her side. She was trying to protect me.'

Relief melted through him. 'I'm glad I didn't cause a permanent rift.'

Valentina shook her head and glanced round. When she located Ezz and found her engrossed in whatever Thea was saying, she turned back. 'It's a shame you live so far apart.'

He realised she knew all she needed to about him and Ezz. 'That's an understatement,' he said ruefully. Then Erik interrupted them, introducing himself to Valentina as their paths had never crossed.

It seemed ages before Ezz's orbit finally coincided with

that of Mats. She'd secured a mug of coffee, probably by wandering into the kitchen and making it herself. He smiled just to have her close. Her perfume, her smile, even the way she held her head, were achingly familiar, and he had to clear his throat before speaking. 'You might be pleased to know that you can expect Mum and Dad to spend nice long summers in Skye from now on. He's not going to work so hard. She's retiring altogether.'

Her beautiful blue eyes lit up. 'That's great.'

But before he could ask how she'd feel if he too visited as often as feasible, someone called Ezz. When she realised her sisters – both adoptive and birth – were proposing a photo together, she flushed, then beamed.

'I'll hold your coffee,' he offered, and returned to his role as spectator.

Ebba had volunteered to take the picture, Ezzie in the centre, with Thea and Valentina posing on one side and Julia and Iona on the other. Ezz made a comment, and they all laughed as Ebba fired off shots, then they clustered around the phone to crane at the screen, four darkish heads and one, tall, willowy blonde.

He nursed her drink, like the saddo in a romcom admiring the popular girl at a party from afar. She looked up and their gazes met. Slowly, she detached herself from the group and headed back his way.

But Kay and Rick managed to arrive just as she reached him. Rick eased his collar. 'We were just thinking, Kay and me. We'd love to know about Maxie and Vince. I don't want to make you feel awkward, but we owe them so much.' He halted uncertainly.

From Ezz's smile, there was nothing more calculated to make her feel kindly towards them. 'I have photos, and a scrapbook about their careers.' Then, after a beat: 'Why don't you come to my place tomorrow? I don't return to work until Monday.'

Mats' heart lurched, though he'd known from emails between his mum and Ezzie that she'd asked to stay off until January 6th. He could understand why she'd felt it easier, but he hadn't yet been able to tell her his news.

Kay looked as if she might cry. 'That would be wonderful. Let me give you my phone so you can put your address in it.'

It would be wrong to barge into such an emotional exchange, and Mats resigned himself to waiting. Then Grete edged in. 'Ezzie, I am so sorry to speak to you about work tonight, but I wanted to tell you myself that the family is leaving on the 2nd. Many need to prepare to return to work or school.' She added a smile. 'And Erik and I need to make appointments ahead of semi-retirement.'

Mats rolled his eyes. *Damn*. He'd wanted to tell Ezz himself.

Ezz's smile faded as she visibly drew on her work persona. 'I can return to work on the 2nd and drive you to the airport.'

Grete glanced at Mats and hesitated, perhaps noticing his black frown. 'Let me talk to Erik.' And, after sending Mats an apologetic look, she melted away.

Kay and Rick were now chatting with Hadley and his wife, so Mats decided it was time to get Ezz's attention. He touched her arm. 'Shall I tell you why Inger isn't here?'

Ezz glanced around the room with a frown. 'I hadn't noticed. There's been a lot going on.'

If it was true that she hadn't noticed Inger's absence, then Mats was sunk. But he didn't think it was true, because Ezz had a way of being aware of everyone and everything, and her reply had been too casual. 'Two days after Christmas, Andreas arrived in the superyacht Inger had been cruising on,' he told her, and felt cheered when she gave him all her attention. 'It anchored in the Sound of Sleat and Andreas was tendered ashore to Armadale, where he telephoned a taxi to get him to Rothach. Inger was suitably impressed and told me afterwards that it had been rough sailing up the west of England and Wales. Everyone was seasick, but he wouldn't hear of turning back. They went off for a heart-to-heart and she returned having accepted her engagement ring back and they've gone to complete their cruise. The children had her here for Christmas, which is the reason she'd given for coming.' He allowed a note of irony into his voice. They both knew there had also been an element of jealousy.

Ezz's eyes were fixed on his face, expression inscrutable. 'How do you feel?'

'Relaxed. Relieved. The children know they'll see her again. For my sake, my family made the best of her being here during the Christmas they'd planned so carefully.' It would be unkind to say, *I was glad to see the back of her,* even to Ezz. 'The three of us talked and put to bed some of the bad feeling and misunderstandings. I was amazed to hear Andreas admit he's felt jealous of me, not just as Inger's ex, but because I'm Astrid and Alvin's father, whereas he's just their stepfather. He gave a pompous speech about me knowing where I am in life.' He laughed. 'That was odd, because when I came here in November I felt as if I'd lost my grip and my life was going to shit. And though I've always pointed out that he's never had to work for his money, I hadn't realised that it made him feel directionless.'

Her smile faded. 'But where you're *going* is back to Sweden.'

She looked so desolate that he jumped in before someone could interrupt again. 'Would you come with me?' Everything else he'd planned to say – about his children knowing and adoring her already and that he'd keep Inger out of Ezz's hair – faded away the instant he saw blank astonishment in her gaze. *Shit*. Despite the long hours of thought and hanging around until he could get her alone, he'd made a complete mess of it.

Her expression shuttered. 'You're asking me to give up my life in favour of yours.'

He considered. 'I suppose I did just do that. But—'

'Your impulsiveness is impressive,' she said drily. 'We've known each other a short time and been "together"—' she made air quotes '—for even less. What if it doesn't work?' She waited, but when he didn't immediately conjure up an answer, she supplied one. 'Your parents would have filled my job, and my landlord would have relet my home.'

With a feeling of doom, he watched her gaze roving over the guests around them and he imagined her ticking them off as reasons not to leave: *Thea* having a baby. *Valentina* buying a holiday cottage in Rothach. *Her first family* living in England, where she could get to know them more easily from Scotland. He blushed. 'I don't have a fully developed plan. I just know how I feel about you.' Desperately, he tempered his request. 'Would you ever visit us in Gothenburg?'

She hesitated. Her gaze returned to him, but her eyes held regret and perhaps disillusionment. 'I want to say yes. But what if it's just like prodding a bad tooth? It won't become less painful unless we let it heal.'

He managed a smile. 'Lovely. I'm a bad tooth, as well as impulsive.' Heavily, he realised his plans didn't have a prayer. Sadly, he said, 'The 2nd is a public holiday in Scotland, so don't come back to work. The family can hire another car to drive to Inverness Airport.'

After a hesitation, she said colourlessly, 'Of course.' She didn't even argue that it was up to Grete and Erik to sanction her hours, not him.

Unable to help himself, he opened his arms, and she stepped in for a long, long hug. He tried to burn the feel of her in his arms into his memory. 'You'll see me again,' he murmured.

Slowly, she disentangled herself. 'Well, yes . . . if you visit Rothach. But our situation will only be the same. I live here, and you live in Sweden.' She gave him a watery smile. 'Say goodbye to the kids for me. I don't want to risk upsetting them.' Then she turned and strode away, to where Valentina was talking persuasively to Barnaby, probably about bedtime. He glanced at his watch. It was nearly ten, and the children were wilting.

Alvin came over rubbing his eyes. 'Barnaby's got to go home,' he complained plaintively, falling into Swedish.

Mats crouched to scoop him up, kissing his head while avoiding the cake crumbs stuck in his hair. 'I'm afraid all the children have to go to bed. It's very late.'

As he watched, Thea and Dev conferred with Ezz and Valentina and they all nodded, then crossed the room to Grete and Erik, plainly taking their leave, pointing at Barnaby, and then Thea pantomiming drooping with exhaustion. She probably wouldn't see his parents until they were back at Rothach, he thought. Or might she be on maternity leave by then? He wasn't clear on the Scottish system.

Then both Ezz's families were lining up to add their thanks and take their leave.

Ezz, of course, knew where the cloakroom was and prepared to lead everybody to their coats. He had to swallow hard when Astrid suddenly noticed Ezzie leaving and flew after her, 'Ezz, Ezz! Goodnight.'

And Ezz dropped to her knees and received his daughter into her arms, giving her the biggest hug, before murmuring something and smiling. Astrid nodded, but looked doleful. He imagined the conversation. *Don't worry. We're enjoying our holidays with our families, aren't we?*

Then Alvin wriggled out of Mats' arms and galloped over to join the hug, and Ezz gave them one last kiss goodbye.

Her leaving seemed to take the light from the room. The guests who remained, Hadley and his wife, Gwen and Caitriona were still cheerful, but it was certainly time for the children to be in bed. He went to round up Alvin and Astrid, hiding his misery behind forced smiles.

For the sake of Grete and Erik he'd return and join everyone in toasting the New Year with good Skye whisky, after Jonas had fulfilled the Scottish tradition of first footing as a dark stranger.

But it seemed an empty gesture now. The New Year didn't look as if it wanted to bring Mats a fresh start at all.

Outside, frost was glittering prettily. While Dev cleared his car windscreen, Ezz turned to Thea. 'Do you think you could drop Valentina and Barnaby at my place in your car? I want to talk to Rick and Kay and everyone before they go.' It was a fib, but Ezz was used to having time alone at home to think, which wasn't possible with Valentina and Barnaby there.

Obligingly, Thea agreed. 'Of course. Pile in, everyone.'

As they clambered into the car, an overtired Barnaby asked grumpily, 'When are we going to see Dad?'

Valentina hesitated. Then, as if just now making her decision, she answered comfortingly. 'Soon, because it's school on Monday, and Dad and I go back to work. We'll drive home on Friday, so we'll have the weekend there.' She didn't betray her own emotions at the prospect of once again sharing the family home with Gary by so much as a flicker.

To make her fib less of one, Ezz wandered over to Rick and Kay's car to call, 'See you tomorrow,' as their car defrosted, and then stooped to wave to Julia and Iona in the back seat.

When they'd driven away, their headlights vanishing around the hall in the direction of the drive, she turned away from the hall, striding into the darkness to breathe in freezing air and contemplate everything that had flipped her life upside down.

It was odd to be both unhappy and happy.

She couldn't do much about the unhappiness over Mats, except wait for it to pass – which felt as if it would take a long time. She remembered the jolt of shock when he'd asked her to return to Sweden with him, but she'd had no hesitation in turning him down. She wasn't impulsive, like him. She needed to think things through, manage situations, see workable solutions. It was not Esmerelda Wynter to say, *Yes, I'll give up my career, home and family, and trail around in your wake,* even if she also wanted to say, *I want you all the time and can't stop thinking about you. I'm falling in love.* Maybe if they'd had longer together . . . but they hadn't.

She gazed up at a sky spangled with stars, winking and twinkling, and blinked back tears.

There was no constellation called Birth Family.

But if there was one called Family, tonight had brought two parts of it into alignment, with her in the centre, and that fuelled the happy part of her heart.

She stood there for a long time under the shimmering stars, until she felt like a pillar of ice. Then she trudged back to scrape the twinkling frost from her own car, nursing her mixed-up heart.

Chapter Twenty-Five

On Friday, the 3rd of January, Valentina and Barnaby piled everything into the car ready to drive home. Barnaby jumped in, eager to see his dad again and tell him about his time in Rothach. Valentina was pale but philosophical, seemingly feeling that, because of Barnaby, her relationship with Gary might be changed but could continue in a new form. Ezz gave her an extra hard hug, grateful that they, at least, were back to their normal loving ways. 'You always know what you're doing, Valentina, so if you think it's right, it's right.'

Valentina joked, 'Admitting I'm right? Do you need to lie down?' Then she hugged Ezz back, murmuring, 'I'm sorry it didn't work out with Mats.'

Throat tight, Ezz nodded. 'He texted yesterday to say the family was overnighting in Amsterdam. They should all arrive back in Sweden today.' She hadn't realised how hard it would be to let Mats leave, but that's what she'd had to do.

Valentina's eyes darkened with concern. 'I'm happy for you about your first family, at least.'

Ezz managed a smile. Their visit to her cottage on New Year's Day for Ezz to share her memories of Maxie and Vince had turned into quite an afternoon. As Valentina and Barnaby had been staying anyway, she'd invited Thea, Dev and Daisy too and, with sofas, kitchen chairs and cushions pressed into service to accommodate so many, they'd finished up the festive goodies in a fine mix of lemonade, Irn-Bru, oat cakes, tablet, chocolate and biscuits. Ezz had wiped a couple of tears because Maxie and Vince hadn't been there in person but knew they would have enjoyed her first family listening to their music while admiring photos of them playing and singing. And being there for their children. 'So am I. You and Thea have been so great about it. They set off towards home very early today, but we'll see each other again.'

So followed a solitary weekend for Ezz, putting the cottage to rights after her visitors and feeling as if she was ordering her mind at the same time. Getting used to the new normal. She waved to Rosamund across the road once as she put out bottles for recycling, and that was the sum of her human interaction.

Monday's return to the office felt alien after two weeks away. Her office smelt of polish as she turned on her computer, feeling very alone, despite the distant grumble of a vacuum cleaner that suggested the housekeeping staff were busy in the – empty – family side of the hall.

To ground herself, she began by listing outstanding tasks. The accountants would be returning to work and would soon expect the year-end figures and statements. A winking red light on her phone meant voice messages awaited. Her inbox was full of routine enquiries and January offers disguised as Happy Hogmanay wishes from suppliers. She'd start with the inbox.

That took an hour. The remainder of the morning crawled by, silent but for the tapping of her keyboard and the cries of gulls outside.

Then the white door opened and Ezz glanced up, ready to say hello to Georgia and Peony with their cleaning things. But it was Astrid and Alvin who bowled out, fighting each other to be first into Ezz's office, coats flying and boots thumping. 'Daddy's taking us to feed the ponies. Will you come?' Astrid panted.

'And the donkey,' Alvin added, grinning. 'Like on my *mössa*.' Proudly, he showed Ezz a hat with a donkey knitted into the pattern.

Ezz couldn't speak. It was as if a time machine had picked her up and transported her back a couple of weeks, before Inger arrived. Her brain couldn't compute what Astrid and Alvin were doing in her office when she knew them to be safely back in Sweden.

Then Mats strolled out, too, his eyes glowing as they alighted on Ezz. 'We've timed it to coincide with your lunchtime,' he said casually. 'It's a lovely day. Would you come? You could put your coat and boots on while I bring the cart round.'

'Can I ride on it?' Alvin demanded.

'Can I stay with Ezz?' Astrid asked.

Mats gave Ezz a dazzling smile. 'Can she?'

'Of course,' Ezz managed, wondering if she was dreaming.

Mats and Alvin went off for the cart, Alvin's piping voice fading away. Astrid gave Ezzie a stern look. 'You said you'd put on your outdoor things.'

'Right.' Ezz rose and went towards her coat hook, giving Astrid's hair a pat as she passed. The little girl felt real enough.

Astrid smiled sunnily. 'We're the only ones left now. The others have gone home, even Farmor and Farfar.'

'Right,' Ezz said weakly. Slowly, she buttoned her coat, wound her scarf about her neck and pulled on her hat. It was the smoky blue with thick faux fur hat that Thea had given her for Christmas. She felt odd as she trod into her boots – numb but shaky.

Astrid skipped to the office door, clearly impatient. 'Ready? C'mon.'

Soon, they were outside in the biting cold, where the grass rippled in the wind and Mats was rounding the house with Alvin kneeling happily in the cart, his arm around the hay. Astrid fell in to trot alongside, chattering to Alvin about Haggis, Scotch, Mary and Clive.

Ezz turned her gaze on Mats. Then she reached out and touched his face. 'Just checking that you're real.'

His familiar, eye-crinkling smile blazed. 'I'm working from here for a bit – at least until Inger's back in Sweden and I have to share the children again. Josefin's on her way back to Rothach. We've had a long talk about her role and her actions generally. I don't think there will be any more . . . misunderstandings. She doesn't want to leave my children and I'm confident in her care of them.' The cart's fat tyres hissed on the driveway, and he puffed from pushing it at the same time as walking and talking. 'She says she wants to apologise to you for carrying tales to Inger. I didn't think you'd bear a grudge.'

Silently, she shook her head.

'Ponies!' shouted Astrid, as they crossed the bridge and

360

the paddock came into sight, the Sound of Sleat glittering in the sunshine beyond and the peaks on the mainland half-covered by snow.

'Clive!' yelled Alvin.

The ponies and Clive met them at the gate, snorting and whickering. Mats wheeled the cart through, and then Ezz helped the children up onto the gate and held on to their coats while they watched Mats flake off hay, before pouring feed from the bucket. When he'd checked the water, he trundled the cart back. The children giggled as the gate opened and closed and they remained astride it, with Ezz ensuring they didn't tumble off.

Then Mats arranged himself behind them, his hands on the top rail either side of his children, which meant Ezz was included in the haven of his arms. All the feelings she'd been suppressing so hard roared back into her, every part of her body fizzingly aware of their coats brushing, his breathing, his warmth and her desire. Her mind leapt to crystal clarity, instead of the bamboozled mush it had been on the way down the slope.

This was good. It had to be, that Mats was still here when she'd thought him gone.

'I'm hoping,' he said, 'that by the time I have to go back, maybe we'll know what we're going to do. Be warned, I'm hoping very much that you'll visit Gothenburg with me at the end of that time to see how you like it. And if you think you could ever live between there and here.'

Her mind flew to logistics and her heart sank. 'That sounds impossible.'

'Different,' he acknowledged. 'But not impossible.'

He lifted the children down and gently turned them back towards the hall. 'Astrid and Alvin, you run for a bit while I push the cart up the worst of the slope. Then you can both ride for the last part.'

'Yeah!' The two little people began running, Astrid holding her hat, Alvin soon lagging behind, though his small legs pedalled furiously.

Mats made no move to follow but let the handle of the cart fall to the ground while he took Ezz's hands. He was bare-headed, and his fair hair blew in the wind. Smile lines radiated from the corners of his eyes yet a cleft dug itself between his brows. 'I'm sorry that I can't live here, but I can't, because the children need a home with me and a home with Inger, and those homes will be in Sweden. But an airline has just announced direct flights between Gothenburg and Inverness that will make moving between the two places a hundred times easier. We could do it in half a day, door-to-door. But even if something happens to stop the new route, what I suggest is possible – just more hassle.' One corner of his mouth tugged up. 'I'm not being impulsive,' he pointed out. 'I've thought through every last detail. I happen to know your employer would let you work remotely as much as possible, once the assistant manager is settled in to see to a lot of the day-to-day – as I think was the case when you were assistant manager and Tavish was manager. We could come here as much as Inger, school and work allowed. There would be weeks where I'm there and you're here, I know, but we could be together for big chunks of each year.'

'Daddy?' Astrid's voice was thready on the wind. 'Are you coming?'

Mats sent her a quick wave. 'In a minute. I'm just talking to Ezz about something important.'

'What about the children?' she asked, dry-mouthed,

hardly daring to examine the plan he'd laid out for them in case she found holes.

'They adore you.' Gently, he squeezed her fingers. 'Of course, you have to want to become part of yet another family and that will make three, but we want you very much. I'm not going to drop down on one knee or even tell you I love you yet because you'll tell me I'm impetuous and dismiss everything I've suggested.'

She stared into his winter-sea eyes, her heart galloping faster than any of the nearby ponies could ever have done. What he suggested could work. She'd be back here often. She didn't have to miss Thea's baby growing up or Valentina's holidays in Rothach. She could visit her birth family.

And she'd have a new family.

And Mats.

No more feeling miserable and hollow without him. A chance to share his children, too – the ones who were now shouting insistently, 'Dad*dee*. Come *on*.'

Her heart felt as if it was soaring over the roofs of Rothach Hall and up into the brilliant blue winter sky. 'I'm glad you'll be here for a month or so,' she said softly.

A huge smile broke over his face. 'So, you'll use it as a chance to decide?'

'No.' She shook her head. 'I've decided already. I want the third family. There are enough stars in the sky.'

'There are,' he declared. 'Though I've no idea what stars have to do with anything.' Then he swept her into his arms and squeezed her so hard she thought her ribs would break, as he planted kisses all over her face, making Ezz laugh and splutter and gasp for breath.

Astrid came panting back. 'What are you doing that for?'

Mats turned a big smile on her. 'Because I love her.'

'Oh.' Astrid's face cleared. 'So do I. But can you bring the cart up the steep bit so we can ride the rest of the way?'

'I can,' said Mats.

'Jump in now,' Ezz invited. 'I can help Dad push.' She gave him a wink. 'That's how we're going to work things, right? We're in it together.'

Epilogue

April

Ezz was in her bedroom at Chapel Road, wardrobes and drawers open and two big blue suitcases on the bed. Since Mats and family had returned to Sweden in early February, Ezz had worked from Gothenburg for two periods of two weeks each, and now the new assistant manager, Alasdair, was going to be tested by her being there for the entire month of April. How weird would it be to leave the on-the-spot management to him, especially over Easter, which would be the start of visitor numbers picking up for the summer?

Very weird, she decided, hearing Mats arriving downstairs. He'd used the newly created direct flight to come to Rothach Hall for a week, but the new family home was waiting for them in Örgryte, a suburb of Gothenburg. A refurbished 1920s villa, it had an apartment on the top floor for Josefin, and on the middle floor a balcony and a semi-circular window like half a wheel. Ezz wasn't sure who was the most excited about the house – her and Mats or the children.

In May, she'd fly back to Rothach, and then Mats, the children and Josefin would follow when Inger and Andreas began their summer tour of places like Monte Carlo, Nice and Ibiza, with a week booked in the Highlands while they took the children for a holiday with them. Then Ezz would give up her cottage in Chapel Road altogether and use Rothach Hall as her UK base, which seemed surreal – but not in the turret room, which Mats used to share with Inger. Ezz, Mats and the children were moving right up in the attics, a conversion already underway, for which they'd chosen the décor.

They'd spend all summer in Rothach, as would Grete and Erik – seriously, Ezz's life could not have changed more – and Jonas, Maja and their families might pay shorter visits. Ezz would be in Rothach for the birth of Thea's baby, who they now knew would be a girl, and for when Valentina and family spent the school summer holiday at Overlook Cottage.

Ezz and Thea hadn't seen Gary since the problems over Christmas, but whenever Ezz asked if she was OK, Valentina always said, 'We're making a go of things.'

Mats arrived in the bedroom. 'Haven't you finished yet? We leave in an hour.' He picked up some new underwear that she was about to pack. 'Mm, pretty. Wear it later when the children are in bed.'

Taking the pink scraps of satin back, though happy to bear in mind his suggestion for later, she pretended to be cross. 'I know we leave in an hour. It was me who wrote the itinerary.'

He slipped his arms around her. 'I can't believe we're finding a way to make our lives together work.'

Her laughter faded. 'I know. It's an incredible adventure for me. It'll be weird to see a football stadium and apartments from the window instead of Rosamund's pub.'

He nestled her against him. 'We won't be far from the sea, and we'll be back here a lot. Inger's much more flexible about the children now, and her having them for a couple of weeks here and there will leave me free to come back to Scotland, even after Astrid begins school in September.'

Ezz shivered at the feel of his hands through the fabric of her clothes. 'Kay and Rick want to take a city break in Gothenburg while we're there. Kay called me this morning.'

'That sounds great.' Mats' mouth travelled down her neck at the same time as his hand slipped up inside her top.

She tipped back her head. 'We don't have time.'

'We do if we just throw everything in your cases instead of doing all that folding up,' he suggested, his tongue hot on her skin.

'You're so impulsive,' she groaned. Then she began tugging at his shirt. 'But, OK. Let's do that.'

They made the flight eventually, but not all of the clothes in Ezz's suitcase were neatly folded. That wasn't what mattered.

What mattered was their life together stretching out before them – unorthodox, perhaps, but *theirs*.

Loved

A Skye Full of Stars?

Then why not try one of Sue's other
cosy Christmas stories or
sizzling summer reads?

The perfect way to escape
the everyday.

LOSE YOURSELF IN THE FIRST BOOK
OF THE SKYE SISTERS TRILOGY

*A Scottish island. A stranger from the
mainland. A summer of possibilities...*

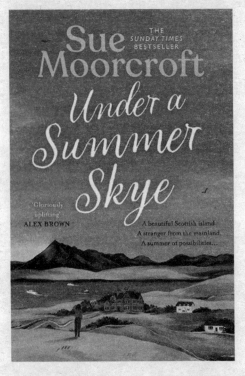

*From old lives to new beginnings, lose yourself on
the beautiful Isle of Skye with Thea as she discovers
how many possibilities life can truly hold if you look
hard enough. A gorgeous, escapist read for fans of
Sarah Morgan and Karen Swan.*

Curl up with these feel-good festive romances...

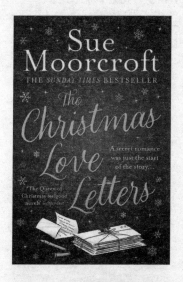

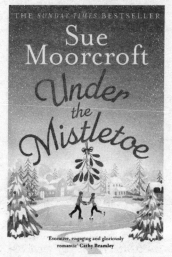

More heartwarming stories of love, friendship and Christmas magic!

Grab your sun hat, a cool glass of wine, and escape with these gloriously uplifting summer reads...

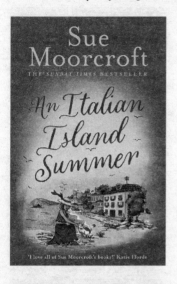

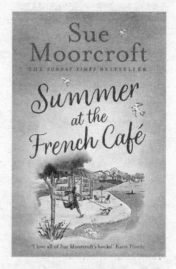

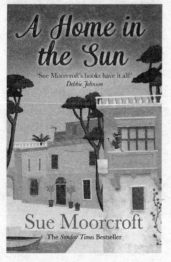

Dive into the summer holiday that you'll never want to end...

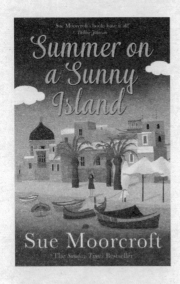